JOURNAL FOR THE STUDY OF THE NEW TESTAMENT
SUPPLEMENT SERIES
37

Executive Editor, Supplement Series
David Hill

Publishing Editor
David E Orton

JSOT Press
Sheffield

PAUL and JESUS

Collected Essays

edited by

A.J.M. Wedderburn

Journal for the Study of the New Testament
Supplement Series 37

To
Christian Wolff

Copyright © 1989 Sheffield Academic Press

Published by JSOT Press
JSOT Press is an imprint of
Sheffield Academic Press Ltd
The University of Sheffield
343 Fulwood Road
Sheffield S10 3BP
England

Printed in Great Britain
by Billing & Sons Ltd
Worcester

British Library Cataloguing in Publication Data

Paul and Jesus
    1. Jesus Christ 2. Bible. N.T. Paul,
    the Apostle, Saint
    I. Wedderburn, Alexander J.M. II. Series
    232

ISSN 0143-5108
ISBN 1-85075-218-4

CONTENTS

PREFACE

It was with some surprise that I found myself in 1983 being invited to join Dr Christian Wolff of East Berlin in chairing a series of seminars on the theme of 'Paulus und Jesus' to be held during the annual conferences of the *Studiorum Novi Testamenti Societas*. This seminar met during the years from 1984 to 1988, covering 'Grundprobleme der Beziehungen Pauli zur Jesustradition' in Basel in 1984, the theme of 'Gesetz und Gottes Wille bei Paulus und Jesus' in Trondheim in 1985, that of 'Die sachliche Entsprechung zwischen Jesus und Paulus in Verkündigung und Verhalten' in Atlanta in 1986, 'Imitatio Christi und paulinische Christologie' in Göttingen in 1987, and 'Geschichte, Geschichtlichkeit und Geschichte Jesu in der Christologie des Paulus' in Cambridge in 1988.

The present volume is in no way an official record of this series of seminars. It is one person's attempt to bring together a series of papers, not all of them delivered at these seminars, which may provide a helpful survey of the state of our present knowledge concerning this central question of the New Testament and at the same time serve to advance further the discussion of some aspects of it.

Some of these papers have been published previously, either in English or in German, and acknowledgement is hereby made that permission to reproduce material was granted as follows:

—Chapter 2, V. P. Furnish, 'The Jesus–Paul Debate: from Baur to Bultmann', in *Bulletin of the John Rylands Library* 47 (1964–5) 342–81, by permission of The John Rylands University Library of Manchester (this is a revised version with certain alterations and supplementary information supplied by Professor Furnish or myself in consultation with Professor Furnish);

—Chapter 3, N. Walter, 'Paulus und die urchristliche Jesustradition', in *New Testament Studies* 31 (1985) 498–522 (with one or two modifications or additions introduced in consultation with the author), Chapter 6, A. J. M. Wedderburn, 'Paul and Jesus: Similarity and Continuity', in *New Testament Studies* 34 (1988) 161–82 (with modifications), and Chapter 7, C. Wolff, 'Niedrigkeit und Verzicht in Wort und Weg Jesu und in der apostolischen Existenz des Paulus', in *New Testament Studies* 34 (1988) 183–96, by permission of Cambridge University Press;

—Chapter 5, A. J. M. Wedderburn, 'Paul and Jesus: the Problem of Continuity', in *Scottish Journal of Theology* 38 (1985) 189–203 (also with modifications), by permission of Scottish Academic Press (Journals) Ltd.

I am deeply indebted, too, to a number of other persons: to Professors Furnish and Walter and to Dr Wolff for their cooperation in this enterprise, which has greatly helped the accuracy of this volume, and for further help with bibliographical and other information; to my research student, Mr W. A. Simmons, who is working on the subject of 'Paul and Jesus', for the stimulus of his contributions to this discussion; to Mr C. B. Bremner, the St Andrews University Cartographer, and Dr. J. R. Ball and Dr P. J. Robertson of the University's Computing Laboratory and my colleague, Dr R. A. Piper for technical assistance and advice in the preparation of material in camera-ready form; and finally to Dr David Hill, Dr David Orton and the staff of Sheffield Academic Press for accepting this collection of essays into their series of Supplements to the *Journal for the Study of the New Testament* and for all their encouragement and help in this project. I have left the contents of all essays but my own untouched save for such changes as were necessary in the interests of uniformity of style or were agreed to be desirable by the original authors; also, to avoid repetition of bibliographical information, I have used cross-references throughout the volume, and have given the references to notes in other essays by the chapter number followed by a stop and the note number (e.g. 'See n. 1.2'); the revisions which I have undertaken in my own essays have largely been undertaken to convert what were in two cases very much seminar papers, written with a view to the needs and the state of discussion in those seminars, into contributions that hopefully make sense within the rather different context of a volume such as this.

Lastly, this volume is dedicated to my co-chairman, Christian Wolff, in deep admiration for his scholarship and for his illuminating and gracious leadership of our discussions in the seminars over the last few years, and in gratitude for his most valued friendship.

St Andrews, Scotland   A. J. M. Wedderburn

ABBREVIATIONS

In general the conventions followed are those of the *Journal of Biblical Literature* 107 (1988) 579–96, and G. Kittel, tr. G. W. Bromiley, *Theological Dictionary of the New Testament* 1 (Grand Rapids: Eerdmans, 1964) xvi–xxxix.

In addition note the following:

Comm.	Commentary/Commentaries
ET	English translation
par(r).	(and) parallel(s)
repr.	reprint(ed)
SNTS	Studiorum Novi Testamenti Societas
Tr.	Translated/translation

Commentaries are, after the first reference to them, referred to by the usual abbreviation for that Biblical work.

1

INTRODUCTION

Alexander J. M. Wedderburn

The theme of 'Paul and Jesus' is one whose importance and centrality to the study of the New Testament and early Christianity should be readily apparent. Indeed, such is the influence which the apostle Paul has exercised on the subsequent history of Christianity and the development of its thought that this might reasonably be claimed to be a central question for all Christian theology; the suggestion that this man was the 'second founder' of Christianity, as William Wrede claimed (thus, as in so many other matters, setting the agenda for the theological discussion of this century),[1] would have far-reaching implications: it would leave open the possibility that one could choose between the two founders, Jesus of Nazareth and Paul of Tarsus; it might even force such a choice upon us if the differences between the two were thought to be irreconcilable.

A historical survey is first necessary to set the scene for the discussion in this volume; although it is now a number of years since its publication in 1964–5, the article by Victor Paul Furnish, now University Distinguished Professor of New Testament at the Perkins School of Theology of the Southern Methodist University at Dallas, Texas, and a widely respected authority on Paul, has stood the test of time as a brief but magisterial survey of the discussion, which is here reprinted unchanged but for one or two modifications. Although he stops his survey with the work of Rudolf Bultmann he recognizes that the discussion is still going on and to the works of Jüngel, Schmithals and Kümmel of 1962–4 further works may now be added.[2]

---

1. *Paulus* (Halle: Gebauer–Schwetschke, 1904) 104, repr. as Religionsgeschichtliche Volksbücher 1, Tübingen: Mohr, 1906, 1907[2], and in (ed.) K. H. Rengstorf, *Das Paulusbild in der neueren deutschen Forschung* (Wege der Forschung 24, Darmstadt: Wissenschaftliche Buchgesellschaft, 1969) 1–97, here 96.

Two pieces of evidence have seemed to favour the case of those who
argue the case for discontinuity between Jesus and Paul: Paul cites
singularly few sayings of Jesus, even where one might have expected him
to, and in 2 Cor 5.16 he seems to disparage a knowledge of Jesus
'according to the flesh'. Professor Nikolaus Walter surveyed the evidence
for Paul's use and knowledge of Jesus-tradition at the first meeting of the
'Paulus und Jesus' seminar at the meeting of the Studiorum Novi
Testamenti Societas in Basel in 1984, a session which had the sub-title
'Basic Problems of the Relations between Paul and the Jesus-Tradition',
and his paper is here translated in Chapter 3.

---

2.   For these three authors see n. 2.1. Among those that have appeared since
mention may be made of the following: A. T. Hanson, *Paul's Understanding of
Jesus, Invention or Interpretation?* (Hull Univ., 1963); J. Blank, *Paulus und
Jesus: eine theologische Grundlegung* (SANT 18, München: Kösel, 1968) and
Paulus: von Jesus zum Christentum: Aspekte der paulinischen Lehre und Praxis
(München: Kösel, 1982); C. F. D. Moule, 'Jesus in New Testament Kerygma', in
(ed.) O. Bocker, K. Haacker, *Verborum Veritas (Festschrift* for G. Stählin,
Wuppertal: Brockhaus, 1970) 15–26, and 'Jesus, Judaism and Paul', in (ed.) G. F.
Hawthorne, O. Betz, *Tradition and Interpretation in the New Testament: Essays
in Honor of E. Earle Ellis for His 60th Birthday* (Grand Rapids: Eerdmans &
Tübingen: Mohr, 1987) 43–52; J. W. Fraser, 'Paul's Knowledge of Jesus: II Cor-
inthians v. 16 Once More', in *NTS* 17 (1970–1) 293–313, and, id., *Jesus and
Paul: Paul as Interpreter of Jesus from Harnack to Kümmel* (Appleford,
Abingdon: Marchan Manor, 1974); F. F. Bruce, 'Paul and the Historical Jesus',
BJRL 56 (1974) 317–35, *Paul: Apostle of the Free Spirit* (Exeter: Paternoster,
1977) ch. 11, and *Paul and Jesus* (London: SPCK, 1977); M. Hengel, 'Zwischen
Jesus und Paulus', in *ZTK* 72 (1975) 151–206, ET in *Between Jesus and Paul:
Studies in the Earliest History of Christianity* (London: SCM, 1983) 1–29,
133–56; F. Regner, *'Paulus und Jesus' im 19. Jahrhundert: Beiträge zur
Geschichte des Themas 'Paulus und Jesus' in der neutestamentlichen Theologie*
(Studien zur Theologie und Geistesgeschichte des Neunzehnten Jahrhunderts 30,
Göttingen: Vandenhoeck & Ruprecht, 1977); P.-G. Müller, *Der Traditions-
prozeß im Neuen Testament: kommunikationsanalytische Studien zur Versprach-
lichung des Jesusphänomens* (Freiburg-i-B., etc.: Herder, 1982); E. P. Sanders,
'Jesus, Paul and Judaism', in (ed.) W. Haase, H. Temporini, *Aufstieg und
Niedergang der römischen Welt* II.25.1 (Berlin & New York: de Gruyter, 1982)
390–450; O. Merk, 'Nachahmung Christi: zu ethischen Perspektiven in der paulinischen Theologie', in (ed.) H. Merklein, *Neues Testament und Ethik (Festschrift* for R. Schnackenburg, Freiburg-i-B., etc.: Herder, 1989) 172–206. To
these may be added two *Festschriften*, that for W. G. Kümmel, *Jesus und
Paulus: Festschrift für Werner Georg Kümmel zum 70. Geburtstag* (Göttingen:
Vandenhoeck & Ruprecht, 1975)—although relatively few articles in this deal
with the relation between Jesus and Paul (but see n. 3.42 below)—, and that for F.
W. Beare, *From Jesus to Paul: Studies in Honour of Francis Wright Beare*, ed.
G. P. Richardson, J. C. Hurd (Waterloo, Ontario: Wilfrid Laurier Univ., 1984).

Chapter 4 faces the second question: what does Paul mean in 2 Cor 5.16 when he refers to no longer knowing Jesus 'according to flesh'. This study was a lecture given by Dr Christian Wolff on the occasion of his installation as Rektor of his college in East Berlin, the Theologische Ausbildungsstätte der Evangelischen Kirche von Berlin–Brandenburg. Obviously the theme of 'Paul and Jesus' was much in his thoughts at the time, but he was also occupied in preparing a commentary on 2 Corinthians for the Theologischer Handkommentar zum Neuen Testament series of which he is joint editor. Thus he was able to set this otherwise enigmatic verse within the context of Paul's whole argument in this section of the letter, and provides a cogent and persuasive counter to Bultmann's interpretation of the verse, an interpretation to which the latter still clung in the text of his own commentary on 2 Corinthians, published in 1976, the year of his death.[3]

The main theme of this volume, however, is the connection, if any, between the thought and practice of Paul and those of Jesus. It is 'the problem of continuity', as the sub-title of the first of my own essays puts it. Yet in their planning in Trondheim in 1985 for the seminar at Atlanta the following year the 'Paulus und Jesus' seminar wished to explore the question of *Entsprechung* ('correspondence' or, to use the term employed in my second essay, 'similarity') rather than *Kontinuität*, 'continuity'. This was because the latter was seen as involving a discussion of the process by which Jesus-tradition was mediated to Paul, and the elucidation of that process had proved an elusive process as we had discovered at both Basel and Trondheim: in particular the study of Paul's use of Jesus-traditions by Dr N. Walter at Basel in 1984, mentioned above, and that of the possibility that the Hellenists were a 'bridge between Jesus and Paul' by Professor H. Räisänen in Trondheim,[4] had, through no fault of the excellent and judicious papers of these two scholars, seemingly shown that the *traditionsgeschichtliche* question implied by the term 'Kontinuität' had proved a blind alley. In addition it is clear that the language used by Jesus and Paul in presenting their respective messages is strikingly different. Yet it remains true that one can point to a number of points at which Paul's message and practice show similar patterns, or, to use the term which Professor Furnish

---

3. *Der zweite Brief an die Korinther* (ed. E. Dinkler, MeyerK Sonderband, Göttingen: Vandenhoeck & Ruprecht, 1976[10]; ET: Minneapolis: Augsburg, 1985).

4. H. Räisänen, 'The "Hellenists"—a Bridge between Jesus and Paul?', in id., *Torah and Christ: Essays in German and English on the Problem of the Law in Early Christianity* (Publications of the Finnish Exegetical Society 45, Helsinki, 1986) 242-306 (an expanded version of the Trondheim paper).

employs in his translation of a passage from an important article by Werner Georg Kümmel, 'material correspondence',[5] as my first two essays and the second one by Dr Wolff argue; one then must raise the question, whether this similarity is a coincidence, and, if not, how it arose, and that may in turn force one to postulate the channels by which Paul inherited these shared patterns.

The first of my essays, which was originally delivered as a lecture to the St Mary's Summer School of Theology in St Andrews in 1984, and the second of Dr Wolff's, presented to the session of the SNTS 'Paulus und Jesus' seminar in Atlanta in 1986, which is many ways a very natural sequel to his paper on 2 Cor 5.16, are more concerned with showing what this 'material correspondence' was; my second paper, delivered at the same meeting in Atlanta, was, despite the fact that its title is so similar to that of the first, rather different: its concern was with the possible chain of tradition and lines of influence that had brought this correspondence about. The assumption that is made here is that such a correspondence was historically and concretely mediated; it did not arise by accident, nor was it the case that Paul just picked up something that was 'in the air' at the time.

Yet it is undeniably true that Paul very rarely appeals explicitly to the earthly Jesus as the source of, or authority for, these patterns; even when there seems to be such an appeal, it turns out that he is appealing more to the entire sweep of the story of the pre-existent Christ who was sent from God into this world. This in turn raises the questions dealt with in the last essay which was presented at the 'Paulus und Jesus' seminar in Cambridge in 1988 in response to problems that had become evident previous year in considering the nature and character of the Christ whom Christians 'put on' according to Gal 3.28: how did Paul's story of the

---

5. 'Jesus und Paulus', in *NTS* 10 (1964) 163–81, repr. in *Heilsgeschehen und Geschichte: Gesammelte Aufsätze 1933–64* 1 (Marburg: Elwert, 1965) 439–56, picked up again in Professor Walter's essay (n. 3.2). I am indebted to Prof. H. Boers for pointing out in a paper on 'The History of Jesus and the Myth of Christ' for the Cambridge meeting of the seminar that this distinction has its at least partial antecedents: R. Bultmann, referring to H. Braun, 'Der Sinn der neutestamentlichen Christologie', in *ZTK* 54 (1957) 341–77, repr. in id. *Gesammelte Studien zum Neuen Testament und seiner Umwelt* (Tübingen: Mohr, 1962) 243–82, makes a distinction between 'historische Kontinuität' and 'Konstanz': 'Das Verhältnis der urchristlichen Christusbotschaft zum historischen Jesus', in *Sitzungsberichte der Heidelberger Akademie der Wissenschaften, philosophisch-historische Klasse, Jahrgang 1960*, 3. Abhandlung (Heidelberg: Winter, 1960) 21; ET: 'The Primitive Christian Kerygma and the Historical Jesus', in (ed.) C. E. Braaten, R. A. Harrisville, *The Historical Jesus and the Kerygmatic Christ* (New York & Nashville: Abingdon, 1964) 15–42.

pre-existent Christ arise, and how is it related to the traditions about the earthly Jesus? Did the early Christians, including Paul, feel free to embellish at will this story and thus the nature and character of the Christ described in it, or were there certain limits, certain bounds, within which the story had to be told? How much scope was offered to the play of 'creative imagination'?[6] What evidence is there that Paul and his fellow Christians felt themselves to be constrained by the actual history of Jesus' earthly life?

Even if the scope of this volume and the nature of the evidence do not permit a final answer to all these different questions, it remains incontestably true that an attempt at an answer must be given, for too much is at stake, too much hangs on this issue for it to be neglected. If Paul has parted from, and even falsified, the message of Jesus, then the claim of Paul to be a Christian witness who must be listened to today is seriously undermined. And, on the other hand, if Paul and his contemporaries had so lost touch with Jesus and what he proclaimed and stood for, what realistic hope is there that we may be able to remain in any sort of continuity with that message, and thus to claim that our faith and our actions are in any way Christian?

---

6. So Boers, ibid. 22.

2

THE JESUS–PAUL DEBATE: FROM BAUR TO BULTMANN

Victor Paul Furnish

The question of the relation of Paul to Jesus has, during certain decades in the last century and a quarter, been the chief preoccupation of biblical criticism and systematic theology alike. The publication in 1962 of E. Jüngel's provocative new book, *Paulus und Jesus*, and of W. Schmithals' Marburg lecture, 'Paulus und der historische Jesus', and the 1963 lecture of W. G. Kümmel 'Jesus und Paulus'[1] suggests that the topic is still alive. But since these recent publications also make it clear that the discussion has taken a new turn, a survey of the course of the preceding debate may help to define the issues which most demand the attention of critical scholarship in our own day.

The Jesus–Paul controversy in its modern form may perhaps be dated from an article published in 1831 by the Tübingen critic, F. C. Baur, who offered an important new hypothesis respecting Paul's place in the earliest church.[2] Baur held that Paul 'had developed his doctrine in complete opposition to that of the primitive Christian community',[3] and

1. E. Jüngel, *Paulus und Jesus: eine Untersuchung zur Präzisierung der Frage nach dem Ursprung der Christologie* (HUT 2, Tübingen: Mohr, 1962); W. Schmithals, 'Paulus und der historische Jesus', in *ZNW* 53 (1962) 145–60. Kümmel's lecture was subsequently published in *NTS* 10 (1964) 163–81 (cf. n. 1.5 above).

2. 'Die Christuspartei in der korinthischen Gemeinde, der Gegensatz des petrinischen und paulinischen Christenthums in der alten Kirche, der Apostel Petrus in Rom', in *Tübinger Zeitschrift für Theologie* (1831) 61–206, repr. in id., (ed.) K. Scholder, *Ausgewählte Werke in Einzelausgaben* 1: *Historisch-kritische Untersuchungen zum Neuen Testament* (Stuttgart & Bad Cannstatt: Frommann, 1963) 1–146.

3. A. Schweitzer, *Paul and His Interpreters* (London: Black, 1912; ET by W. Montgomery of *Geschichte der Paulinischen Forschung von der Reformation bis*

that the early church was divided into 'Pauline' and 'Petrine' wings. Using the pattern of Hegelian dialectic, Baur identified the emergence of the early catholic church as the adjustment of these two antithetical streams of earliest Christianity. Along with this novel interpretation of the character and development of earliest Christianity went a radical sifting of the New Testament evidence. Not only were the Synoptic Gospels carefully—sometimes drastically—pruned, and thereby thrown into question as reliable historical sources, but the Pauline Corpus as well felt the sharp knife of Tübingen surgery. Only Romans, Galatians, and 1, 2 Corinthians were admitted as primary sources for Pauline thought. In 1845 Baur published the first edition of his work on Paul,[4] and in 1853 the first edition of his study of the first three centuries of church history.[5] In the latter he raised the question 'how the apostle Paul appears in his Epistles to be so indifferent to the historical facts of the life of Jesus', and answered that Paul's 'whole Christian consciousness is transformed into a view of the person of Jesus which stands in need of no history to elucidate it' (1, 49–50).

In reaction to Baur's emphasis on Paul's religious consciousness and his spiritual view of Christ, Heinrich Paret published a lengthy article devoted exclusively to the Jesus–Paul problem.[6] Paul's religious consciousness, he claimed, rested nonetheless on historical facts (9), and apart from the 'Geschichte Jesus' one cannot discern the 'Geschichte des Herrn' (6). In the mission field Paul was in contact with persons for whom the names 'Jesus' and 'Christ' had no meaning, and both needed clarification and development before faith in Jesus as the Christ could be commended (8–9). Paret then scoured Paul's letters (he did not confine himself to the Tübingen four, but also used 1 Thessalonians, Philippians, and Colossians) to prove not only that the apostle knew and valued the historical facts of Jesus' life, but that he also quoted, used, and alluded to the teachings of Jesus. If materials we should expect to find there are omitted, that may be explained, Paret held, by Paul's major intention

---

auf die Gegenwart, Tübingen: Mohr, 1911) 12.

4. *Paul: His Life and Work* (2 vols, rev. A. Menzies, London: Williams & Norgate, 1875–6; ET of *Paulus, der Apostel Jesu Christi: sein Leben und Wirken, seine Briefe und seine Lehre: ein Beitrag zu einer kritischen Geschichte des Urchristentums*, Stuttgart: Becher & Müller, 1845, 1866-7[2]).

5. *The Church History of the First Three Centuries* (2 vols, London: Williams & Norgate, 1878; ET of *Das Christentum und die christliche Kirche der drei ersten Jahrhunderte*, Tübingen: Fues, 1853, 1863[3]).

6. 'Paulus und Jesus: einige Bemerkungen über das Verhältnis des Apostels Paulus und seiner Lehre zu der Person, dem Leben und der Lehre des geschichtlichen Christus', in *Jahrbücher für deutsche Theologie* 3 (1858) 1–85.

which was to emphasize the high points of dogma, while presupposing the groundwork previously laid in his missionary preaching (11).

In later editions of his *Church History* Baur took the opportunity to respond to Paret's article, and thus the issue was joined. Said Baur,

The attempt to make out quotations is very defective and unsatisfactory, and it is impossible to help thinking that had the apostle himself felt the need of such credentials for his teaching, he would have expressed himself quite differently in his epistles (1, 50–1 n. 2).

Meanwhile, Baur's volumes on Paul and on church history were being translated into English (the former appeared in English in 1873–5, the latter in 1878ff), and shortly thereafter the Britisher, George Matheson, published a series of studies in response.[7] He was particularly disturbed at Tübingen's scepticism with respect to the four gospels as historical sources, and turned to Paul's letters (he was more circumspect than Paret, and used only the four letters Tübingen would acknowledge as authentic) for confirmation of the Synoptic material. Passage by passage Matheson found in Paul material about the earthly Jesus: his teachings, his character, the events of his life. Matheson's purpose was not to 'save' Paul but to 'save Jesus' as portrayed by the four gospels, and this he was confident he had done.

In the light of St. Paul's Epistles the facts recorded in these Gospels are proved, beyond the shadow of a doubt, not only to belong to the first Christian century, but to be the product of the first Christian age, and the objects of implicit belief with the first Christian converts. The questions, therefore, of the genuineness, the authenticity, and the date of our canonical Gospels no longer stand in the foreground; the citadel can be saved apart from them (2, 369).

But one may perhaps discern Baur's influence in Karl von Weizsäcker's *The Apostolic Age*, originally published in German in 1886.[8] Weizsäcker held that Paul's theology was guided neither by the primitive church nor by the teaching of Jesus, but by 'his own thought and spiritual life...' (1, 135). When Weizsäcker speaks of Paul's 'intuitions' as the basis for 'the final and supreme principles of his theology' (137) he seems simply to be echoing Baur's earlier discussion of Paul's 'Christian consciousness'. Some of these ideas are further expanded in later works by Paul Wernle[9] and Heinrich Weinel.[10]

7. 'The Historical Christ of St Paul', in *The Expositor* 2nd ser. 1 (1881) 43–62, 125–38, 193–208, 264–75, 352–71, 431–43; 2 (1881) 27–47, 137–54, 287–301, 357–71.

8. *The Apostolic Age of the Christian Church* (tr. J. Millar, London: Williams & Norgate, 1894; ET of Freiburg-i-B.: Mohr, 1886, 1890[2]).

9. *The Beginnings of Christianity* 1 (tr. G. A. Bienemann, London: Williams

I

Although the first skirmishes of the Jesus–Paul controversy were
prompted by the radical criticism of the Tübingen School in the years
following 1831 and were in general fought on German soil,[11] the article
which marks the beginning of the major battles and ushers in the period
of world-wide conflict was written by Hans Hinrich Wendt of Jena, and
published in 1894.[12] On the one hand Wendt acknowledged an essential
integrity between the message of Jesus and the preaching of Paul, and
ascribed this to Paul's having taken up Jesus' 'religious ideal'—man's
destiny as a child of a loving Father-God (75). But on the other hand
Wendt asserted that in taking over this ideal Paul had re-formed it under
the influence of his own Pharisaic presuppositions. Thus, the simple,
popular, pictorial teaching of Jesus was cast into a theological mould by
Paul 'the learned Jewish theologian' (77). Whereas Jesus preached a pure
piety, Paul speculated about the means of salvation (77–8). When Wendt
summarized his conclusions he acknowledged Paul's contribution in
universalizing the gospel and developing Christian teaching especially in
the direction of Reformation insights, and readily admitted that Paul's
system was, 'from a human point of view', more interesting than Jesus'
preaching. But therein, he concluded, was Paul's greatest weakness.

> We know it to be certain that the teaching of Jesus, if it is only grasped and
> preached in its original strength, can and will exert in a yet much higher measure
> vital and ennobling influences upon the further development of Christendom than
> have proceeded so far from the teaching of Paul (78).

& Norgate, 1903; ET of *Die Anfänge unserer Religion*, Tübingen & Leipzig:
Mohr, 1901, 1904[2]).

10. *St. Paul: the Man and His Work* (tr. G. A. Bienemann, London: Williams
& Norgate, 1906; ET of Tübingen: Mohr,1904).

11. Notice may also be given to an article published in this period in the United
States by J. H. McIlvaine, 'Christ and Paul' (*BSac* 25 [1878] 425–60) which,
however, seems not to have been specifically prompted by the discussion on the
Continent. McIlvaine acknowledges that Paul differed in many 'particulars of
form' from Jesus, explained by Paul's intention to present the 'truths' taught by
Jesus in 'forms especially adapted to meet Jewish difficulties, and to convince the
Jewish mind' (431). Later, in England, J. S. Banks ('St Paul and the Gospels',
ExpTim 5 [1893–4] 413–15) acknowledged these differences, but contended that
the harmony between the *substance* of Paul's thought and the gospels is 'beyond
question' (413).

12. 'Die Lehre des Paulus verglichen mit der Lehre Jesu', in *ZTK* 4 (1894)
1–78.

These final words of Wendt's essay were but the opening words of a furious debate. Adolf Hilgenfeld responded directly to Wendt.[13] Whereas Wendt's final assessment of Paul had been essentially negative, Hilgenfeld stresses much more Paul's positive contributions to Christianity, and argues that Paul had simply developed what was present already in Jesus' teaching in embryonic form. The contrast between the old and new covenants is sharper in the epistles, the single point of Jesus' death is emphasized above all, and Jesus' simple, straightforward sayings about man's sinfulness are developed into an 'epoch-making' ('bahn-brechende') theory about man's need for redemption (541), but of the basic integrity of Jesus' message and Paul's gospel, Hilgenfeld has no doubt. Appearing in the same year with the articles by Wendt and Hilgenfeld was one by Otto Schmoller.[14] He is concerned with the more radical problem as to whether there ever was a historical person, Jesus of Nazareth. Bruno Bauer, in his *Kritik der Evangelien und Geschichte ihres Ursprungs*,[15] after considering the Pauline as well as the Synoptic evidence, had come to the explicit conclusion: 'there never was any historical Jesus'.[16] It is to this question that Schmoller's article is addressed, for he attempts to show how a study of Paul can shed light on the historic Christ (664). After surveying the Pauline materials he concludes that they confirm the essential reliability and historicity of the portrait of Jesus in the Gospels (700–1, 705). Like Matheson some thirteen years earlier, Schmoller sees Paul not as contributing to our problem about the Jesus of history, but really as solving it.[17]

In 1895 there were still more contributions to the Jesus–Paul debate, among them articles by Heinrici,[18] Nösgen,[19] and Gloatz.[20] This last

13. 'Jesus und Paulus', in *ZWT* 37 (1894) 481–541.

14. 'Die geschichtliche Person Jesu nach den paulinischen Schriften', in *TSK* 67 (1894) 656–705.

15. 2 vols, Berlin: Hempel, 1850–1.

16. A. Schweitzer, *The Quest of the Historical Jesus: a Critical Study of Its Progress from Reimarus to Wrede* (tr. W. Montgomery, London: Black, 1910, 1954³; ET of *Von Reimarus zu Wrede: eine Geschichte der Leben-Jesu-Forschung*, Tübingen: Mohr, 1906) 157.

17. It is also noteworthy that Julius Wellhausen, in the first edition of his *Israelitische und jüdische Geschichte* (Berlin: Reimer, 1894), held that Paul 'was really the man who best understood the Master and carried on His work' (quoted by Schweitzer, *Paul* [n. 3] 159 n. 1).

18. C. F. G. Heinrici, 'Jesus und Paulus', in *Neues Sächsisches Kirchenblatt* (1895) 749–52, 765–70, 783–6,797–802, 817–20.

was a detailed reply to Wendt, and carried through the increasingly emphasized idea that Paul and—said Gloatz—also John had been the ones who most deeply grasped the real meaning of Jesus' message. The same point was made by two British writers in separate articles a little later. Arthur Hoyle[21] declared that Paul was by no means the 'second founder' of Christianity, and that he had simply developed Jesus' teachings; he had not departed in any crucial way from them. Alexander Mair[22] also argued in this vein, contending that Paul had supplied the technical statement of Christianity's creed, but had in no way substantially altered it. However, Mair's case is weakened because he uses quite indiscriminately and without any real critical sense material from all four Gospels and Acts.

Meanwhile, two more Germans, W. Sturm and Richard Drescher, added articles to those of Hilgenfeld, Gloatz, and others defending the essential agreement of Paul's gospel with the teaching of Jesus. Sturm[23] made the important observation that the mere paralleling of verses from the Synoptic Gospels with verses from the Pauline letters is both questionable methodologically and of slight help. One must proceed, he said, by taking the leading ideas, the 'salvation words', from both texts, and comparing them. Thus, for example, he compares Mark 10.45 ('For the Son of man also came not to be served but to serve, and to give his life as a ransom for many') with Romans 5.19 ('For as by one man's disobedience many were made sinners, so by one man's obedience many will be made righteous'); and again Matthew 11.29 ('Take my yoke upon you, and learn from me; for I am gentle and lowly in heart, and you will find rest for your souls') with 2 Corinthians 10.1 ('I, Paul, myself entreat you, by the meekness and gentleness of Christ...'). Drescher[24] made the more general point that Paul, in the four major letters as well as in

---

19. K. F. Nösgen, 'Die apostolische Verkündigung und die Geschichte Jesu', in *Neue Jahrbücher für deutsche Theologie* (1895) 46–94.

20. P. Gloatz, 'Zur Vergleichung der Lehre des Paulus mit der Jesu', in *TSK* 68 (1895) 777–800.

21. 'Paul and Jesus', in *ExpTim* 8 (1896–7) 487–92.

22. 'The Modern Overestimate of Paul's Relationship to Christianity', in *The Expositor* 5th ser. 6 (1897) 241–57.

23. *Der Apostel Paulus und die evangelische Ueberlieferung* (Wissenschaftliche Beilage zum Jahresbericht der 2. Städtischen Realschule zu Berlin, Ostern, 1897, 1900, Berlin: Gaertner, 1900).

24. R. Drescher, 'Das Leben Jesu bei Paulus', in *Festgruß Bernard Stade zur Feier seiner 25jährigen Wirksamkeit als Professor...* (Gießen: Ricker, 1900) 99–162.

Philippians, supports an ethic of intention in opposition to an external legalism, and must surely have been influenced therein by Jesus himself. The letters in fact provide 'an imposing amount of material' on Jesus' life.[25] This seems to have remained the dominant view, even in Germany, for the next several years, and the names of Arthur Titius,[26] Adolf Harnack,[27] Paul Feine,[28] A. Resch,[29] and, in the United States, R. R. Lloyd[30] may be mentioned as its exponents. Of course, exponents of what Schweitzer calls 'the usual view'[31] were also to be found, the most notable being Maurice Goguel.[32] Goguel believed that there was a fundamental doctrinal difference between Jesus and Paul and that Paul's theology of redemption had gone far beyond the scope of the preaching of Jesus.[33]

25. The articles of Sturm and Drescher were not directly available to me, and for a knowledge of their contents I am dependent on H. J. Holtzmann, 'Zum Thema Jesus und Paulus', in *Protestantische Monatsheften* 4 (1900) 463–8, and Schweitzer, *Paul* (n. 3) 159 n. 1.

26. 'Der Paulinismus unter dem Gesichtspunkt der Seligkeit', pt 2 of *Die neutestamentliche Lehre von der Seligkeit und ihre Bedeutung für die Gegenwart* (Freiburg-i-B. & Leipzig: Mohr, 1895).

27. *What Is Christianity?* (tr. T. B. Saunders, London: Williams & Norgate, 1901; ET of *Das Wesen des Christentums: sechzehn Vorlesungen*, Leipzig: Hinrichs, 1900). Said Harnack: 'Those who blame [Paul] for corrupting the Christian religion have never felt a single breath of his spirit, and judge him only by mere externals, such as clothes and book-learning; those who extol or criticise him as a founder of religion are forced to make him bear witness against himself on the main point, and acknowledge that the consciousness which bore him up and steeled him for his work was illusory and self-deceptive. As we cannot want to be wiser than history, which knows him only as Christ's missionary, and as his own words clearly attest what his aims were and what he was, we regard him as Christ's disciple, as the apostle who not only worked harder but also accomplished more than all the rest put together.' In sum, Paul 'was the one who understood the Master and continued his work' (176).

28. *Jesus Christus und Paulus* (Leipzig: Hinrichs, 1902).

29. *Der Paulinismus und die Logia Jesu in ihrem gegenseitigen Verhältnis* (TU neue Folge 12, Leipzig: Hinrichs, 1904). Resch found 925 allusions to Jesus' sayings in nine Pauline letters, 133 more in Ephesians, 100 in the Pastoral Epistles, and 64 in the Pauline speeches in Acts. See M. Goguel, *Jesus and the Origins of Christianity* 1 (tr. O. Wyon, Harper Torchbooks, New York: Harper, 1960; ET of Paris: Payot, 1932) 127 n. 2.

30. 'The Historic Christ in the Letters of Paul', in *BSac* 58 (1901) 270–93.

31. *Paul* (n. 3) 159.

32. *L'apôtre Paul et Jésus-Christ* (Paris: Fischbacher, 1904).

Goguel's position was temperate and hardly earth-shaking. But this can by no means be said of an explosive monograph which opened the debate afresh, William Wrede's *Paulus*, published in German in 1904 and translated into English in 1907.[34] Wrede began by stressing Paul's conversion experience whereby he had been transformed from a hater of Jesus into his apostle (25). The essence of this experience was a new conviction that Jesus was Messiah, 'the germ of a dogma' from which Paul's whole theology subsequently evolved (76). The apostle's belief in Jesus' messiahship, Wrede claimed, came not from his impression of Jesus' personality, nor was it the result of his deifying Jesus. Rather, 'Paul believed in such a celestial being, in a divine Christ, before he believed in Jesus', and his conversion consisted in an identification of the two (151).

Wrede carries forward Wendt's insistence that Paul was essentially rabbinic in his theological background and impulses, contrasts this with Jesus' Pharisaic background, and criticizes both Wellhausen and Harnack for regarding Paul as Jesus' expounder and successor (157). Wrede believes that Jesus' emphasis on the fatherly providence of God 'scarcely finds an echo in Paul', and doubts 'whether the Pauline picture of the future can be considered a propagation of the original thoughts of Jesus' (158). Also with respect to morality and ethics Wrede finds Paul departing from Jesus' teaching.

Great as is Paul's ethical interest, there is no doubt that he subordinated the moral

33. For comments on Goguel's position see Schweitzer, *Paul* (n. 3) 159f. In 1903 the fourth edition of Paul de Lagarde's *Deutsche Schriften über das Verhältnis des deutschen Staates zur Theologie, Kirche und Religion* had appeared (the first edition was published in 1878—Göttingen: Dieterich), contending in very radical terms that no bridge could be built backwards from Paul to Jesus. Paul Wernle (see n. 9 above) was on Lagarde's side so far as positing a sharp disparity between Jesus and Paul, although at the same time he held that Paul understood Jesus better than some of his predecessors. Wernle also contended that Paul surely knew more about Jesus than his letters reveal, 'but his theology intentionally ignores the biography of Jesus, as we know it from the gospels'. (Cited by E. Vischer, 'Jesus und Paulus', in *TRu* 8 [1905] 129–43, 173–88, here 177.)

34. Cf. n. 1.1; the ET is *Paul* (tr. E. Lummis, London: Green, 1907 & Boston: American Unitarian Association, 1908; repr. Lexington KY: American Theological Library Association on Reprinting, 1962); page-reff. are to the ET. A discussion of Wrede's position, as well as of the contributions to this topic by Wernle, Brückner, and Goguel, may be found in W. G. Kümmel, *Das Neue Testament: Geschichte der Erforschung seiner Probleme* (Orbis academicus 3.3, Freiburg-i-B. & München: Alber, 1958, 1970²; ET: London: SCM, 1973) 367–82.

virtues of character to something else, and not only in polemic; to faith or belief, that is, to a conviction with a quite definite, formulable content, at bottom belief in a dogma. ...(164)

Wrede's conclusions were more radical than Wendt's and certainly more sharply stated. Moreover, because Wrede's book was popularly written, its effect was far greater than the scholarly article of Wendt published a decade earlier. 'In comparison with Jesus', said Wrede,

Paul is essentially a new phenomenon, as new, considering the large basis of common ground, as he could possibly be. He stands much farther away from Jesus than Jesus himself stands from the noblest figures of Jewish piety (165).

And, finally: 'It follows conclusively from all this that Paul is to be regarded as the second founder of Christianity' (179). 'This second founder of Christianity has even, compared with the first, exercised beyond all doubt the stronger—not the better—influence' (180).[35]

An early but only partial response to Wrede's book appeared in the following year in an article by Eberhard Vischer which summarized and commented upon the major recent contributions to the debate (viz. Wellhausen, Harnack, Lagarde, Wernle, Feine, Deißmann, Resch, and Brückner, as well as Wrede).[36] Vischer insisted that Paul's letters had been called forth by particular historical situations and that his theology was thus basically polemical. Since Paul writes to congregations where his gospel is already known, said Vischer,

one is not permitted simply to identify what stands in his letters with his missionary preaching. So it is possible, indeed probable, that Paul had imparted more about the life of Jesus and his words in the oral proclamation than one is able to infer from his letters. A passage like 1 Cor 11.23 presupposes that the congregations are acquainted with at least a part of the history of Jesus (131).

Martin Brückner, whose earlier work, *Die Entstehung der paulinischen Christologie* (1903), was a more detailed and in some ways sounder presentation of the position represented by Wrede, responded to Vischer in an article published the year after his.[37] Brückner's article focused chiefly on the question of a legitimate methodology for research

---

35. One may compare Nietzsche's comments that, but for the superstitious and crafty Paul, 'there would be no Christianity; we should scarcely have heard of a small Jewish sect whose master died on the cross'; Paul was 'the first Christian, the inventor of Christianity. Until then there were only a few Jewish sectarians' (*Morgenröthe*, Chemnitz: Schmeitzner, 1881. These quotations are from excerpts translated in *The Portable Nietzsche*, tr. and ed. W. Kaufmann [New York: Viking, 1954] 76–7, 79.)

36. See n. 33 above.

37. 'Zum Thema Jesus und Paulus', in *ZNW* 7 (1906) 112–19.

into the Jesus–Paul question. He agreed with Vischer that the attempt to compare the Pauline letters with individual passages in the Gospels is not very fruitful. The same point had been made by Sturm in 1900, as noted above, but Brückner's reasons for insisting on it are his own: (1) the gospel tradition itself is uncertain; and (2) the discovery of parallels does not necessarily mean that one has proved the dependence of one source on another, as shown by history of religions' research and the many parallels uncovered in ancient but genetically unrelated texts. Brückner holds that the controlling questions for research ought not to be 'What does Paul know about Jesus?' and 'What parts of the Pauline Christ picture stem from the historical Jesus?' but rather, 'How has Paul presented the earthly life of Jesus?' and 'In what relationship to Paul's whole viewpoint do the particular parts of his Christ picture stand?' Do they grow out of that, or have they been imported from outside (112–13)?

With respect to the first of these questions Brückner answers that Paul, in the main, disdains the earthly life of Jesus, considering it not a 'revelation' but an abrogation of the messianic nature of Christ, an 'emptying', a time of 'weakness' which leads to death (114). Paul's picture of Jesus thus has a half-historical, half-dogmatic character because for the apostle historical and dogmatic ideas are closely conjoined and often cannot be separated (115). Brückner concludes, thereby answering the second of his two questions, that Paul's letters themselves reveal no influence of the personality of Jesus upon the apostle's Christology. His Christology is entirely and more clearly explicable in terms of Paul's own theological perspective (117) which, as Brückner had in his earlier work already sought to demonstrate, consisted of Paul's combining the ideas of incarnation and dying–rising with the Jewish messianic idea. Therefore, he concluded, the deep kinship between Paul and Jesus in matters of theology, eschatology, and ethics, was not just an 'accident'. Both shared the common ground of Judaism and the common 'ideal kernel of religion'— belief in the fatherhood of God and the infinite worth of the individual (118–19).

In spite of Brückner's temperate and learned support of the general position represented by Wrede, it was the latter's book which remained the centre of the controversy and to which dissenting scholars felt obliged to respond. Attacks on Wrede came, within the three years following publication of his book, from Julius Kaftan,[38] Paul Kölbing,[39] Arnold

---

38. *Jesus und Paulus* (Tübingen: Mohr, 1906).

39. *Die geistige Einwirkung der Person Jesu auf Paulus* (Göttingen: Vandenhoeck & Ruprecht, 1906).

Meyer,[40] and Adolf Jülicher.[41] Kaftan sought to expose Wrede's falsely-conceived scholasticizing interpretation of Paulinism. He insisted that, although Paul's Pharisaic training led him to certain distinctive statements of the gospel, the apostle had much more in common with Jesus than Wrede had allowed.[42] Jülicher was particularly concerned with Wrede's bold assertion that Paul had been Christianity's 'second founder', and sought to refute that particular statement of the case.

Arnold Meyer's volume was also addressed to this specific question, as its German title indicated: 'Who Founded Christianity? Jesus or Paul?' But it is characteristic of Meyer's book that he does not try to minimize the differences between Jesus and Paul as many others had. In fact, he speaks of the 'vastness of the gulf' separating Jesus and the 'strange speculations of St. Paul' (23). Paul's system was essentially Gnostic, Meyer argued (24); as opposed to the directness and simplicity of Jesus, Paul's thought was dialectic and complex (77ff), his conception of God retained 'traits of Oriental despotism and caprice' (80); and in distinction from the pure piety of Jesus, Paul offered 'a mythological drama' of redemption realized in personal experience (83). Echoing Wendt and also Wrede, Meyer speaks about 'the warping influence [upon Paul] of the Rabbinic schools...' (87); he contrasts the urban Paul with the rural Jesus (87–8); he emphasizes Paul's pathological tendency to see everything in sharp contrasts (88–9); and believes that his holding aloof from those who had known the historical Jesus 'was in every sort of way fatal for the Apostle' (90). Moreover, Meyer is quite ready to acknowledge that there were certain crucial differences between Jesus and Paul concerning the Gentile mission. But on the central point of Paul's gospel—the proclamation that Christ died for our sins—Meyer finds decisive agreement, although with an important qualification.

> This conception can scarcely have been derived from Jesus Himself; but the disciples of Jesus could not have ascribed it to Him and could not have so interpreted His death unless Jesus had lived His own and God's forgiving love before their eyes. Hence it was the Spirit of Jesus that came over St. Paul, and in so far he rightly regarded Jesus as his Lord, and rightly called himself an apostle of Jesus (103).

Thus, Meyer's own answer to the question posed in the title of his

40. *Jesus or Paul?* (tr. J. R. Wilkinson, London: Harper, 1909; ET of *Wer hat das Christentum begründet, Jesus oder Paulus?*, Tübingen: Mohr, 1907).

41. *Paulus und Jesus* (Religionsgeschichtliche Volksbücher 1.14, Tübingen: Mohr, 1907).

42. Since Kaftan's monograph was not directly accessible to me, I am dependent for this statement of his position upon James Moffatt, 'Paul and Jesus', in *Biblical World* 32 (1908) 168–73, here 171.

book is not simply formulated. On the one hand he insisted: '*Our religion in its essence is derived from Christ*' (125). But on the other hand he could still say that 'St. Paul, ...though not the sole founder was still the principal founder of that form of Christianity which alone proved capable of subduing the wide world to Christ...' (132). Meyer here develops what had been implicit in Wendt's presentation of the case in 1894, and which, following Meyer, became more and more the position of liberal Protestant theology: that Paul's function was necessary in its day, but that it was essentially apologetic, polemical, and organizational, and that the present-day motto of the Christian ought to be: 'Back through Paul to Jesus and God!' (134)

While each of the writers who attacked Wrede scored certain points in the debate with him (his interpretation of Paul's view of faith as belief in dogmas was particularly susceptible to attack), the force and effect of Wrede's work was by no means dissipated. Johannes Weiß correctly observed that, while some details of Wrede's thesis had been refuted, the general impression was left that his overall point remained standing.[43] This impression Weiß now earnestly seeks to dispel. He admits one basic difference between Jesus and Paul—the latter's exaltation of Jesus to the status of God, his 'religious veneration' of him (4ff); and from the outset Weiß acknowledges his own preference for a 'Jesus of Nazareth religion' as distinguished from the 'exalted Christ religion' of Paul and the earliest church. Paul's Christology and doctrine of reconciliation could not have been simply 'developments of Jesus' teaching'—thus far Weiß supports Wrede (13–14); but against Wrede, Weiß holds that Paul's doctrinal formulations were necessitated by the requirements of the age (Meyer's point also) and were 'the theological expression...of a religious attitude directly derived from the teaching of Jesus' (14). Here is the key to Weiß's solution of the Jesus–Paul problem. Paul was influenced by Jesus' *personality*, by his fundamental religious consciousness and attitudes. Thus, Weiß does not concentrate on the collection of parallels between Paul's letters and the Gospels, but is chiefly concerned to establish the content of Paul's conversion experience which, according to him, was 'psychologically inconceivable except upon the supposition that he had been actually and vividly impressed by the human personality of Jesus' (31). The exegesis of 2 Corinthians 5.16 ('From now on, therefore, we regard no one from a human point of view; even though we once regarded Christ from a human point of view, we regard him thus no longer') is, in this connection, crucial for Weiß, and he believes the

---

43. *Paul and Jesus* (tr. H. J. Chaytor, London: Harper, 1909; ET of Berlin: Reuther & Reichard, 1909)

passage proves that Paul had indeed known Jesus 'after the flesh', i.e. 'from a human point of view' (41–54).[44]

In defining the relation of Jesus and Paul, Weiß thus differs, on the one hand, from those who had seen Paul's theological system as a simple development of Jesus' teaching and, on the other hand, from those who had viewed it as a product of Paul's rabbinic and Jewish (messianic-apocalyptic) presuppositions. Paul's Christology represented a *correction* of his Jewish view of the Messiah, said Weiß —a correction based on a 'past experience'.

> Paul must have been convinced by the narratives of the first disciples or by personal impression that Jesus was entirely devoted to the task not merely of preaching the love of God, but of acting as its incarnation in His every deed and word and of preaching it so attractively that sinners were able to take courage in view of that love (93).

This 'impression of the person of Jesus' Weiß identified as 'the profound and decisive influence of Jesus upon Paul' (94). Particularly before Paul was the 'self-renouncing love' of Jesus (118), on which point 'Paul "understood" Jesus inwardly, deeply, and correctly' (121). Weiß begins and concludes with the assertion that, because Paul and the early church regarded Jesus as an object of religious veneration, they represented 'a new type of religion' (130). But the idea that this new religious type had no 'living tie with the historical figure of Jesus' Weiß firmly rejects (131).

Meanwhile, how were British and American scholars responding to the questions being debated in Germany? Wrede's book was translated into English in 1907, and the volumes by Meyer and Weiß were translated two years later. From some quarters there were anguished cries against the 'anti-Paul' writers, but without a critical evaluation of the texts which had for so long been under discussion in Germany (and France).[45] The earliest notable contributions in English came from James

---

44. Throughout the various periods of the Jesus–Paul debate many articles dealing with the exegesis of this passage have appeared. Among them are the following: H. F. Perry, 'Knowing Christ after the Flesh (2 Cor. 5:16)', in *Biblical World* 18 (1901) 270–86; V. Weber, 'Wann und wie hat Paulus "Christus nach dem Fleische gekannt" (2 Kor. 5,16)', in *BZ* 2 (1904) 178–87; S. T. Lowrie, 'Exegetical Note on 2 Cor. v.16, 17', in *Princeton Theological Review* 4 (1906) 236–41; A. D. Martin, 'Knowing Christ κατὰ σάρκα', in *ExpTim* 24 (1912–13) 334–5; A. M. Pope, 'Paul's Previous Meeting with Jesus', in *The Expositor* 8th. ser. 26 (1923) 38–48; F. C. Porter, 'Does Paul Claim to Have Known the Historical Jesus?', in *JBL* 47 (1928) 257–75. Cf. also the remarks of A. S. Peake, 'Paul the Apostle: His Personality and Achievement', in *BJRL* 12 (1928) 368 n. 1.

45. Cf. W. H. Johnson, 'Was Paul the Founder of Christianity?', in *Princeton*

Moffatt and William Morgan in 1908. Moffatt does little more than review the work of Wrede, Kaftan, Bousset, Meyer, and Jülicher.[46] With the last he agreed that Paul was not even the 'second founder' of Christianity, but at the same time conceded that Paul's theological interpretation of Christ's death bears the marks of rabbinic dialectic. 'But this admission', Moffatt concluded, 'still leaves the core and centre of Paul's gospel to be accounted for. Jesus did not preach justification; Paul did.' Moffatt 'accounts for' this gospel by referring to Paul's 'religious experience' which was 'the direct outcome of the impression made by Jesus Christ upon him' (173). Thus far Moffatt's emphasis on Paul's religious experience and the 'impression' Jesus made on him recalls Weiß's book (to which Moffatt does not refer); but in another respect Moffatt goes beyond Weiß when he suggests that Pauline thought was, in fact, 'a genetic development of [Jesus'] original gospel' (ibid.).

Morgan's article also is mainly a review of the German discussion, and considers primarily Wrede, Kaftan, Jülicher, and Meyer.[47] Morgan's own conclusion is essentially that of Meyer. 'Paul did not pervert Jesus' gospel, although he brought into the foreground elements that were foreign to it' (58). But this was necessitated by apologetic considerations: 'The gospel had to be presented in the thought-forms of the time', says Morgan (ibid.), and then concludes as Meyer had concluded: 'Therefore the cry should be, not away from Paul back to Christ; but rather, through Paul back to Christ and to God' (ibid.).

More original than the articles of Moffatt and Morgan is the essay on 'Jesus and Paul' by C. A. A. Scott.[48] Scott challenges Wrede, as many of his German critics had, on his view of Paul's doctrine of faith (358), and contends against him (and with Wellhausen, Harnack, etc.) that Paul's thought represents a development of Jesus' teachings but no contradiction of them (359). There is indeed, he insists, substantial agreement between the two on such key issues as the Fatherhood of God and ethics (360ff). Scott acknowledges that Paul shows little interest in Jesus' earthly career (335), but ascribes this to the apostle's anticipation of Jesus' parousia, 'an expectation which would tend at least to suspend interest in the record of

Theological Review 5 (1907) 398–422, and W. Sanday in (ed.) J. Hastings, *A Dictionary of Christ and the Gospels* 2 (New York: Scribner, 1908) 888: 'That there is a real connexion, and a close connexion between the ideal laid down by Christ and that inculcated by St. Paul cannot be denied; it is really one and the same'.

46. 'Paul' (n. 42).

47. 'The Jesus–Paul Controversy', in *ExpTim* 20 (1908) 9–12, 55–8.

48. In (ed.) H. B. Swete, *Essays on Some Biblical Questions of the Day by Members of the University of Cambridge* (London: Macmillan, 1909) 329–77.

Jesus of Nazareth' (340–1). In so far as Paul's thought did differ from Jesus' teaching (Scott has reference to the two points of distinction discussed by F. C. Baur: nomology and Christology), these differences are to be explained by 'three distinctions of experience' (343): (1) Jesus never knew the sense of dependence on the authority of another, whereas Paul lived as one 'under authority'; (2) Jesus never knew a sense of guilt such as was crucial in Paul's experience; (3) Jesus, unlike Paul, never sensed the Law as an intolerable tyranny (343–4). Nevertheless, concludes Scott, 'Paul shews just that harmony with Jesus, with His aim and method, which in another we should put down to intimacy' (375). 'The thought of Jesus reaches us through Paul as well as in the records of the Gospels...' (377).

One other article in English deserves notice here. In 1909 Arthur Cushman McGiffert summed up the discussion for American readers, and then presented his own point of view.[49] To Christianity, McGiffert concluded, Jesus contributed a deep, religious piety, a 'vivid realization of God as his father and the father of his brethren, and [an] attitude of perfect trust and joyful devotion...' (18). In these respects Paul was profoundly influenced by Jesus. But, as far as the fundamental doctrines of Christianity, its ideas of redemption, salvation, atonement, the church, and the sacraments, McGiffert concluded: 'All of these had their origin ultimately in the experience of Paul and not in the teaching of Jesus' (ibid.).

Of three major articles published in the year 1912,[50] the most original and important was by Wilhelm Heitmüller.[51] Heitmüller proposes two points for discussion. First, he wishes to emphasize Paul's conscious and deliberate self-reliance and independence in his religious life and theology. He takes account of the arguments of those who insist that Paul, due to his contacts with the twelve disciples, must have known more about Jesus than his letters reveal, but insists that there is nothing in his letters which leads us necessarily to postulate that possibility (322). The frequent assertion that Paul's missionary preaching contained more about

---

49. 'Was Jesus or Paul the Founder of Christianity?', in *AJT* 13 (1909) 1–20.

50. In the interim Arthur Drews had published his book, *The Christ Myth* (tr. C. D. Burns, London: Unwin, 1910; ET of 3rd German ed. of Jena: Diederichs, 1910; the first German ed. was published in 1909), much indebted to the radical scepticism about Jesus' historicity which was characteristic of several studies published by Bruno Bauer in the 1840's. See H. J. Holtzmann, 'Paulus als Zeuge wider die Christusmythe von Arthur Drews', in *Christliche Welt* 24 (1910) 151–60.

51. 'Zum Problem Paulus und Jesus', in *ZNW* 13 (1912) 320–37, repr. in Rengstorf, *Paulusbild* (n. 1.1) 124–43.

Jesus' life and personality than we find in his letters Heitmüller regards as a conjecture which the sources do not really permit (ibid.), and concludes that, on the basis of our sources, we must only suppose Paul's missionary preaching to have centred on Jesus' incarnation, obedience, crucifixion, and resurrection (324). Paul's theology, according to his own testimony, came not from a revelation in the historical Jesus but through the living, exalted Lord (ibid.). Heitmüller's second point was, in 1912, even more original. A second factor in Paul's departure from the historical Jesus is the apostle's dependence not upon Christianity in its Palestinian-Jewish form, but in its Hellenistic form (325–6). 'Paul is separated from Jesus not only by the primitive community, but also by a second factor. The line of development reads: Jesus—the primitive community—Hellenistic Christianity—Paul' (330). In proposing Hellenistic Christianity as the background and chief factor in the formulation of Paul's thought, Heitmüller is not only criticizing those who had dealt with the Jesus–Paul problem as if there were no third term to consider, but he is also criticizing those who, like Wendt, Brückner, Wrede and many others, had described the major influence on Paul's theology as Jewish-rabbinic-apocalyptic. Heitmüller now insists that Paul was dependent on a form of Christianity which was already far from Jesus and that Paul's theology had not been an innovation, but could be explained in terms of historical origins.

The other two articles published in 1912, one by a German, one by an American, attack Wrede on the basis of conservative presuppositions and theological interests and do not significantly advance the discussion. Gerhard Kittel[52] disputes Wrede's ascription to Paul of a doctrine of Christ's pre-existence and a magical view of the sacraments (373–90, 390–8). Like others before him Kittel remarks that Paul's letters are somewhat silent about the historical Jesus because the first readers were already acquainted with the facts of his life and teaching (394). Yet Kittel finds many Pauline passages which seem to him to give much more of a picture of Jesus' character, individuality, and 'moral personality' than Wrede had acknowledged (397). Even Paul's use of κύριος and ἐν Χριστῷ are often, if not always, in contexts where the historical Jesus is in mind (e.g. 1 Cor 11.27)—399. Thus, concludes Kittel, the historical Jesus stands more in the foreground of Paul's though than is often supposed (400).

In America, J. Gresham Machen led the conservative attack against Wrede.[53] For him the 'value' of Wrede's book was the demonstration

52. 'Jesus bei Paulus', in *TSK* 85 (1912) 366–402.

53. 'Jesus and Paul', in *Biblical and Theological Studies by the Members of*

that 'Paul was no disciple of the liberal Jesus', for modern liberalism had 'produced a Jesus who [has] really but little in common with Paul' (549). The liberals, then, had created their own problem by liberalizing Jesus, and given their presuppositions, there was indeed a Jesus–Paul problem. But this liberal picture of Jesus Machen sharply attacks: 'As a teacher, ... Jesus was not the founder of Christianity. He was the founder of Christianity not because of what he said, but because of what he did.' 'Paul was a disciple of Jesus, if Jesus was a supernatural person; he was not a disciple of Jesus, if Jesus was a mere man' (577). Machen also criticized the liberals' habit of making a distinction between Paul's practical religion (or 'religious attitudes') and his doctrinal formulations. It is impossible, said Machen, 'to separate Pauline piety and Pauline theology...' (550). He also insisted that the very sparsity of information about Jesus in Paul's letters, and the casual way he includes what information they do contain, supports the view 'that for him such factual knowledge was a matter of course' (563). 'A missionary preaching', Machen said, 'that included no concrete account of the life of Jesus would have been preposterous. The claim that a crucified Jew was to be obeyed as Lord and trusted as Saviour must surely have provoked the question as to what manner of man this was' (562).

II

After World War I the Jesus–Paul debate was not resumed with anything like its prior intensity. It is significant that, in the period between 1920 and 1945, the articles and books bearing on the topic are primarily in English, not in German[54]—indicating perhaps, that only now was

the *Faculty of Princeton Theological Seminary* (New York: Scribner, 1912) 547–78.

54. An 'Appendix' in Emil Brunner's *The Mediator* (tr. O. Wyon, Philadelphia: Westminster, 1947; ET of Tübingen: Mohr, 1927) 536–46, denies the alleged contradiction between Paulinism and the message of Jesus. Although Brunner believes that 'the uniting factor between the witness of the Apostle Paul and the Message of Jesus Himself can, in the nature of the case, only be like a very slight thread, a minute point' (545), it is nonetheless real, and to be found in Jesus' eucharistic words which Paul claims to have 'received' from the master himself (543–5). German publications on this topic in the decade prior to World War II should be read in the light of the popular appeal of Alfred Rosenberg's *Der Mythus des 20. Jahrhunderts: eine Wertung der seelisch-geistigen Gestaltenkämpfe unserer Zeit* (München: Hoheneichen, 1930). Rosenberg claimed that Paul was the sole creator of the gospel of faith and grace, so much so 'that the churches are not Christian but Pauline...' (235), and that Paul the Pharisee had falsified (i.e. Judaized!) the gospel by identifying Jesus as the Jewish Messiah (605). Rosenberg's position (influenced by Paul de Lagarde and H. S. Chamber-

biblical scholarship in Britain and America taking full account of the
debate which had been raging on the Continent. However, with only a
few exceptions the articles and books produced have little original to
contribute. For example, the article by Fred G.
Bratton, 'Continuity and
Divergence in the Jesus–Paul Problem', is virtually the only contribution
to this debate appearing in the pages of the American *Journal of Biblical
Literature*.[55] He begins by noting that since such diametrically opposed
solutions have been proposed to the problem, one must conclude that a
synthetic answer is the valid one. Yet Bratton's conclusion simply
follows in the line of those who separate Paul's 'theology' from his
'religion'.

> Paul's spiritual *élan vital* was identical with that of Jesus—the creative power
> which is derived from personal fellowship with the divine. Paul's continuity with
> Jesus is seen in the realm of spiritual values (159).

In 1923 Adolf Deißmann had published some English lectures under
the title, *The Religion of Jesus and the Faith of Paul*,[56] in which he
reaffirmed the position he had already taken in his earlier volume on
Paul.[57] In that work, completely revised and published in a second
German edition in 1925, Deißmann had concluded:

> The Christ-centered Christianity of Paul is...neither a breach with the Gospel of
> Jesus nor a distortion of the Gospel of Jesus. It secures for many the evangelical
> experience of God which had been the possession of the One, and it does so by
> anchoring these many souls in the soul of the One (258).[58]

This view also characterizes the 1923 volume:

> To Paul Christ is not a person of the past, with whom he can have intercourse only
> by meditating on his words as they have been handed down. To Paul Christ is not
> a great 'historic' figure, but a reality and power of the present, an 'energy' whose
> life-giving power is daily made perfect in him (188–9).

lain) is of course properly discussed in relation to the rise of Naziism, and does
not deserve serious consideration in a discussion of the Jesus–Paul debate *per se*.
See A. R. Chandler, *Rosenberg's Nazi Myth* (Ithaca NY: Cornell Univ., 1945),
esp. 42–8.

55. 48 (1929) 149–61.

56. Tr. W. E. Wilson (London: Hodder & Stoughton, 1923); the volume had
not been previously published in German.

57. *Paul: a Study in Social and Religious History* (New York: Harper, 1957;
ET of 1925[2]; the first German ed. appeared in 1911 [Tübingen: Mohr], and the ET
was made in 1927).

58. In this citation I have slightly altered Wilson's translation where this alteration seemed to me necessary.

In England[59] J. Ernest Rattenbury also emphasized Paul's Christ-faith, the 'Jesus of personal experience', in a special section on this topic in his book, *The Testament of Paul: Studies in Doctrines Born of Evangelical Experience*.[60] 'Paul's letters', he said, 'portray the Christ whom he experienced' (61), and this 'not after the flesh, but after the Spirit' (60). However, Rattenbury cautions, Paul plainly identified this Christ of faith with Jesus of Nazareth:

> The vagueness of mysticism is avoided by Paul's identification of the Christ of his experience with the Jesus of history, and all attempts to break down such an identification endanger Christianity (71).

Therefore, the antithesis 'Jesus or Paul?' misses the point, for it fails to see beneath Paul's doctrines to his experience (93).

Meanwhile, the 'Chicago School' of social-historical research was dominating American biblical studies, and its chief spokesman, Shirley Jackson Case, had brief but significant comments on Paul's view of the historical Jesus. Paul 'could have written a gospel that would have been quite as accurate and extensive as the Gospel of Luke', he opined, but he unfortunately 'had no interest in such an enterprise'.[61] Case mentions several factors which resulted in Paul's indifference to the matter: his supreme concern for 'the heavenly Christ'; his eschatological expectation; and his need, in the face of attacks upon his apostleship, to minimize the significance of historical contact with Jesus (85–7). One who, like Paul, claims to possess the mind of Christ, need have no concern for seeking out 'traditional information about the life and teaching of the earthly Jesus' (87).

Brief notice may also be given here to an arresting article in which Hans Windisch insists that the apparent paradox of continuity and divergence between Jesus and Paul is due to a mixing, in Paul's letters, of a 'Jerusalem Gospel' and a 'Damascus Gospel'.[62] Windisch maintains that the alternative, 'historical Jesus/preached Christ', is false.

> In the Synoptic Gospels we have a Christ other than the one met in Paul. It is Christ Jesus, the one met by the earliest disciples, the authentic disciples, in Galilee and Jerusalem, and who were there forced to a decision in a completely different manner than Paul had been forced to a decision. It is the Christ who was

59. In *History and the Gospel* (New York: Scribner, 1938) C. H. Dodd does not deal with the Jesus–Paul problem, but he does use the Pauline letters as a source for the life and teaching of the historical Jesus, and even believes that 'Paul has a definite conception of the character of Jesus' (65).

60. London: Epworth, 1930, 49–93.

61. *Jesus: a New Biography* (Chicago: Univ. of Chicago, 1927) 85.

62. 'Paulus und Jesus', in *TSK* 106 (1936) 432–68.

living before there was an apostolic kerygma concerning him, before Paul, before the gospel which originated in Damascus (467).

Windisch's attempt to forge a link between Jesus and Paul by saying that the two were the same 'religious type' (Windisch compared the apostolic and messianic offices) was later regarded by W. G. Kümmel as so far-fetched as to warrant no response.[63] Kümmel himself strives to take account of both the similarities and differences in Jesus' preaching and Paul's gospel, but like Windisch is critical of the way in which Rudolf Bultmann had been stressing the historical discontinuity between Jesus and Paul.

It was, indeed, during this period between the Wars that Bultmann's initial contributions to the Jesus–Paul debate were published. In the first of two important articles Bultmann poses three questions: (1) Is Paul's thought-structure influenced by the historical (*historische*) Jesus, and is that influence direct or mediated through the primitive community? (2) What is the material relation of Paul's theology to Jesus' preaching? (3) What significance for Pauline theology has the fact of the historical (*geschichtliche*) Jesus?[64] In responding to the first question Bultmann contends that Paul first met Christianity in its Hellenistic form (the influence of Heitmüller, to whose Marburg chair Bultmann succeeded in 1921, is apparent here) and concludes: 'When one focuses on the

---

63. 'Jesus und Paulus', in *TBl* 19 (1940) 211. Ernesto Buonaiuti's attempt to define the relationship of Jesus and Paul deserves notice here ('Christus und Paulus', in *ErJb* 1940–1 [Zürich: Rhein, 1942] 257–94). Like Windisch he seeks to identify Jesus and Paul as belonging to the same religious type, although this is defined in a different way. 'The agreement of attitude between Christ and Paul presupposed by the orthodox tradition does not exist, but just as little does the unbridgeable, impenetrable distinction assumed by liberal criticism prevail. Christ and Paul are inseparably connected in the same programme: to make out of religion an enduring dynamism of "conversions" and "rebirths" which occur from moment to moment and which permit escape from the enclosing wall of tangible values into the sphere of spiritual values' (283).

64. 'Die Bedeutung des geschichtlichen Jesus für die Theologie des Paulus', in *TBl* 8 (1929) 137–51, later repr. in *Glauben und Verstehen* 1 (Tübingen: Mohr, 1933) 188–213; ET in *Faith and Understanding: Collected Essays* (London: SCM, 1969) 220–46. Page reff. herein are to the latter. Kümmel, in his most recent discussion of Jesus and Paul (see above n. 1), criticizes this threefold division of the problem as methodologically untenable 'because the questions of the *influence* of the person and teaching of Jesus on Paul and of the *meaning* of the person of Jesus for Paul are in reality only different aspects of the *one* problem of the continuity between Jesus and Paul' (171). Kümmel's reformulation of the problem has two foci: '(1) The historical connection between Jesus and Paul (i.e. the problem of continuity), (2) the material correspondence or difference between Jesus and Paul (i.e. the problem if identity)' (ibid).

essential Pauline ideas, it is clear that in them Paul is not dependent upon
Jesus. Jesus' preaching is for him—at least in essentials—irrelevant'
(191). With respect to the second matter, he affirms a far-reaching
material similarity between Paul's theology and Jesus' preaching about
the Law (for both the love-commandment is basic—191–5). Yet the two
are significantly different in that the decisive event for which Jesus
waited is proclaimed by Paul as having already *occurred* (200–1).
Bultmann criticizes Wrede and Jülicher for having, each in his own way,
interpreted Paul's theology as a theological *development* of Jesus'
message.

> The significance of Pauline theology is not that in it views of Jesus are further
> developed, but rather that in it the fact of Jesus 'having-been-there' [*Dagewesen-
> seins*] is understood in a specific manner (202).

For Paul, 'the situation of the world is fundamentally another, new, since
Jesus was there' (ibid.). [65]
 These observations lead on to Bultmann's major concern in the article,
to discover the meaning of the historical (*geschichtliche*) person of Jesus
for Paul's theology. This can be answered, he says, in a single sentence:

> ...the historical [*geschichtliche*] *person of Jesus makes Paul's preaching a
> gospel*. For Paul proclaims neither a new God-idea nor a new messianic concept,
> but rather an act of God in history [*Geschichte*], the coming of the Messiah, who
> is identical with the person of Jesus (202–3).

Bultmann does not intend to posit a complete disjunction between Paul
and Jesus even at this point, for he acknowledges that already in Jesus'
preaching there is an *implied* Christology (204) which is then formulated
in the earliest church's preaching of Jesus as God's decisive *word*
spoken, his decisive *action* (205). But the church's preaching—and
Paul's—was centred not on the 'what' (*Was*) of Jesus' life (his
character, ministry, teaching) but on its 'thatness' (*Daß*), the fact of it
(ibid.). This means that for Paul Jesus was a teacher only in so far as he
was first of all *Kyrios*; that he was an example only in so far as he was

---

65. Here Bultmann is in some accord with Albert Schweitzer whose book, *The
Mysticism of Paul the Apostle*, while begun in 1906, was published in the same
year as Bultmann's article. Says Schweitzer: '...Paul shares with Jesus the
eschatological world-view and the eschatological expectation, with all that these
imply. The only difference is the hour in the world-clock in the two cases. To use
another figure, both are looking towards the same mountain range, but whereas
Jesus sees it as lying before Him, Paul already stands upon it and its first slopes
are already behind him' (tr. W. Montgomery, London: Black, 1931 [ET of
Tübingen: Mohr, 1930], 113).

first of all acknowledged as the pre-existent Christ. And certainly Paul did not preach Christ as a 'hero', for he declared

> that the cross of Christ is a devastating judgment against all human achieving in work and wisdom, against all *kauchasthai*, all heroism, and that precisely therein lies the liberating act of God (206).

Bultmann's solution of the Jesus–Paul problem represents a sharp break with many of the most frequently recurring ideas in the previous literature on the subject. For one thing he stresses the importance of acknowledging a third factor—the primitive community—as Paul's immediate background, and like Heitmüller he suggests that Paul's inheritance was from the Hellenistic, not the Jewish side (against Wendt, Schweitzer, and many others). For another thing he refuses to separate Paul's theology from his religious experience, to interpret his theology as a dogmatic, mechanical salvation-history, or to define Paul's relationship to Jesus in terms of a common idea of God or ethical ideal. Basic to Bultmann's viewpoint is his emphasis on the *kerygma* by which Paul had been converted and of which he had become a preacher. Bultmann's remarks on this are important enough to be quoted in full.

> The kerygma does not proclaim general truth, a timeless idea, be it a God- or a Redeemer-idea, but rather a historical [*geschichtliche*] fact. But it does that not in such a manner as to make itself superfluous when it has mediated the knowledge of this fact to the hearer (in that case it would have only the role of a mediator); but rather the kerygma itself belongs to the fact.
> Therefore, one must not attempt to go behind the kerygma, using it as a 'source', in order to reconstruct a 'historical [*historische*] Jesus' with a 'messianic self-consciousness', his 'inwardness', or his 'heroism'. That would be precisely the *Christos kata sarka* which is gone. Not the historical [*historische*] Jesus, but Jesus Christ, the proclaimed, is Lord (208).

In the mid thirties Bultmann published a second article[66] in which the central question is not whether Paul's theology was dependent upon Jesus' message (he regards a negative answer to this as 'a sure result of research'—185), but whether and in what way 'the actual subject matter of Paul's theology is related to Jesus' proclamation...' (186). Bultmann argues that with respect to the Law, man's sinfulness, the transcendence of God, and even the Reign of God, Paul and Jesus were in essential, if not verbal accord. 'Thus,' says Bultmann, 'whoever finds Paul offensive und uncanny must find Jesus equally so' (194). Finally, then,

---

66. 'Jesus und Paulus', in *Jesus Christus im Zeugnis der Heiligen Schrift und der Kirche* (BEvT 2, München: Kaiser, 1936) 68–90; repr. in id., *Exegetica: Aufsätze zur Erforschung des Neuen Testaments* (ed. E. Dinkler, Tübingen: Mohr, 1967, 210–29; ET by S. M. Ogden in *Existence and Faith* (New York: Living Age Books, 1960) 183–201.

one cannot flee from Paul and return to Jesus. For what one encounters in Jesus is the same God who is encountered in Paul. ...All that one can do is to go to Jesus *through* Paul; i.e., one is asked by Paul whether he is willing to understand God's act in Christ as the event that has decided and now decides with respect both to the world and to us (201).

Schniewind's 1937 Herford lecture, which took particular note of Bultmann's essays, sought from the standpoint of a more conservative handling of the sources to show that much of what is called 'Pauline theology' is 'nothing other than the collected preaching of the first community', and that Paul himself had emphasized the unity of the church's tradition from Jesus on down. Schniewind seeks to maintain the probability that Paul's missionary preaching had contained more about the earthly Jesus than did his subsequent letters, by comparing the differences in content between the First Epistle and Gospel of John, and Acts and Luke.[67] But the character of and relationships between these writings are not sufficiently analogous to the character of and relationships between Paul's letters and preaching to lend much credibility to Schniewind's argument.

III

The years since the close of World War II yield a few scattered articles on the Jesus–Paul question, but until recently most of these have been simply restatements of positions articulated, attacked, and defended many years before. At one extreme is an ultra-liberal tirade against historic Christianity which holds that the Gospels were second century, mythological, literalizing corruptions of the profounder mystery ('trance-experience') proclaimed non-literally by Paul to and for *educated* men.[68] 'Paul knew nothing of good tidings newly preached in Galilee', says this writer; 'he spoke of Hidden Wisdom and a revelation vouchsafed to Moses long centuries before'.[69] At the other extreme are the Roman Catholics, Lattey and Stanley, who are still at work cataloguing Paul's quotations of and allusions to Jesus' sayings,[70] and

---

67. 'Die Botschaft Jesu und die Theologie des Paulus', in id. (ed. E. Kähler), *Nachgelassene Reden und Aufsätze* (Berlin: Töpelmann, 1952; repr. Gießen & Basel: Brunnen, 1987) 16–37, here 23, 34, 35.

68. R. Knight, 'Gospels and Epistles', in *Hibbert Journal* 45 (1947) 304–8, and 'Jesus or Paul? In Continuation of Gospels and Epistles', in ibid. 47 (1948) 41–9.

69. Id., 'Jesus' 47.

70. C. Lattey, 'Quotations of Christ's Sayings in St. Paul's Epistles', in *Scr* 4

the conservative Protestant, H. E. Turlington, who maintains that Paul
accurately describes Jesus' moral character, reflects his ethical teachings,
and records numerous details of his earthly career.[71] Turlington believes
he can find evidence that Paul's missionary preaching had dealt fully with
the historical Jesus, and that it was Paul's preaching especially which
influenced and made possible the writing of the canonical Gospels
(56–64)!

Anton Fridrichsen takes a position highly reminiscent of that assumed
by Machen. Fridrichsen criticizes those who describe Paul as having no
or little knowledge of and interest in the historical Jesus. They are guilty,
he says, of overlooking and denying the messianic features in the person
and work of Jesus, and of seeking 'to put together on the same level Jesus
the Messiah in his historical situation and the apostle in his'.[72]
Fridrichsen evidently seeks thus to emphasize what Machen had called
the 'supernatural Jesus'. Paul was not a disciple in the sense that he
sought to transmit and interpret Jesus' teachings; indeed, Jesus had *no*
'disciples' in that sense (245). Rather, Paul, like the Gospel writers,
sought 'to fulfil the intention of Jesus' (244–6), and this was
accomplished by preaching his death and resurrection.

> Whoever heeds the watchword: Back to Jesus! [Fridrichsen means: in the 'liberal'
> sense] will find himself further back than he foresaw. He will have to go back
> beyond Jesus to the synagogue. He stops at the Sermon on the Mount and the
> parables and thinks he is then in the company of Jesus. But even in the Sermon on
> the Mount and the parables Jesus is on the way to Calvary and the glory of the
> Father (246).

Paul's gospel, then, was 'immediately derived' from the preaching of
Jesus, and 'the origin of the Easter faith and of the Pentecost experience
lay in the person and deeds of Jesus' (253). Essentially in accord with
Fridrichsen's conclusions, but with varying emphases and critical
methodologies, are Duncan, Ridderbos and Beare.[73]

The most significant current contributions to the Jesus–Paul debate are
related to the recently re-opened and redefined 'quest of the historical

(1949) 22–4; D. M. Stanley, 'Pauline Allusions to the Sayings of Jesus', in *CBQ*
23 (1961) 26–39.

71. 'The Apostle Paul and the Gospel History', in *RevExp* 48 (1951) 35–66.
See esp. p. 55. Cf. E. Stauffer, *Jesus, Paulus, und wir* (Hamburg: Wittig, 1961).

72. 'Jesus, John, Paul', in *LQ* 3 (1951) 243–54, 353–65, here 243–4.

73. G. S. Duncan, 'From Jesus to Paul', in *SJT* 2 (1949) 1–12; H. Ridderbos,
Paul and Jesus: Origin and General Character of Paul's Preaching of Christ (tr.
D. H. Freeman, Philadelphia: Presbyterian & Reformed Publishing Co., 1958: ET
of Dutch of Kampen: Kok, 1952); F. W. Beare, 'Jesus and Paul', in *CJT* 5 (1959)
79–86.

Jesus', and the attendant discussion of hermeneutics and historical research.[74] This converging of the Jesus–Paul problem and the 'new quest' has resulted in a new formulation of the old question. Now it is not so much the question of the relationship of Jesus and Paul as it is the more inclusive question of the relation of Jesus and the kerygma. Bultmann's work has directly influenced this reformulation of the question, and it is to this issue that Bultmann's Heidelberg lecture, 'Das Verhältnis der urchristlichen Christusbotschaft zum historischen Jesus',[75] is directed. There Bultmann re-emphasizes, in fact sharpens, a distinction he had made previously between two questions—on the one hand, the question of the historical continuity between Jesus and the kerygma, and on the other, the question of the material, or substantial relationship between them (15–16).

With respect to the first of these questions Bultmann is prepared to acknowledge a historical continuity between Jesus and the kerygma only in so far as one may say it is the historical Jesus who was preached as the Christ. But there are two important qualifications on which Bultmann insists. First, this historical continuity is not between the Jesus of history and the Christ of the kerygma, but between the Jesus of history and the primitive Christian proclamation of the kerygma (18). Second, this proclamation of the Christ of faith need not go beyond the 'that' of Jesus' historicity; Bultmann does not acknowledge any historical continuity between the kerygma and the 'what' and 'how' of the historical Jesus (20).

In discussing the second question Bultmann distinguishes two types of approach which have been followed in an effort to establish a material correspondence between Jesus' teaching and the Christian gospel (20–1). One focuses on the kerygma and attempts to prove by historical-critical analysis that it presupposes the objective historicity of Jesus' person and ministry. Bultmann is critical of this attempt not only because he believes it impossible to separate scientifically 'faith' and 'fact' in the kerygma (e.g. in the Gospels), but also because he fears that its practitioners (e.g. Althaus) think thereby somehow to 'legitimize' the kerygma. But the kerygma itself, Bultmann contends, offers no such objective (historical) legitimation of the faith it proclaims (21–6).

The second approach focuses on Jesus' preaching and ministry and attempts to find there the kerygma *in nuce* (27–30). That Jesus' message

74. See, e.g., Braun, 'Sinn' (n. 1.5) esp. 342–7, 364–8. Braun believes there is a factual, but not a historical connection between Paul and Jesus, and that this is in the area of anthropology, not Christology.

75. See n. 1.5. The following reff. are to the English version.

had a certain 'kerygmatic character' Bultmann does not deny, nor even that one may find there an implied Christology. 'How far does all this take us?' he asks. 'The argument that the kerygma goes back to the claim of Jesus contained in his activity does not yet demonstrate the material unity between the activity and preaching of Jesus and the kerygma' (30). In the kerygma, he says, not the historical but the exalted Jesus speaks.

> The Christ of the kerygma has, as it were, displaced the historical Jesus and authoritatively addresses the hearer—every hearer. So how can we speak of an identity of Jesus' activity with the kerygma in the sense that in Jesus' deed and word the kerygma is already contained *in nuce*? (Ibid.)

That Bultmann's questions and answers have been influential in setting the stage for the most recent discussion is demonstrated in Jüngel's monograph where he summarizes at the outset the questions most important to discuss:[76]

> 1. To what extent does the historical ['historische'] Jesus belong to the theology of the New Testament?
> 2. To what extent had Paul to be a theologian in his preaching of the historical ['historischen'] Jesus as the crucified and risen Lord?
> 3. What does that mean for the relationship of the Pauline teaching about righteousness to the preaching of Jesus?
> 4. How far are eschatological themes determinative for this relationship?
> 5. To what extent does the historical ['historische'] Jesus himself become an eschatological theme and to what extent is he this?
> 6. In what eschatological mode is the historical ['historische'] Jesus expressed ['zur Sprache kommt'] in Paul's teaching about righteousness?
> 7. What relationship between the preaching of Jesus and faith in Jesus Christ follows from this?

IV

Jacques Barzun has keenly distinguished 'intellect' on the one hand, and 'intelligence' on the other.[77] While intelligence is 'an individual and private possession' which 'dies with the owner unless he embodies it in more or less lasting form' (5), intellect, he says,

> is the capitalized and communal form of live intelligence; it is intelligence stored up and made into habits of discipline, signs and symbols of meaning, chains of reasoning. ...Intellect is at once a body of common knowledge and the channels through which the right particle of it can be brought to bear quickly, without the effort of redemonstration, on the matter in hand (4).

---

76. *Paulus* (n. 1) 16.

77. *The House of Intellect* (New York: Harper, 1959) 1–6.

And so it is appropriate and necessary that we ask with respect to the continuing debate which has been the subject of this survey: What has it taught us? To what relatively firm conclusions has it come? To what extent has it directed us to meaningful questions? At what points has it served to caution us against travelling 'dead end' streets? Or, to put the matter into a single question, and in terms of intellectual history: What is the residue of 'live intelligence' which remains as 'community property', which has been built into our 'House of Intellect' as a result of the Jesus–Paul debate? And what does all this portend for the future?

Let us begin by observing three relatively firm conclusions at which the debate may be said to have arrived. *First*, one must acknowledge that the Pauline letters (whether we accept Tübingen's four, Bultmann's seven, or even all thirteen) contain only fragmentary materials about the life and teaching of Jesus. This fact is most dramatically apparent when one asks what, for example, would be known about Jesus' life if, of the New Testament materials, only Paul's letters had survived. One would know that Jesus had been born under the Law as a Jew (Gal 4.4), of the line of David (Rom 1.3), that he had at least two brothers (1 Cor 9.5), one of whom was James (e.g. Gal 1.19), and twelve disciples (1 Cor 15.5), of whom he mentions by name only Peter (Cephas) and John (e.g. Gal 2.9); that he ate a last meal with them, and on that same night was betrayed (1 Cor 11.23ff); that as a consequence of his obedience to God's will Jesus gave himself up to death (Gal 1.4; Phil 2.8), was executed on a cross (Gal 3.1; 1 Cor 2.2, *et passim*), and was buried (1 Cor 15.4; Rom 6.4). These are the only 'biographical' data that Paul's letters yield. One finds there no details about Jesus' birth, no direct mention of Jesus' teaching or healing ministry, no confession at Caesarea Philippi, no transfiguration, no cleansing of the Temple, no conflict with the authorities, no Gethsemane scene, no trial, no thieves crucified with Jesus, no last words from the cross, no soldiers, no weeping women, no word about the place or time of the crucifixion, no mention of Joseph or Mary, or of John the baptizer, or of Judas, or of Pilate.

The situation is not very different when we inquire into the matter of the teachings of Jesus reported in Paul's letters. Of course it is true that the phrase 'teachings of Jesus' is not to be found in them at all. Paul refers, rather, to 'the word' or 'charge' of the 'Lord', and this is of the greatest significance. Moreover, there are only three certain instances in the Pauline homologoumena where Paul cites a 'word of the Lord', all of these in 1 Corinthians. In 7.10–11 he cites a saying about divorce ('To the married I give charge, not I but the Lord, that the wife should not separate [or: be separated] from her husband...'), in 9.14 he cites a saying about financial support ('...the Lord commanded that those who proclaim the gospel should get their living by the gospel'), and in 11.23ff, drawing on the liturgical tradition, he quotes the words which institute the eucharist. (References in 1 Cor 14.37 and 1 Thess 4.15 to, respectively, a 'word' or 'command' of the Lord are generally regarded as references to 'prophetic' words, not to traditional sayings of the earthly Jesus.)

The sparsity of biographical material and direct reference to Jesus' words has prompted interpreters from the earliest (Paret) to the most recent (Lattey, Stanley) years of the debate to search out *allusions* to Jesus' personality, ministry and words. The search for allusions to Jesus' personal moral character and to his career has never been very successful, in spite of repeated references to such passages as 2 Corinthians 10.1 ('the meekness and gentleness of Christ'), Philippians 2.1–11 (Christ's humility and obedience), and 2 Corinthians 12.12 (where Paul's statement that 'the signs of a true apostle were performed among you in all patience, with signs and wonders and mighty works' is supposed to prove that Paul attached significance to Jesus' miracles).

The most probable instances of Pauline allusions to Jesus' teachings are Rom 12.14; 1 Cor 4.12 (see Luke 6.28*a*; cf. Matt 5.44) and Rom 14.14 (see Mark 7.15; Matt 15.11). Possible instances are Rom 13.8–10; Gal 5.13–14 (see Mark 12.31; cf. Matt 22.39; Luke 10.27). Much less likely, but worth noting, are 1 Cor 13.2 (cf. Mark 11.23; Matt 17.20; 21.21) and Rom 13.7 (cf. Mark 12.17; Matt 22.21; Luke 20.25). The identification of all allusions, however, is a very subjective and therefore problematic enterprise, and may be said to have reached the point of no return in the *tour de force* of Resch in 1904,[78] and it is remarkable that this search still has its practitioners. Thus, one may readily identify as a *second* relatively firm conclusion, that the Jesus–Paul debate has not ever been significantly advanced, nor will a solution to the Jesus–Paul problem ever be finally achieved, by locating parallel passages in Paul and the Gospels. This was seen already by F. C. Baur and repeatedly emphasized in the thick of the debate by Sturm, Vischer, and Brückner. This is so, as Brückner observed, partly because of the difficulties necessarily involved in recovering the 'ipsissima verba Jesu', and partly because such parallels, even where they are established, do not necessarily prove genetic dependence.[79]

But there is yet another flaw in this hunt for parallels, indicated by a *third* relatively firm conclusion one may draw from the history of the Jesus–Paul debate: the issue cannot be fruitfully discussed so long as a

---

78. See above n. 29.

79. For a recent criticism of the scholarly disease, 'parallelomania', see S. Sandmel, 'Parallelomania', in *JBL* 81 (1962) 1–13.

narrowly bifocal concern is retained. The most significant contributions
to the discussion have been those which have seen that the problem is far
broader than the relation of the individual, Jesus of Nazareth, to the
individual, Paul of Tarsus. Schweitzer saw this clearly and thus criticized
Maurice Goguel for posing the issue in an unreal form: 'The statement of
the problem which is here presupposed leaves out the middle term,
primitive Christianity'.[80] Heitmüller, making a similar point, had,
however, inserted an additional factor: *Hellenistic* Christianity. That this
insight has been appropriated by the most recent discussants is shown by
the way in which the problem is now more broadly defined in terms of
Jesus and the earliest kerygma (Bultmann, *et al.*). Thus, Schmithals is
perfectly correct when he describes the problem as having to do
essentially with the origins of Christianity.[81]

But new results always raise new issues, and that is certainly the case
with each of the three points just recorded. First, granting the sparsity of
biographical and teaching material relating to Jesus found in Paul, what
accounts for this? The radical answer that Paul had no such historical
information because there was none to be had, although it has a recent
exponent,[82] does not deserve serious consideration. Chapters 7 and 11 of
1 Corinthians supply firm evidence that, at the very least, Paul was
acquainted with Jesus' words as mediated in the catechetical and
liturgical traditions; and Galatians (1.18 *et passim*) requires us to
acknowledge that, in his contacts with Jesus' disciples, Paul at least had
the *opportunity* for learning about the historical Jesus.[83] The custom of
conservative interpreters (e.g. Paret, Vischer, Kittel, Machen, Turlington,
but also Kümmel) has been to hold that Paul is so silent about the
historical Jesus because he can presuppose his readers' knowledge of
Jesus' life and teaching. This knowledge, it is asserted, had been relayed
to them in the apostle's missionary preaching. But Heitmüller was correct
in criticizing such a point as pure conjecture,[84] and beyond this one must
ask whether it is not true that, even though the letters in general pre-

80. *Paul* (n. 3) 160.

81. 'Paulus' (n. 1) esp. 153.

82. Ray Knight, 'Gospels' (n. 68) 368.

83. G. D. Kilpatrick's attempt to show that Gal 1.18 refers specifically to the
dissemination of information about the historical Jesus is hardly successful
('Galatians i:18: ἱστορῆσαι Κηφᾶν', in [ed.] A. J. B. Higgins, *New Testament
Studies in Memory of Thomas Walter Manson, 1893–1958* [Manchester Univ.,
1959] 144–9), and Heitmüller's point that contact with Jesus' disciples does not
necessarily prove Paul's knowledge of his career and character is still valid.

84. Above, p. 31.

suppose the apostle's missionary preaching, they nonetheless provide some clues as to its probable content. One thinks immediately of 1 Corinthians 2.1–2 ('When I came to you, brethren, I did not come proclaiming to you the mystery of God in lofty words or wisdom. For I decided to know nothing among you except Jesus Christ and him crucified') and 1 Thessalonians 1.9–10 (where Paul refers to his initial visit and 'how [the Thessalonians] turned to God from idols, to serve a living and true God, and to wait for his Son from heaven, whom he raised from the dead, Jesus who delivers us from the wrath to come'). There is nothing in these summaries of his missionary preaching in Corinth and Thessalonica to support the conjecture that the narration of Jesus' earthly life or instruction into his sayings was the central, or even an essential part of it. Moreover, in Romans Paul cannot presuppose a knowledge of his own previous message, and, although he strives to summarize its essential points, he says no more there (if as much) about the earthly Jesus than he does in the letters written to congregations of his own founding. Scott's suggestion that Paul's anticipation of the parousia precluded any substantial interest in Jesus' career, and Case's additional one that Paul had to minimize his historical contacts with Jesus for polemical reasons, are at least worthy for discussion.

The second conclusion, that the collection of parallel passages is not ultimately very helpful, leads us only to the new question, whether and how more substantial *material correspondences* may be detected between Jesus and Paul. That there are material correspondences almost every participant in the debate has been willing to agree. But there has been large disagreement as to how these are to be defined and detected. Some speak in terms of common 'religious ideals' (the Fatherhood of God, the brotherhood of man, etc.) or 'spiritual values'. One may list here the names especially of Wendt, Brückner, Sanday, Scott, McGiffert, and Bratton. Since Bultmann, however, this particular way of defining the correspondence has been increasingly attacked. Bultmann himself defines the essential correspondence between Jesus' preaching and Paul's gospel in terms of the kerygma, the coming and present-ness of God's Word addressing man and calling him to decision. And now in Jüngel's vocabulary the concept of speech-event ('Sprachereignis') seems to be the key for establishing a material correspondence between the two.

Our third point was that the debate needs to be broadened so as to include more than Jesus and Paul as isolated figures. Here again new questions arise, and indeed were already being raised in the first decade of our century. They concern the religio-cultural milieu not only of Jesus and Paul, but of earliest Christianity as a whole. Is Jesus to be viewed as a unique phenomenon in world history, or against his background in

Judaism? If the latter, what *kind* of Judaism? Is Paul to be viewed against a rabbinic-Jewish-apocalyptic background (Wendt, Wrede, Brückner, Schweitzer, etc.) or in terms of a Hellenistic one (Bousset, Heitmüller, Morgan, Bultmann, etc.)? How important a role did Oriental and Gnostic tendencies play within the earliest church? To what extent did they figure—either positively by the contribution of new categories and concepts, or negatively as the objects of the church's polemic—in the formation of early Christian doctrine?

In stating these 'new' questions we must not lose sight of a very fundamental issue which has been a central matter for discussion at least since Wendt's article in 1894: what accounts for the distinctive features of Paul's gospel? What is the origin of the differences between Jesus and Paul? This, of course, thrusts us back upon the prior question which asks about the kind and extent of the differences between the two. Most of the scholars here surveyed would agree that there are *formal* differences, at least, between Jesus' preaching and Paul's gospel relating to vocabulary, style, etc. But there is widespread disagreement as to whether these are 'only' formal differences, and as to the extent of them. Six distinguishable positions may be listed.

1. First, the view that Paul simply provided the 'technical' statement of Jesus' religion (Mair, Hoyle), and that there is therefore a virtual identity between the preaching of Jesus and Paul. This is certainly also the basic position of Matheson, Schmoller, and Turlington, each of whom regards the Pauline letters as actually *confirming* the preaching of Jesus as it is present in the gospel tradition.

2. Only a short step removed from this view is the one shared by Gloatz, Wellhausen, Harnack, and Deißmann, that Paul was the *interpreter* of Jesus, perhaps even—as some of these men held—the one who best understood Jesus. Although Jüngel represents a perspective in some ways very different from that of these earlier men, his final assessment of Paul's relationship to Jesus is not dissimilar to theirs. For he too insists that Paul's doctrine of righteousness is but the interpretation—indeed the necessary interpretation—of Jesus' preaching about the Kingdom of God.

3. Diametrically opposed to the notion that Paul simply continues, or at most interprets, the message of Jesus, is the radical assertion that Paul was essentially an *innovator*. This concept is present in its most un-refined and unacceptable form in Nietzsche (who called the apostle 'crafty' and 'superstitious') and Knight (who called him 'profound'), but it also appears in F. C. Baur, Weinel, and Wernle.

A term which constantly recurs in the Jesus–Paul discussion as a description of Paul's theology in relation to Jesus is: 'development'. Paul, it has been said very often, was the 'developer' of Jesus' message. Here, however, one must be careful to distinguish between two very different views of this development.

4. On the one hand Wendt, Wrede, and Goguel regarded Paul's theology as an essentially *illegitimate* development of Jesus' message: thus the 'Back to Jesus' slogan.

5. But, on the other hand, Hilgenfeld, Kaftan, Meyer, Weiß, Moffatt, Morgan, Scott, Fridrichsen, Duncan, and Beare all regard Paul's doctrinal teaching as a *legitimate* extension and development of Jesus' message.

6. Finally, Bultmann may be listed as the most prominent present exponent of the view that Paul's theology is not identical with Jesus' message, nor explicitly an interpretation of it, nor historically a development from it, either in the positive or negative sense. Rather, for Bultmann, Paul's theology is an explication of the kerygma of the Hellenistic church, and its subject-matter is neither the message nor the deeds of Jesus, but the present-ness of God's address to men in the Risen Lord.

But now we must return to the question of how one is to account for the distinctively Pauline traits. What factors determined the form and content of Paul's theology? This is a question whether one regards it as a continuation of Jesus' message, an interpretation of it, a development from it, or a unique innovation. Our literature provides instances of three possible answers, no two of which need necessarily be regarded as mutually exclusive. Each of these answers usually involves its exponent in some particular view of Paul's place and function within the developing Christian church, and one may perhaps venture to speak of them as stressing, respectively, the historical, psychological, and theological origin of Paul's gospel.

First is the view that Paul's contribution to the church was in universalizing the gospel and that his theological statement of it was called forth by the apologetic and polemical needs of his day. Here one meets a *historical* explanation for Paul's theology, and it is the position taken, for example, by McIlvaine, Wernle, Vischer, Meyer, and Morgan.

This perspective on Paul is not absent from Wrede's interpretation, but neither is it determinative for him. Wrede refers Paul's theology basically to his own unique piety, and particularly to the transforming event of his conversion, the essence of which was the conviction, 'Jesus is Messiah'. This was the 'germ' from which his theology supposedly evolved. Wrede, however, did not develop this 'theology of experience' motif as much as some others. Weizsäcker, for example, spoke of Paul's 'intuitions' in a way reminiscent of F. C. Baur's 'principle of Christian consciousness', and similar passages can be found in the books of Wernle and Weinel.

The emphasis on the *psychological* origins of Paul's theology is most apparent, however, in the works of Weiß and Deißmann, both of whom take Paul's conversion experience as the key to the structure and scope of his gospel. One also encounters British and American exponents of this view, notably Moffatt, Scott, McGiffert, and Rattenbury.[85] Along with this stress on the psychological importance of Paul's conversion often goes the insistence that Paul's doctrine is not only separable, but necessarily to be separated from his personal piety, that his theology is distinct from his religion (so, for example, Hilgenfeld, Mair, Meyer, McGiffert, and Bratton). This arbitrary separation of the two was rooted in nineteenth-century presuppositions and was characteristically used as a way of relating the 'religious ideals' of Jesus and Paul. Machen and Bultmann, although of course with very different results, have rightly sought to maintain the integrity of these two.

Finally, there is the attempt to explain the origin of the distinctively Pauline gospel in a *theological* way. This is perhaps the appropriate term for describing Bultmann's position as he sets it forth in his *Theology of the New Testament*.

> Standing within the frame of Hellenistic Christianity [Paul] raised the theological motifs that were at work in the proclamation of the Hellenistic church to the clarity of theological thinking; he called to attention the problems latent in the Hellenistic proclamation and brought them to a decision; and thus—so far as our sources permit an opinion on the matter—became the founder of Christian theology.[86]

Here one may also refer to Jüngel's recent book, although between the positions represented by Bultmann and Jüngel there is an important difference: Bultmann describes Paul as a theologian of the Hellenistic church, that is, one who develops theologically the faith of the post-Easter community, while Jüngel describes Paul as a theologian of the preaching of Jesus, one who develops theologically the motifs already present in his teaching about God's Reign.[87]

---

85. See also S. M. Gilmour, 'Paul and the Primitive Church', in *JR* 25 (1945) 119–28, who maintains that 'it is difficult to overemphasize the importance of Paul's conversion experience for his life and thought as a Christian' (122). 'Paul's gospel was determined by his conversion experience, and there was little place in it for a heroic Christ, a didactic religion, or a nonmystical faith' (125). Gilmour also lists Paul's Hellenistic environment and upbringing and his 'own genius' as having significantly influenced his theology.

86. 1, 187 (tr. K. Grobel, New York: Scribner, 1951; ET of Tübingen: Mohr, 1948–53).

87. *Paulus* (n. 1) esp. 281–3.

This brings us to a final issue, and the one which seems to be at the centre of the Jesus–Paul question as it is now being formulated: To what extent are the questions of historical and material correspondence in theology distinct? Or, to put it another way, How important is the historical element in the church's kerygma? Bultmann urges a clear distinction between history and kerygma, and wants to keep the questions of historical continuity and material correspondence strictly separate. With this Jüngel disagrees,[88] and holds that the very essence of the kerygma is its identification of the *eschaton* and *history* ('Geschichte').[89]

It is not easy to consolidate all these issues of the past and present into any single project for the future. Further research will necessarily and properly be carried on at many points simultaneously. But it is at least clear from this survey and analysis of the discussion so far, that in the future scholars must concentrate not on what or how much Paul knew about the historical Jesus, but rather on the way he employed and applied the knowledge he did have, and what place the Jesus of history had in relation to the heart and centre of his preaching.

---

88. Ibid 273 and n. 1 (273–4).

89. Ibid. 272 *et passim*. For an important critique of Jüngel's book, see J. M. Robinson, 'The New Hermeneutic at Work', in *Int* 18 (1964) 346–59.

3

PAUL AND THE EARLY CHRISTIAN JESUS-TRADITION

Nikolaus Walter

I

Are there any new aspects of this much-discussed topic which merit renewed consideration? What has made the theme once more of such interest that a series of seminars of the SNTS should be devoted to it? Within the context of the tradition- and form-critical study of the early Christian Jesus-tradition we usually work with the picture of a tradition that developed and took shape gradually and in different ways; it was eventually gathered up by various groups and finally took on a literary form in the (Synoptic) Gospels.[1] From such a perspective Paul's sparing use of Jesus-tradition in his letters, in other words in that part of his work that is directly accessible to us, is noteworthy and gives us food for thought. But this observation has not been regarded as too surprising historically, and was not felt to be a grievous problem theologically— especially not when, in the tradition of the church's faith in Christ as formulated in the Apostolic or Nicene Creeds, one could easily show that even Paul certainly 'taught' that which was essential for our salvation in the Christ-event—the incarnation, the passion, the crucifixion and the resurrection of Christ. In addition the hermeneutical debate at the start of the 'New Quest of the Historical Jesus' in the 60's made it quite clear that the theologically decisive question of continuity in *substance* between Jesus' preaching of the kingdom of God and Paul's gospel of justification was not dependent on particular assumptions about the history of *tradition*, but could be approached and answered in other ways.[2]

---

1. One may mention as representative of this way of viewing things the volume edited by H. Köster and J. M. Robinson, *Trajectories through Early Christianity* (Philadelphia: Fortress, 1971).

The situation now seems to have altered. Or perhaps it would be more correct to say that another starting-point for the investigation of the early Christian Jesus-tradition has again come into the limelight. Increasingly a picture is painted of the post- or even pre-Easter beginnings of the Jesus-tradition which tends to assume that the pre-Synoptic tradition was already formed and gathered together to the widest possible extent *before* the post-Easter beginnings of the history of the church. Of course the tradition of Jesus' sayings is primarily in view here.[3] Now for such a starting-point it is certainly a serious problem that Paul's letters display so scanty a knowledge of Jesus-tradition, especially when one supposes that Paul three years after becoming a Christian at the latest (Gal 1.18) not only became acquainted with the entire extent of the Jesus-tradition, but also naturally received it as something which he was to be actively involved in passing on. The problem becomes particularly pressing theologically if with this view of the tradition there is linked a further presupposition (admittedly one that is far from being openly discussed nowadays, but which rather is operative beneath the surface): the continuity in substance between Jesus' ministry and that of Paul can only be assured if one can show as extensive as possible a continuity of tradition between the two. At any rate that can be the only explanation of the earnest zeal with which some are again concerned to extend as far as possible the scope of the Jesus-material that can be detected within the Pauline corpus.[4]

2.   In my view the following works point the way ahead: in German Jüngel's *Paulus* (n. 2.1), in English J. M. Robinson, *A New Quest for the Historical Jesus* (SBT 25, London: SCM, 1959—also in a revised German ed. as *Kerygma und historischer Jesus*, Zürich: Theologischer, 1960). Rightly, too, W. G. Kümmel in his presidential address to the General Meeting of the SNTS in 1963 emphasized the distinction between the two questions of the 'historical connection between Jesus and Paul' and of the 'agreement or difference in substance' between them: 'Jesus' (n. 1.5) 171=*Heilsgeschehen* 447.

3.   Among earlier works that show this tendency are B. Gerhardsson's *Memory and Manuscript: Oral Tradition and Written Transmission in Rabbinic Judaism and Early Christianity* (ASNU 22, Uppsala & Lund: Gleerup, 1961) and *Tradition and Transmission in Early Christianity* (Lund: Gleerup, 1964), summarized and developed in German in id., *Die Anfänge der Evangelientradition* (Wuppertal: Brockhaus, 1977). As an important more recent example we may mention R. Riesner, *Jesus als Lehrer: eine Untersuchung zum Ursprung der Evangelien-Überlieferung* (Tübingen: Mohr, 1981). However, Riesner too—despite the sub-title of his work—in practice concentrates only on the beginnings of the sayings-tradition; only peripherally (pp. 487ff) does he touch on the first beginnings of the narrative-tradition.

Any who are unwilling simply to retreat from this set of problems with a 'non liquet' have to resort to hypotheses and will always be compelled to include hypothetical assumptions in some form or other among their deliberations. The question is just what scope one should give to such hypotheses, what range one is able to allow them, before one strays from the field of arguable views into the realm of pure fantasy.

So we can, of course, on the one hand assume as a hypothesis that Paul knew the entire early Christian Jesus-tradition in a fixed form and took it with him on his missionary journeys. The other extreme would be the view that Paul only knew that Jesus-tradition of which he gives evidence in his extant letters, or not significantly more. This too is of course a hypothesis; it must employ an argument from silence. The first hypothesis on the other hand has to come to terms with the fact that it cannot adduce any strong argument in its support apart from prior hypotheses (concerning how Jesus-tradition was handed down); rather it is very rapidly involved in severe internal tensions *vis-à-vis* the Pauline texts: for it is then necessary, if it is postulated that Paul knew 'all', first to find hypothetical reasons (yet further hypotheses) for the absence of any trace of considerable portions of the Jesus-tradition in Paul's letters.[5]

It therefore seems to me that a more useful starting-point for this study is the 'minimal hypothesis'—as long as one, in holding this assumption, remains open to the possibility that Paul may have known more sayings of Jesus than are directly attested in his letters. On this understanding I hope in the following to base myself as far as possible directly on the texts and to interpret them.

---

4.   As the latest examples may be mentioned D. C. Allison, 'The Pauline Epistles and the Synoptic Gospels: the Patterns of Parallels', in *NTS* 28 (1982) 1–32, and P. Stuhlmacher, 'Jesustradition im Römerbrief? Eine Skizze', in *TBei* 14 (1983) 240–50.

5.   A peculiar solution to this problem is found in L. Goppelt, *Theologie des Neuen Testaments* 2 (Göttingen: Vandenhoeck & Ruprecht, 1976) 370–1 (ET: Grand Rapids: Eerdmans, 1981–2), to which Stuhlmacher, ibid. 242 and n. 12, expressly appeals. It is Goppelt's view that the silence of the early Christian letters (including Paul's) can be satisfactorily explained by the 'observation that the activity of the earthly Jesus is strictly related to his special eschatological situation. ...As such it cannot be transferred to the Church's situation.' Thereby any interest in Jesus-tradition is so deprived of its decisive motivation that the emergence of a collection of sayings of the Lord (like Q) is really unintelligible, even if on the other hand it can thus be more easily explained why Paul was not particularly interested in the Jesus-tradition.

II

Any treatment of this subject should start from the really *obvious stock of traditional Jesus-material* in those Pauline letters that are generally recognized as 'genuine'.[6] It is true that this stock is not entirely uncontroversial, but its general outlines can still be sketched.

A

The *explicit references* to 'words of the Lord' by Paul can be quickly listed:

	(Synoptic parallels:)
1 Thess 4.15ff (to 5.3?)	Matt 24.30–1, 43, 39 (partly with parr.)
1 Cor 7.10–11	Mark 10.12 + 11; also Matt 5.32 par.
1 Cor 9.14 (cf. Gal 6.6?)	Luke 10.7 (Matt 10.10*b*)
1 Cor 11.23–5	Luke 22.19–20; Mark 14.22–4 par.

We may also mention 2 Cor 12.9 as a further 'word of the Lord'; at this point it is of course made plain by 12.8 and 9*a* that Paul does not know of this 'word' from some tradition or other, but has had it spoken directly to him by the Lord. But we should also be clear that neither here nor anywhere else does Paul lay any weight on the distinction which we are wont to draw between the 'earthly' and the 'exalted' *Kyrios*.

It is certainly harder to decide whether or not we should include amongst the express quotations of sayings of the Lord those sayings whose connection with the tradition of the sayings of Jesus can be fairly reliably established, and in citing which Paul is clearly aware of uttering something that is connected with the *'Kyrios* Jesus'. I am thinking particularly of Rom 14.14*a* (with its 'variants' in 1 Cor 6.13 and 8.8*a*); however Gal 5.14 and Rom 13.8–10 could also be considered here. Yet these passages should preferably be discussed under the heading of 'indirect references'.

In quoting the tradition of the Lord's Supper in 1 Cor 11.23–5, where he uses the language of tradition ('receive—hand down'), Paul himself draws attention to the fact that here he is dealing with a piece of tradition that exists in a fixed form even in its wording (although it can remain an

---

6. As far as I can see to all intents and purposes the position would not be altered in the discussion if one were to include, say, 2 Thess, Col, Eph or the Pastorals in our investigation. Amongst the letters generally recognized as genuine Phil, Gal and Philemon scarcely provide any relevant material.— Questions of the unity and integrity of the Pauline letters assumed to be genuine can be left to one side in the context of the present discussion.

open question whether this tradition is written or oral). But that can in no way be immediately assumed to be true of the other 'quotations' of sayings of Jesus. In most cases a fixed form of words is out of the question, let alone one fixed in a written form; that can be adequately shown by comparing the available parallels from the Synoptic Gospels or by pointing to the difficulty which we have in declaring a particular Synoptic passage to be a true parallel. Paul's having tradition in the shape of fixed formulae to hand in the case of 1 Cor 11.23–5 is quite obviously connected with its use in liturgical rites (or in catechetical instruction about rites). The same is true of 1 Cor 15.3–5 which is also introduced with the explicit language of tradition. Neither passage allows us to draw conclusions as to the way in which Paul learnt and transmitted tradition about Jesus in general.

Yet we may compare the way in which Paul deals with texts from the 'scriptures' (of the Old Testament). In this case he clearly had a fixed traditional text, and yet many questions remain unanswered, and not only in the notorious case of 1 Cor 2.9.[7] Here too a distinction should be drawn between (1) explicit quotations with quotation formulae, which are meant to be verbatim quotations (even if one then too must in some instances grant that liberties have been taken with regard to accuracy in quoting), then (2) references to particular Old Testament texts even though they are not 'quoted' in the strict sense, and finally (3) the non-specific use of Old Testament phrases and ways of speaking without any specific or intentional reference to a particular text; in this last case the exegete can yet demonstrate that this passage or that is echoed; this is not being unfair to Paul, but at the same time it cannot be assumed that Paul himself had precisely this passage in mind. So, where there is no explicit reference to a saying of the Lord, one can neither exclude *a priori* a deliberate reference to a saying of Jesus, nor on the other hand can one assume such a reference to be self-evident without giving more precise reasons for the assumption.

B

So we come to passages where connections with traditional sayings of Jesus may be discerned, but where these *connections are not made directly* by Paul himself. The scope of this essay does not allow us to deal with all the passages where a relationship of this sort to Jesus-traditions could at least be suggested.[8] I will therefore mention only

---

7. To my knowledge the most recent treatment of this text is by K. Berger: 'Zur Diskussion über die Herkunft von 1 Kor ii.9', in *NTS* 24 (1977–8) 271–83; he adduces a wealth of instances of the maxim quoted by Paul, but does not suggest Paul's literary dependence on one of these 'sources'. Cf. also now D.-A. Koch, *Die Schrift als Zeuge des Evangeliums* (BHT 69, Tübingen: Mohr, 1986) 36–41, as well as the treatment of Paul's use of 'scripture' throughout this book.

those cases which seem to me to be to some extent clear; these will form a minimum (which can be expanded) which our discussions can with some confidence use as a starting-point.

It seems fairly clear that a whole network of connections with sayings of Jesus is to be found in the paraenesis of Rom 12.9–21; in particular the following may be mentioned:

Rom 12.14	—Luke 6.28*a* (Matt 5.44*b v.l.*)
Rom 12.17*a* (1 Thess 5.15*a*)	—Luke 6.29/Matt 5.39*b*–41
Rom 12.18	—Mark 9.50/Matt 5.9
Rom 12.19–21	—Luke 6.27*a* + 35/ Matt 5.44*a*.

A similar 'nest' seems to occur in 1 Cor 4.11–13; cf.

1 Cor 4.11*a*	—Luke 6.21*a*/Matt 5.6; 10.9–10; 11.19
1 Cor 4.12*b*–13	—Luke 6.22–3/Matt 5.11–12; Luke 6.27–8 (Matt 5.44)

In these two instances we can assume that there is a connection with the tradition of Jesus' sayings, since the sayings are clearly connected in the case of the Jesus-tradition too (in the basic components of the 'Sermon on the Plain' or the 'Sermon on the Mount'). But we still have to leave the question open whether Paul, in using these sayings, did so in the consciousness that these were sayings *of Jesus*.[9] There is no indication that he did so.[10] Stuhlmacher's opinion, that the readers of each of these letters would have been in a position to identify 'allusions and references' to Jesus-tradition 'inasmuch as they had been instructed in the Jesus-tradition by Paul himself and other early Christian teachers'

---

8. Apart from the articles mentioned in n. 4 cf. also: H. Schürmann, '"Das Gesetz des Christus" (Gal 6,2): Jesu Verhalten und Wort als letztgültige sittliche Norm nach Paulus', in (ed.) J. Gnilka, *Neues Testament und Kirche (Festschrift* for R. Schnackenburg, Freiburg-i-B., etc.: Herder, 1974) 282–300, here 285f. Stuhlmacher ('Jesustradition' [n. 4] 240) remarks of Allison's list of parallels ('Epistles' [n. 4] 20) that they will 'unfortunately only partly pass a careful critical scrutiny'. That will always be the case when one is concerned to expand the range of parallels as far as possible and another author then subjects the results to a 'critical scrutiny'.

9. Schürmann, ibid. 283 n. 12, expresses a similar reservation which raises a further possibility that is worth considering: for a number of passages we must first 'ask with greater critical rigour whether the elements in common between Paul and the Synoptic sayings cannot be explained by the paraenetic traditions in Judaism which lie behind both of them'.

10. Or perhaps there is a hint at least in 1 Cor 4 in the introduction in v 10 which refers to the relationship to Christ of this catalogue of the apostles' afflictions (*Peristasenkatalog*)?

(245)[11] is a vague hypothesis that has to proceed on the basis of several unknown factors: in the first place it presupposes that Paul himself handed down Jesus-tradition to his churches *as Jesus-tradition*; on the other it claims to know what Paul must have known of the manner in which missionaries taught who worked completely independently of him (e.g. in Rome).

The matter is somewhat different in the case of Rom 14.14*a* (cf. also v 20*b*) which has already been mentioned. Here we have what Paul clearly thinks of as a specifically 'Christian' maxim when he says that 'nothing (relating to food-stuffs) is unclean in itself'. Yet we cannot say with any certainty whether the introduction οἶδα καὶ πέπεισμαι ἐν κυρίῳ Ἰησοῦ, 'I know and am persuaded in the Lord Jesus' (RSV), means that Paul is here basing himself upon a saying of Jesus that has been handed down to him (Mark 7.15 would be the most likely parallel),[12] or whether he is thinking of an insight that seems to him a necessary corollary of his gospel of Christ. Its importance for him is shown not only by his quarrel with Peter in Antioch (which was a matter of the alleged 'uncleanness' of Gentile table-companions—or of their food-stuffs—Gal 2.12), but also by the fact that he also cites this maxim in two 'variant forms' in 1 Cor 6.13 and 8.8*a*, where it is a matter of (Gentile) Christians' attitude to their pagan surroundings, and thus a matter of fundamental importance for the way of life of 'his' churches.

We may also assume a connection between Gal 5.14/Rom 13.8–10 and the tradition of Mark 12.28–34 par. Both the fact that Paul names love of one's neighbour as a summary of the Torah in such a similar fashion in two letters, and the basic nature of this formulation in both cases, show that here too it was for him a matter of a thoroughly 'Christian' insight which he would certainly not have formulated thus in his pre-Christian days as a Pharisee.[13] It is true that here too we must

---

11. Or does the 'inasmuch' indicate a real limitation? But cf. also 248. Contrast the to my mind thoroughly appropriate caution of U. Wilckens, *Der Brief an die Römer* (EKKNT 6, Neukirchen–Vluyn: Neukirchener & Zürich: Benziger, 1978–82) 3, 23!

12. On the question whether Mark 7.15 (and 20ff) can be traced back to Jesus cf. W. G. Kümmel, 'Äußere und innere Reinheit des Menschen bei Jesus' (1973), in id., *Heilsgeschehen und Geschichte* 2 (Marburg: Elwert, 1978) 117–29; H. Hübner, 'Mk VII. 1–23 und das "jüdisch-hellenistische" Gesetzesverständnis', in *NTS* 22 (1975–6) 319–45; contrast K. Berger, *Die Gesetzesauslegung Jesu: ihr historischer Hintergrund im Judentum und im Alten Testament* 1: *Markus und Parallelen* (WMANT 40, Neukirchen–Vluyn: Neukirchener, 1972) 461ff, and others, who regard Mark 7.15 (and its context) as not going back to Jesus.

13. A. Nissen, *Gott und der Nächste im antiken Judentum* (Tübingen: Mohr,

leave open the question, whether Paul intended to reproduce a saying that went back to Jesus himself (that is not necessarily the same as a 'thoroughly Christian' saying!), since even cautious critics of the Jesus-tradition are very wary of attributing Mark 12.28–34 or just 12.29–31 to Jesus himself.[14] At any rate more careful attention must be paid than is usually done to the difference between the *double* commandment of love of God and one's neighbour as a 'two-headed' summary of the Law in Mark 12.29–31 and the summing up of the Law in the *single* commandment to love one's neighbour in Paul (see below).

I will leave aside other cases like the oft-discussed relations between Rom 13.6–7 and Mark 12.13–17 par.[15] Rather I want here briefly to raise the question whether Mark 10.45 (Matt 20.28) is echoed in the letters of Paul, perhaps in Rom 3.25–6 and 4.25 (or also in 5.15, 19), as P. Stuhlmacher in particular has sought to prove.[16] In Mark 10.45, as is well known, we have the only saying within the Synoptic Jesus-tradition,

---

1974), has shown that there was in all of ancient Judaism neither evidence of the Law being summed up as in Mark 12.29–31 nor the ways of thought that would lead to this. In contrast C. Burchard (see next n.) and K. Berger (see n. 12) considered this possible in Hellenistic Judaism. Yet cf. here the critical remarks of W. G. Kümmel, 'Ein Jahrzehnt Jesusforschung (1965–75)', in *TRu* 41 (1976) 197–258, 295–363, here 332–7. For the rabbinic area cf. also P. Schäfer, 'Die Torah der messianischen Zeit', in *ZNW* 65 (1974) 27–42, and also in id., *Studien zur Geschichte und Theologie des rabbinischen Judentums* (Leiden: Brill, 1978) 198–213: there is no evidence in rabbinic sources of the idea of concentrating the Torah in *one* (double) commandment.

14. Cf. C. Burchard, 'Das doppelte Liebesgebot in der frühen christlichen Überlieferung', in (ed.) E. Lohse *et al.*, *Der Ruf Jesu und die Antwort der Gemeinde: exegetische Untersuchungen Joachim Jeremias zum 70. Geburtstag gewidmet von seine Schülern* (Göttingen: Vandenhoeck & Ruprecht, 1970) 37–62. He traces the saying to the Hellenistic Jewish wing of early Christianity. (I too am sure that this wing had an active interest in such a saying; see below pp. 74–5)

15. On this cf. most recently P. Stuhlmacher, 'Jesustradition' (n. 4) 248, referring above all to L. Goppelt, 'Die Freiheit zur Kaisersteuer' (1961), in id., *Christologie und Ethik* (Göttingen: Vandenhoeck & Ruprecht, 1968) 208–19 (towards the end of the article), and also the Romans commentaries of O. Michel (MeyerK, Göttingen: Vandenhoeck & Ruprecht, 1966[13]) and U. Wilckens (n. 11).

16. Ibid. 246 (and 250); cf. also P. Stuhlmacher, 'Existenzstellvertretung für die Vielen: Mk 10,45 (Mt 20,28)', in (ed.) R. Albertz, *Werden und Wirken des Alten Testaments* (*Festschrift* for C. Westermann, Göttingen: Vandenhoeck & Ruprecht, 1980) 412–27, repr. in id., *Versöhnung, Gesetz und Gerechtigkeit* (Göttingen: Vandenhoeck & Ruprecht, 1981) 27–42, and other passages in this volume of essays.

apart from the words of Jesus uttered at the Lord's Supper, which gives a soteriological significance to Jesus' offering up of his life.[17] For that reason it would be of particular importance if we could on the one hand show that Paul knew this saying, and if on the other we could assume that this saying went back to Jesus himself. Now it is well known that Luke (22.26–7) has included amongst his account of Jesus' parting words a version of the saying that must be reckoned to represent an earlier stage in the transmission of Mark 10.45. Thus it could be the case that Paul in Rom 3.25–6 and 4.25 (cf. also 1 Cor 15.3*b*) shares the same tradition— perhaps Antiochene—of the soteriological interpretation of Jesus' crucifixion (influenced by Isa 43.3–4 and 53.11–12); the further elaboration of Jesus' saying in Luke 22.26–7 in the direction of the version of Mark 10.45[18] also draws on this interpretation;[19] yet Paul may still not have known or used this saying as a saying of Jesus.

On the other hand I would have no hesitation in tracing the addressing of God in prayer as 'Abba' which Paul cites as a mark of the Spirit (Gal 4.6/Rom 8.15) back to Jesus-tradition. Even if there are doubts about the historicity of the Gethsemane scene in the account in Mark 14.32–42 par., the Lord's Prayer (Luke 11.2ff/Matt 6.9ff) together with general considerations[20] may suffice for this assumption, even if we cannot cite a specific saying of Jesus to the effect that addressing God as Abba and the gift of the Spirit are connected.

III

What implications have these findings which we have only outlined briefly for the relation of Paul to the Jesus-tradition?

---

17. We cannot go further into the questions of the tradition lying behind Mark 10.45. Mention should be made of the important contribution to the discussion by J. Roloff, 'Anfänge der soteriologischen Deutung des Todes Jesu (Mk. x.45 und Lk. xxii.27)', in *NTS* 19 (1972–3) 38–64, and the essay by P. Stuhlmacher cited in the previous n.

18. In my opinion Mark is responsible for inserting the Son of Man title red-actionally in Mark 10.45.

19. Likewise R. Pesch in his comm.: *Das Markusevangelium* 2 (HTKNT 2.2, Freiburg-i-B., etc.: Herder, 1977, 1980²) 162–4.

20. On this cf. particularly J. Jeremias, *Abba* (Göttingen: Vandenhoeck & Ruprecht, 1966), esp. 15–57.

A

In the first place it can be stated that we can detect no hint that Paul knew of the narrative tradition about Jesus. For we have already said that 1 Cor 11.23–5 stems from liturgical and ritual tradition and so is in a special position (cf. on this the excursus below on pp. 62–3).

That is—and still is![21]—basically a surprising statement, since Paul should in no way be supposed to be disinterested in the 'earthly Jesus'. (There is widespread agreement today that such a disinterest cannot be inferred from 2 Cor 5.16.)[22] On the contrary! Paul reminds the Galatians that when he first preached to them he 'portrayed' Jesus Christ 'before their eyes' (Gal 3.1). How exactly may this 'Jesus-portrait' have appeared? Gal 3.1 focuses exclusively on the crucifixion, even if it is true that this does not refer to 'a loving, pious depiction of the *passio Jesu* and in particular his crucifixion'.[23] The same concentration is found in 1 Cor 1.23; 2.2; see too Gal 4.14, 17 and Phil 2.8*c* (I am assuming that 'even to death on a cross' is an addition by Paul to the hymn which he is quoting). If we supplement the picture from other letters, then we can say that Paul finds the following things important about the earthly Jesus: God sent him—we should understand this to mean 'from heaven'—(Gal 4.4); he was a human being, born of a woman (like every human being), subject to the Law (like every true Jew—he was after all descended from the people of Israel τò κατὰ σάρκα, Rom 9.5); he was 'poor', that is, without divine power and might (2 Cor 8.9—Paul is not saying that he was specially poor in a social sense); following on from his laying aside of his divinity he subjected himself even to the human fate of death (Phil 2.6–8; from the Christ-hymn Paul apparently also infers Jesus' humility towards other human beings; compare the context of Phil 2.3 and 12). In short, then, he suffered (2 Cor 1.5; Phil 3.10; Rom 15.3), gave himself up to death[24] (Gal 2.20*b*; 1 Cor 11.23), and died a death on the cross (see

---

21. I cannot regard the widespread silence of Paul's letters about concrete Jesus-tradition as 'supposedly' striking (as does Stuhlmacher, 'Jesustradition' [n. 4] 241)—it *must* strike the exegete!

22. Here it is enough to cite two authors who otherwise hold very different opinions: Stuhlmacher, ibid. 242, and W. Schmithals, *Jesus Christus in der Verkündigung der Kirche* (Neukirchen–Vluyn: Neukirchener, 1972) 41–2 =*ZNW* 53 (1962) 145–60, here 150. Cf. also n. 57 below.

23. F. Mußner, *Der Galaterbrief* (HTKNT 9, Freiburg-i-B., etc.: Herder, 1974, repr. Leipzig, 1974) 207.

24. Or 'he was given up to death by God'? See below p. 63 (nn. 32–3) on 1 Cor 11.23.

above; Gal 3.13). As far as we can see from Paul's letters, Jesus' actions played no role in this picture, and certainly not his actions as a performer of miracles;[25] nor is his teaching activity emphasized in the relevant statements. At any rate nowhere in Paul's Christological or soteriological statements is there any other reference to the 'earthly Jesus' than to him as the one who suffered, died and was crucified.

Of course, despite all the range of contrary indications, one can still insist that Paul 'self-evidently' knew the narrative Jesus-tradition which has been collected in the Synoptic Gospels and that he passed it on to his churches (these two are of course not the same thing!). But such a thesis cannot be substantiated; no one can really say more than that 'it cannot be ruled out that Paul...'.[26] However it is perhaps worthy of note in this respect that R. Riesner hardly mentions the whole area of the narrative Jesus-tradition in his investigation of the origins of the Jesus-tradition. So he does not suppose that it is also true of this area that here too there existed very early tradition in a fixed form. Riesner's study even leaves open the possibility that W. Schmithals may be correct in his hypothesis that the stories of Jesus—above all the 'Novellen' ('tales') in the sense used by M. Dibelius—were poetic literary texts containing a narrative proclamation of Jesus from the 60's, composed by the author of the pre-Markan 'basic text'.[27] Yet it is not my purpose to speak up for this hypothesis here.[28]

25. On the related thesis of H.-W. Kuhn cf. the next note.

26. So we really must ask whether H.-W. Kuhn's interesting attempt to come to terms with the problem which confronts us here has an at all satisfactory basis. Kuhn ('Der irdische Jesus bei Paulus als traditionsgeschichtliches und theologisches Problem', in *ZTK* 67, 1970, 295–320) takes up and develops further theses put forward by D. Georgi, J. M. Robinson and H. Köster, and supposes that Paul quite deliberately made no use of the very extensive Jesus-tradition with which he too was familiar—he is thinking primarily of the stories of Jesus the miracle-worker, but also of a collection of sayings, in which Jesus was seen above all as the incarnation of Wisdom; Paul did this to give no further support to the per-verted Christology of the rivals opposing him in Corinth, which did not really have any place for the crucifixion of Jesus.

27. Cf. W. Schmithals, Art. 'Evangelien, synoptische', in *TRE* 10 (1982) 570–626, esp. 623–4; also id., *Das Evangelium nach Markus* (Ökumenischer Taschenbuchkommentar zum Neuen Testament 2.1, Gütersloh: Siebenstern, 1979) 1, 43–51, id., 'Kritik der Formkritik', in *ZTK* 77 (1980) 149–85, and id., *Einleitung in die drei ersten Evangelien* (Berlin: de Gruyter, 1985) 260–84, 298–328, 410–21.

28. Schmithals' thesis corresponds, despite a different starting-point, to the old criticism levelled against the form-critical school: to do away with the postulate of

Excursus 1
The Relation between the Words of Institution
of the Lord's Supper and the Passion Narrative

The quotation of the words of institution of the Lord's Supper in 1 Cor 11.23-5 is no evidence that Paul was familiar with the passion narrative in the form known to us from the Synoptics or in a recoverable pre-Markan or even pre-Lukan version. Of course this is not to say that Paul had no knowledge at all of the event of Jesus' suffering and execution.[29] It is rather a matter of his acquaintance with those versions of the text which we have in the Gospels or which can be reconstructed from them. There is no passage in Paul's letters which can be regarded as a reference to one of the versions of the passion narrative. For the words of institution of the Lord's Supper, for which 1 Cor 11.23-5 is the oldest evidence, are an independent piece of traditional material of liturgical or catechetical character which functions as an aetiology for ritual;[30] it is not a part of, or section from, the (pre-)Synoptic passion narrative. By the time of the Synoptics, i.e. more than 25 years since the writing of 1 Cor, the words of institution still formed no integral part of the passion narrative, as is clearly shown by the fact that the passage Mark 14.22-4 can be detached from its present setting and by the redactional re-working of the context by Luke (22.14-23).[31] The words quoted by Paul refer in their

---

an anonymous 'community' that was yet responsible for producing tradition. Schmithals postulates an author, who likewise cannot be named, but yet whose literary profile is recognizable; at *one* literary stroke this author is supposed to have created a mass of individual stories as well as the framework of the pre-Markan 'basic text' that went with them. Yet it is precisely this combination which makes me doubtful of Schmithals' hypothesis.

29. The role that Jesus' suffering, apart from his crucifixion, played in the apostolic self-understanding is of course well-known; cf., e.g., E. Güttgemanns, *Der leidende Apostel und sein Herr: Studien zur paulinischen Christologie* (FRLANT 90, Göttingen: Vandenhoeck & Ruprecht, 1966).

30. In this context we need not seek to determine more precisely the form and function of the passage. However one should speak of an 'aetiology for ritual' rather than the usual 'aetiology for cult', since the early Christian Lord's Supper was certainly a rite, but not a cultic act; cf. my article 'Christusglaube und heidnische Religiosität in paulinischen Gemeinden', in *NTS* 25, 1978-9, 422-42, esp. 436-41.

31. On this, apart from R. Bultmann, *Geschichte der synoptischen Tradition* (Göttingen: Vandenhoeck & Ruprecht, 1957[5]; ET: Oxford: Blackwell, 1963, 1968[2]) 285-6 and 300-1, cf. the very full treatment in J. Jeremias, *Die Abendmahlsworte Jesu* (Göttingen: Vandenhoeck & Ruprecht, 1960[3]; ET: London: SCM, 1966) 83-99 and 106.—Contrast however now Pesch, *Markusevangelium* 2 (n. 19) 354ff, esp. 362 (and further publications quoted there). According to Pesch the view that the words of institution have first been inserted into their Markan context at the stage of redaction is a 'widespread error' (354); rather the version quoted by Paul is a secondary 'cult-aetiological' version of the tradition of the institution of the Lord's Supper which is derived from the pre-Markan passion

introduction to 'the night in which the Lord Jesus was offered up (or handed over)'; this is—apart perhaps from the mention of 'insults' in Rom 15.3—the only mention which we find in Paul's letters of an incident from the passion. The word παρεδίδοτο here should not be taken of the 'betrayal' (by Judas); yet, because of the temporal reference in the phrase ἐν τῇ νυκτὶ ᾗ..., the 'historical' interpretation in terms of Jesus' being 'handed over', his transference into the judicial authority (of the Sanhedrin? or through the Sanhedrin to the authority of the Romans?—that remains undecided), seems to me more likely than the 'theological' interpretation, which sees in this verb an expression of the 'offering up' of Jesus to death (by God)[32] as found in Rom 8.32 or 4.25 (or of Jesus' self-offering as in Gal 2.20).[33] So that means that Paul certainly knew something about the event of the passion of Jesus—how could he not!—; but Paul's knowledge of the passion narrative in the (or a) pre-Synoptic version cannot be shown and 1 Cor 11.23–5 is no evidence for it.

B

Secondly, it is of considerable significance that *at no point in his letters does Paul quote any saying of Jesus* or plainly allude to one, *in which he is expounding the central content of his gospel*, in making important Christological or soteriological statements. It is precisely in his decisive theological statements that Paul adduces no Jesus-tradition. The reverse is true too: in expounding the gospel of Christ Paul shows no trace of the influence of the theologically central affirmations of Jesus' preaching, in particular of his characteristic 'Jesuanic' interpretation of the kingdom of God.[34] Since the first part of this observation becomes all the more

account and which has been separated from its true setting (369–76). Pesch has once again defended this view very recently: 'Das Evangelium in Jerusalem: Mk 14.12–26 als ältestes Überlieferungsgut der Urgemeinde', in (ed.) P. Stuhlmacher, *Das Evangelium und die Evangelien* (Tübingen: Mohr, 1983) 113–55.

32. J. Jeremias argues vigorously for this interpretation (ibid. 106).

33. On the meaning of the verb cf. now W. Popkes in *EWNT* 3, 42–8 (with further literature); Popkes would indeed like to see the 'historical' and 'theological' interpretation combined in the *one* word (45 and 47–8).

34. That can easily be shown in the relatively few passages in which Paul speaks of the βασιλεία τοῦ θεοῦ (1 Thess 2.12; 1 Cor 4.20; 6.9–10; 15.50; Gal 5.21; Rom 14.17). For Paul the βασιλεία τοῦ θεοῦ is a (heavenly) 'entity' which exists permanently and which can serve as a norm for a way of life corresponding to the will of God; 'kingdom of God' is here an appropriate translation. In the message of Jesus, on the other hand, the 'reign of God' is that event whose realization commences with and in his appearance. G. Haufe showed in his article, 'Reich Gottes bei Paulus und in der Jesustradition', in *NTS* 31 (1985) 467–72, which had been delivered as a seminar-paper at Basel, that there is also within the Jesus-tradition a series of βασιλεία-sayings which are closer to Paul's concept (particularly those about 'entering' the kingdom of God); he regards this stratum

critical—not to say fraught with with problems—the more extensive one wants to regard Paul's acquaintance with the Jesus-tradition as having been, so the second part basically excludes any deeper familiarity with what we know from the Synoptics of Jesus' message; or alternatively we can say that this evidence renders highly questionable Paul's ability to understand and assimilate these central ingredients of the Jesus-tradition.

That Paul continually interprets theologically Jesus' death on the cross in Christologically and soteriologically important passages is just as clear as the fact that in doing so he makes use of interpretations drawn from earlier kerygmatic or credal formulations (Rom 3.25–6; 1 Cor 15.3–4;[35] apparently not in Gal 3.13–14). On the other hand, the allusions to Mark 10.45 which P. Stuhlmacher in particular has espoused, and which are supposed to be found in Rom 3.25–6 and 4.25 (and in Rom 5.15 and 19 too),[36] are highly questionable. They possibly point to a common background in the (post-Easter) interpretation of Jesus' death on the cross, perhaps in the pre-Pauline communities of Syria which were under the influence of Hellenistic Judaism. We have already referred to the relative isolation of Mark 10.45 (Matt 20.28) in the pre-Synoptic traditional material; just for this reason alone it would be questionable to trace this saying back to an early stage of the Jesus-tradition. At any rate neither the antiquity of Mark 10.45 nor—turning the argument round— the dependence of Paul's interpretation of the cross upon this saying when regarded as an early one can be supported by the allusions in Paul to this saying which have just been mentioned and which are at best indeterminate.[37]

Excursus 2
On the Interpretation of Ἱστορῆσαι Κηφᾶν in Gal 1.18

What had Paul sought to obtain from Peter on his first visit to Jerusalem three years after becoming a Christian? In relation to Gal 1.18 P. Stuhlmacher, 'Jesustradition' (n. 4) 241 n. 10, refers to the noteworthy article of J. D. G. Dunn, 'The Relationship between Paul and Jerusalem according to Galatians 1 and 2', in

---

as stemming from (post-Easter) baptismal teaching.

35. Cf. here esp. P. Stuhlmacher, 'Zur neueren Exegese von Röm 3,24–26' (1975), in id., *Versöhnung* (n. 16) 117–35.

36. Stuhlmacher, 'Jesustradition' (n. 4) 246 and 250. Particularly elusive are the supposed 'traces of Son of man tradition' (since by that Stuhlmacher in fact means traces of pre-Synoptic, Christological Son of man sayings, not pre-Christian Jewish Son of man tradition) in Rom 5.12ff and 8.34.

37. In Stuhlmacher (ibid.) both conclusions seem to be meant to support each other.

NTS 28 (1982) 461–78. Unfortunately the latter's interpretation of ἱστορῆσαι Κηφᾶν (463–6) is philologically inexact and needs to be made more precise. (1) It must be stated that the translation 'to get to know Cephas' is always a philologically sound one too.[38] (2) Dunn's view of the words involves not only the translation 'to get information from Cephas', but also 'to question Cephas about his view on, about his interpretation of...' as well. This understanding of the phrase is perhaps best illustrated by the example which Dunn cites (464) from Herodotus 2.19; there it is a matter of the question whence, in the view of the Egyptian priests, comes the 'power' of the Nile when it overflows its banks. (3) Above all it needs to be noted that for the rendering which Dunn prefers one would normally expect a second accusative or an equivalent relative clause which would explain with what the enquiries or consultations were concerned. Such a reference is lacking in Gal 1.18 (and this may be why a Greek like John Chrysostom emphatically rejects this proposed interpretation; see Dunn 463). It needs to be supplied from the context—from the context and not, as in Dunn's case, from general considerations ('That Paul would have had a natural curiosity about this Jesus...is *prima facie* obvious', 465). If such a general motive were Paul's reason for going to see Cephas, one must yet at least raise the question why Paul still more than 20 years later sets store by the fact that he could initially suppress this 'natural curiosity' for three years. In fact the context afforded by Gal 1.16 and 2.2, which Dunn interprets in a very illuminating fashion both before this and after (462–3 and 466–8), affords us a far more precise answer. Dunn states that in the context of this passage Paul is concerned with the question whether he had rightly understood the call to apostleship, and that an apostleship to the Gentiles, which he had experienced. If at first everything seemed to him to be clear, so that he regarded as unnecessary any contact with those who were 'apostles before him' (1.17)—a fact of which he is still glad more than 20 years later!—, yet apparently after 17 years (Gal 2.1ff) some uncertainty on this matter showed itself, an uncertainty whose ambivalence Dunn analyses so well (466ff). Something similar would then apply to Gal 1.18, the first contact with Peter: Paul wished 'to discover the view of Cephas', 'to take counsel with Cephas on the question', whether in his preaching of the gospel to the Gentiles he was on a course that was also an acceptable one in the view of Peter. In this the question whether Paul's missionary activity did not run counter to what Peter could tell of Jesus' own work or teaching will also certainly have played an important role. If it had been a matter of 'background information about the ministry of Jesus while on earth' in a *general* sense (so Dunn 465), then his contact with James the brother of the Lord would also have had a bearing, since with him—in contrast to Peter—he shared the twofold perspectives of one who formerly rejected Jesus and then subsequently followed him. But he contented himself merely with 'seeing' him (1.19; Dunn too ponders this change of terminology on pp. 465–6). James had for Paul no competence in the question that was exercising him, or Paul fought shy of conversing with him more deeply, since he was surely already aware then of James's reservations (to say the

---

38. This has subsequently been emphasized by O. Hofius, 'Gal 1,18: ἱστορῆσαι Κηφᾶν', in *ZNW* 75 (1984) 73-85. Dunn has accepted this, but otherwise sticks to his interpretation of Paul's visit to Peter: 'Once More—Gal 1,18: ἱστορῆσαι Κηφᾶν. In Reply to Otfried Hofius', in *ZNW* 76 (1985) 138-9.

least) concerning his missionary work among the Gentiles; perhaps this attitude of
James's was even the reason for his uncertainty. Then fourteen years later, in view
of the increased influence of James in the Jerusalem church and beyond (Gal
2.12*a*), he could no longer avoid discussing such basic matters with James
himself. But on the first occasion he only wanted to consult Peter, who unlike
James was himself active in mission—even if principally among Jews (Gal 2.7)—
and of whose more open attitude *vis-à-vis* the Antioch church's policy in mission
and church order Paul was aware (e.g. through Barnabas, who according to Acts
11.22–6 introduced him into the Antioch church).

C

A *prophetic saying of Jesus* seems to lie behind 1 Thess 4.15ff; here it
seems clear that Paul undertakes a reapplication in so far as the sayings of
Jesus which can be suggested as possible parallels (most clearly Matt
24.43/Luke 12.39 with 1 Thess 5.2) originally served the purpose of
eschatological exhortations to watchfulness, while Paul employs them in
eschatological instruction in order to reassure his readers. It has long been
disputed how much in the verses which follow the introductory τοῦτο γὰρ
ὑμῖν λέγομεν ἐν λόγῳ κυρίου (4.15*a*) is to be regarded as a 'quotation' in
the narrower sense and where Paul's own development of what he has
taken over from tradition begins. P. Stuhlmacher (appealing to O.
Hofius)[39] has now made this discussion that much easier by observing
that Paul's apparent citation formula λέγομεν ἐν λόγῳ κυρίου is in actual
fact not an appeal to a particular saying of the Lord, but is making known
'by whose commission and authority he speaks'.[40] So 1 Thess 4.15ff
should be dropped from the list of quotations of sayings of the Lord and
should be assigned to those sayings containing important 'Christian'
insights, that is, it can be set alongside sayings like Rom 14.14*a* or Gal
5.14/Rom 13.8–10 (see above pp. 57–8); in the present case it can

---

39. O. Hofius, in his article on 'Agrapha', in *TRE* 2 (1978) 104. That was also
the view of, amongst others, E. von Dobschütz, *Die Thessalonischer-Briefe*
(MeyerK 10, Göttingen: Vandenhoeck & Ruprecht, 1909) 193.—U. B. Müller,
Prophetie und Predigt im Neuen Testament (SNT 10, Gütersloh: Mohn, 1975)
220–5, describes the saying in 1 Thess 4.13–14 as a 'salvation oracle' (for the
purpose of encouragement), which Paul then backs up by quoting a saying
(4.15ff) which he supposes to be a saying of the earthly Jesus but which is in fact
the product of early Christian prophesying.—G. Löhr, '1 Thess 4,15–17: das
"Herrenwort"', in *ZNW* 71 (1980) 269–73, has recently attempted to reconstruct
the 'saying' of the Lord used by Paul especially from vv 16–17 (adducing 1 Cor
15.51–2, but with no reference to pre-Synoptic sayings of Jesus). Cf. also H.-H.
Schade, *Apokalyptische Christologie bei Paulus* (GTA 18, Göttingen: Vandenhoeck & Ruprecht, 1981) 159–62.

40. Stuhlmacher, 'Jesustradition' (n. 4) 243.

assuredly also be assumed that at least in 5.2–3 Paul takes up sayings from the Jesus-tradition. Stuhlmacher derives an important insight from this evidence: 1 Thess 4.15ff is not a saying of Jesus newly created with full prophetic authority,[41] but the prophetic application by Paul of extant Jesus-material. But it is true that we can then no longer be sure that Paul was conscious that he was applying *Jesus*-tradition; similarly we can no longer deduce from the ἀκριβῶς οἴδατε of 5.2 that he was referring the Thessalonians 'to their knowledge of the Gospel-tradition' (what is meant is 'to their knowledge of sayings from the *pre*-Synoptic tradition'); we cannot infer more from the words than a reference back to instruction that they had earlier received. Thus Stuhlmacher's conclusion that '1 Thess 4.15ff show that Paul quite clearly distinguishes (his own) prophetic utterance and Jesus-tradition' (243) does not follow—it is indeed practically impossible to distinguish the two from each other in the passage we have been discussing—; it is asking a bit too much to expect the Thessalonians as the first readers of the letter to have understood this particular point (ibid.). Rather Stuhlmacher's analysis also shows a more fluid blending of Jesus-tradition, such as is recognizably in the background of the present passage, with its prophetic application, here by Paul himself (although one cannot rule out the possibility even in the present case that other prophetic applications preceded the present one).[42]

---

41. In contrast to form-critics' view that apparent Jesus-material was formulated by prophetic plenipotentiaries for the first time in the post-Easter church; Stuhlmacher, ibid. n. 16, cites G. Bornkamm as representative of this view; but cf. also U. B. Müller, *Prophetie* (n. 38), etc.

42. In other words the form-critical way of approach which presupposes just such a fluid blending of (Jesus-)tradition and new creations effected by the Spirit is not at all such a bad one, despite all sorts of objections since, say, F. Neugebauer, 'Geistsprüche und Jesuslogien', in *ZNW* 53 (1962) 218–28. And that in the process new sayings formulated on the authority of the Lord (ἐν λόγῳ κυρίου, 1 Thess 4.15) should circulate under the name of Jesus (the 'earthly' Jesus) can be ruled out by no one who does not *a priori* hold every single saying of Jesus in the Synoptics (and the non-Synoptic tradition) to be genuine.—W. J. Houston has shown recently that no case can be made out either against the form-critical approach on the basis of 1 Cor 7.10ff at any rate ('The Words of the Lord and Christian Prophecy: the Irrelevance of I Cor. 7', in *Studia Evangelica* 7 [TU 126, Berlin: Akademie, 1982] 261–4): 1 Cor 7.10ff is located in a context which is such that the form-critical approach would not at all expect to find there the formation of new sayings of the Lord under the leading of the Spirit (it is a paraenetical rather than eschatological context). On the other hand that would apply far better to 1 Thess 4.—Unfortunately I did not yet have access to the apparently important study of M. E. Boring, *Sayings of the Risen Jesus:*

D

The main stock of demonstrable material from the Jesus-tradition in the Pauline letters occurs in connection with *ethical paraenesis*.[43] First of all it should be noted that Paul does not only quote the words of institution of the Lord's Supper in the context of (church) paraenesis, but also other traditional formulations which are highly significant Christologically. This is so obvious that it is enough to remind ourselves of it with a couple of examples: the words of institution of the Lord's Supper are cited in order to give the Corinthians clear guidance in the matter of the conduct of some of their church-members (1 Cor 11.17–34); the Christ-hymn of Phil 2.6–11 is quoted in order to urge the Philippians to be humble towards one another (Phil 2.1–13); Paul uses the statement about the pre-existent Christ who became poor in order to make us rich (2 Cor 8.9) as the basis for his appeal for generous giving in the collection for Jerusalem (2 Cor 8). Jesus' suffering on the cross can also be seen as a model for conduct (Rom 15.2–3). Particularly in Phil 2 the obvious 'playing down' of the Christological riches of the hymn in Paul's paraenetical use of it has been a constant source of wonder, indeed a matter for surprise, for the thoughtful exegete; for Paul himself it seems to have presented no problem.

However let us turn now to Jesus-tradition in the narrower sense. There the paraenetic reference is immediately plain in the network of allusions within Rom 12.14–21. The same is true, but less immediately, of 1 Cor 4.11–13, where the allusions to sayings of Jesus (here especially the Beatitudes) occur in the context of a 'catalogue of afflictions' (*Peristasenkatalog*); but it is true that this speaks of an apostolic way of life that is in keeping with the gospel, which the Corinthians should take as their model (v 6). In 1 Cor 9.14 too it is a matter of an aspect of the apostolic way of life, in which Paul introduces one of the Lord's rules of service for his messengers, only to go on to state that he himself does not conform to it, but lives more unpretentiously than the rule envisaged.[44]

Christian Prophecy in the Synoptic Tradition (SNTSMS 46, Cambridge Univ., 1982)—cf. on this A. Lindemann, 'Literaturbericht zu den Synoptischen Evangelien 1978–1983', in *TRu* 49 (1984) 223–76, 311–76, here 274–6.

43. In itself that is of course no new insight. Cf. the essay of H. Schürmann mentioned above (n. 8); also E. Gräßer, 'Der Mensch Jesus als Thema der Theologie', in *Jesus* (Kümmel *Festschrift*—see n. 1.2) 129–50, esp. 133–6.

44. G. Theißen has clearly shown the sociological background for Paul's departure here from the traditional way of doing things—a change from an itinerant apostolate, as presupposed in Luke 10.7, to stationary missionary activity in the setting of the large Hellenistic cities—: 'Legitimation und Lebensunterhalt:

Clearly 1 Cor 7 is dealing with questions of the Christian way of life; there Paul cites Jesus' saying about the impossibility of divorce (7.10–11). It is nonetheless important to note that the saying, in the form that Paul quotes it here, in two parts (v 10*b* and 11*b*), corresponds most closely to the version in Mark 10.11–12; as far as v 12 is concerned it is generally regarded—and quite rightly in my view—as an expansion of older tradition on the basis of Hellenistic laws regarding marriage.[45] So it is beyond question that here we have a saying of Jesus which has been expanded and 'applied' after Easter and in an 'alien' environment and that furthermore this new version has been attributed to Jesus; this was the form with which Paul was familiar. It is indeed the only case in which Paul appeals *explicitly* to a saying of the Lord to provide the basis of ethical instructions; here the quotation formula itself in no way makes a distinction between the 'earthly' and the 'exalted' *Kyrios* (see above p. 54);[46] that does not mean that there is any question here that Paul means the 'earthly' one—if our distinction were put to him. But it is correct that he draws a very clear distinction in 1 Cor 7 (10–11, 12–13, 25) between a saying of the Lord and his own words. Stuhlmacher is quite right to affirm that 'Paul's freedom, with which he interprets Jesus' prohibition of divorce...for the church and even modifies it, is remarkable' (244). However one should not then say that 'the words of the earthly Jesus guide him in his argument in 1 Cor 7' (ibid.). Paul rather makes use of a saying of the Lord where one is available to him, since he doubtless accords it higher authority than his own words. But where he cannot adduce any instructions of the Lord, he speaks without hesitation on his own authority too (and gives reasons for so doing: 7.25 and 40). And where the situation demands it, he can act so freely towards the saying of the Lord that he 'even modifies it' (see above).

ein Beitrag zur Soziologie urchristlicher Missionare', in *NTS* 21 (1974–5) 192–221, repr. in id., *Studien zur Soziologie des Urchristentums* (WUNT 19, Tübingen: Mohr, 1979) 201–30; ET in id., *The Social Setting of Pauline Christianity: Essays on Corinth* (Studies in the New Testament and Its World, Edinburgh: Clark, 1982) 25–67.

45. Cf. here, e.g., R. Pesch, *Markusevangelium* (n. 19) 120 and 125–6; there is a fuller discussion in B. Schaller, 'Die Sprüche über Ehescheidung und Wiederverheiratung in der synoptischen Überlieferung', in *Der Ruf Jesu und die Antwort der Gemeinde* (*Festschrift* for J. Jeremias, Göttingen: Vandenhoeck & Ruprecht, 1970) 226–46.

46. Contrast Stuhlmacher, 'Jesustradition' (n. 4) 243–4. He emphasizes the difference between 'sayings of the earthly Jesus' and those of 'the exalted Lord' (without any basis in the text); but Paul writes alike κύριος both here and in 2 Cor 12.8–9 (where it is certainly a saying of the 'exalted Lord').

The question of how 1 Cor 7.12–13 is to be evaluated in this respect seems to me an open one. As far as I can see, exegetes do not distinguish between the situation in 7.25 and that in 7.12–13. But Paul's formulation is different. That he 'regrets that he has no word of the Lord available' only clearly applies to 7.25, although most give a summary paraphrase of 7.25 and 7.12–13 together in these terms. In 7.12–13, on the other hand, Paul's language leaves it open whether he knows of no relevant saying of Jesus or whether he does not want to make use of a saying which he knows, since he is of a mind to depart from it. Any who reckon with an extensive knowledge of sayings of Jesus on the part of Paul must, if they are to be consistent, paraphrase his words thus: 'To the rest, that is, the married—to be more precise, those married to an unbelieving partner—I say, departing from a known saying of the Lord: ...' (there follows the advice that the believing marriage-partners should not for their part think of divorce). For Jesus' saying in Luke 14.26 ('He who does not hate father, mother, wife, children, brothers, sisters for my sake...'), understood as ἐπιταγὴ κυρίου, would certainly suggest the dissolution of the ties of marriage and family—and that by the believer himself—, in so far as the members of the family mentioned did not all share a common faith. And so, if one assumes that Paul knew this 'saying of the Lord' too, along with all the rest of the Jesus-tradition, then that would mean that for the sake of a better insight granted to himself Paul could ignore a specific 'command' of the Lord (and suggest that he was doing so by his form of words in 7.12 *a*); moreover he would be doing so while implying very different and more far-reaching general validity for what he was doing compared to the situation in 1 Cor 9.7–15; there he certainly also departs from the Lord's 'instructions' regarding provision for missionaries (v 14), yet only does so in relation to his own person and without casting doubt on the validity of that ruling in other cases. 1 Cor 7.12–13 would then be evidence of a surprising independence even when confronted with a saying of the Lord. But if one supposes that the usual interpretation of 7.12–13, which certainly fits 7.25, is also correct in the former passage, then one can no longer claim that in 1 Cor 7.10ff Paul speaks in the light of a knowledge which he possessed of the whole body of early Christian Jesus-tradition. At any rate the 'chapter on marriage', 1 Cor 7, shows as a whole that, where Paul had a saying of the Lord to hand, he gladly used it, to decide a matter quickly and clearly, but that he was not at all dependent upon such support. He did not allow his ability to give concrete instructions as to how Christians should lead their lives to be governed by whether or not a saying of the Lord was available to him.

In all, the evidence of Rom 12; 1 Cor 4; 1 Cor 7 and other passages points to the following preliminary conclusion: when issuing specific instructions Paul handles sayings of the Lord in part just as teachers would handle traditional wisdom sayings giving rules for life: they use them without reflecting upon those who formulated them before them or had already used them too. Partly, too, he treats them much as a rabbi would treat the statements of a colleague: he quotes them either in order to endorse them or to set another view over against them. Yet, whenever he expressly names the 'Lord' as the author of an instruction, there is still a clear difference to rabbinic discussions of *halakah*: the author of the instruction is the *Kyrios* and Paul does not on principle put himself on the same level as him as if he were his colleague.

The problem takes a rather different form where it is a matter of *basic questions as to how Christians should live their lives* and where there are more or less clear points of contact with the Jesus-tradition.

In Rom 14.14*a* Paul states as his firm conviction 'in the Lord Jesus' that no foodstuffs are unclean in themselves. In such a statement—which is echoed in 1 Cor 6.13*a* and 8.8*a*, again as a basic principle—there is displayed a freedom *vis-à-vis* a whole set of concrete instructions of the Torah which were taken very seriously by Jews (and particularly by the Pharisees), a freedom that is quite astonishing in a Jew who had formerly been of the Pharisaic persuasion.[47] But it is at least as surprising too that Paul does not think it necessary either to justify or defend this conviction of his either to the readers of 1 Corinthians or those of Romans; this is especially surprising when one considers that (a) the readers contained at least *some* Jews who had become Christians, and (b) the so-called 'Apostolic Decree' of Acts 15.28–9 with its specific obligation to keep certain food regulations might also have had some sort of currency in Paul's time among Gentile Christians in the churches which he had founded. For Paul this was at any rate a basic insight of whose truth he was convinced 'in the Lord Jesus' and which was of decisive importance for the way of life of Christians in a pagan environment. To put it briefly, it settled the question whether or not the Christian church should or must shut itself off from the world around it in a sort of ghetto existence as the Jewish community did. This is precisely the issue that was involved when Paul declared that in principle Christians could buy in the market meat that had been offered to idols and could likewise accept invitations to meals that also brought them into contact with such meat (1 Cor 8 and also 10.23–33 and Rom 14).[48] With the words ἐν κυρίῳ Ἰησοῦ Paul

---

47. Cf. U. Wilckens, *Römer* 3 (n. 11) 90–1.

48. To be sure, this freedom was for Paul limited solely by consideration of the 'weak' conscience of some brethren. In contrast a quite different problem is found

indicates that he regards this as a matter of a specifically 'Christian' viewpoint and on this point he has altered fundamentally his own earlier view. It is clear that there is here substantial agreement with sayings in the Jesus-tradition (Mark 7.2–8 and 15–23)—and in my view with Jesus himself—;[49] perhaps it even extends to the basis of this viewpoint in the theology of creation although it is true that this is only in the background in Mark 7; however, it emerges more clearly when Paul mentions thanksgiving for food in Rom 14.6*b* and when he quotes Ps 24.1 in 1 Cor 10.26. But it is not immediately clear from Paul's words how he came to this new Christian insight: was it through identifying himself with the Jewish-Hellenist group of Christians whom he had previously combatted and with their views, which made it possible for them to enjoy full fellowship with converted Gentiles, or was it—only secondarily?— through familiarity with the relevant sayings of Jesus? It is true that, since precisely this point is so decisive for his missionary work, it would be nice to think that he also assured himself expressly when he met Peter that he was in agreement on just this point with the sayings of Jesus,[50] so that he was confident that he could also then sustain his position on this matter in the face of opposition from James and even from Peter and Barnabas (Gal 2.2–10 and then 2.11–14).[51]

A still more important point of contact with the Synoptic tradition, which concerns not just rules of conduct in a specific area but the Torah in its entirety, is doubtless to be found in Rom 13.8–10 and Gal 5.14. Yet, as was mentioned already above (p. 58), one cannot immediately assume that the Synoptic 'parallel' in Mark 12.28–34 goes back to Jesus himself; the Synoptic saying too could be evidence of a similar concern to formulate a 'summary of the Torah'—a concern which may show that, in the view of the Hellenistic Jewish-Christian church, criticism of the Torah in respect of specific details was not to be identified with rejection or even censure of the Torah as a whole (as which criticism of the Torah would almost inevitably be regarded from the Jewish side). Rabbinic Judaism is far from regarding such a 'summing up' of the Torah as

εἰδωλολατρία (so 10.14), that is, in actual pagan religious ceremonies. To this Paul's answer is an unreserved No, and there is no room here for any differentiation between 'strong' and 'weak'. Often, however, the particular problems of 1 Cor 10.1–22 within the context of 1 Cor 8–10 is played down too much in exegesis; cf. my article mentioned in n. 30 above, esp. 425–36.

49. Cf. n. 12 above.

50. On Gal 1.18 see Excursus 2 above, pp. 64–6.

51. According to Acts 10.12–15 Peter must have been filled with a very similar conviction; but he shows no trace of it in his conduct as described in Gal 2.12.

possible; yet even the instances cited from the sphere of Hellenistic Jewish literature are nowhere characterized by being thus reduced to a single formula and thus being in such a 'programmatic' form as is the case in the New Testament statements[52] (amongst which Matt 22.35–40 also underlines further the fundamental nature of this formulation by adding, in comparison with Mark 12, the closing statement that 'Upon these two commandments the entire Law and the prophets are centred'— cf. also Matt 5.17). For Paul it is also clear in the case of Gal 5.14 and Rom 13.8–10 that this is an explicitly 'Christian' new insight gained by him in the context of his message about Christ; for, in the passages mentioned, he articulates one side—the positive one—of his new Christian evaluation of the Torah which he had inferred from his message about justification. How far he thought that in so doing he was referring to a traditional saying of Jesus or could refer to one must remain an open question for the reasons which I have stated. At any rate, apart from this, it is to be noted that for the 'saying of Jesus' in Mark 12.29–31 the Torah is also of permanent, indeed pre-eminent relevance with regard to one's relationship with God (here Matt 22.39 evens things up compared with Mark 12, in that it expressly sets 'the second' commandment on the 'same' level as the first—the 'same' in importance but not in content); Paul, on the other hand, by *his* 'summary statement' limits the Torah's sphere of relevance entirely to the sphere of inter-personal relations as covered in the 'second table' of the Decalogue and passes over the commandments of the 'first table' in Rom 13.8–9—and certainly not just by oversight! Thus Paul removes the position of humanity before God entirely from the sphere of that 'fulfilling of the Law' which could be possible for us or according to God's will. In so far as this represents a deliberate decision contrary to the (Jesus-)tradition, we would then have to assume that Paul had derived it from his theology of justification. Yet Pauline statements about the (new) 'law of Christ' (Gal 6.2; cf. 1 Cor 9.21) could also indicate that here he was taking up and developing further the theological reflections of that group of early Christians with which his life and his theology were linked, namely that Hellenistic Jewish-Christian movement which followed Stephen.[53] If, despite the doubts mentioned already, the 'double commandment of love' can yet be traced back in its essentials to Jesus himself, then certainly that would

---

52. Cf. the studies mentioned above in nn. 13 and 14, esp. the views on this of W. G. Kümmel (n. 13). But nevertheless cf. Philo, *Spec. leg.* 2.63 (Burchard, 'Liebesgebot' [n. 14] 56).

53. Such an idea (mentioned by Stuhlmacher, 'Jesustradition' [n. 4] 248 n. 31) is expressed by M. Hengel, 'Jesus' (n. 1.2) 191 n. 137 (ET 151).

suggest that Paul had learnt this saying of Jesus—passed on to him either by that early Christian movement or by Peter—; but then we should also have to note the freedom with which Paul handles so important a saying of Jesus, in that he reformulates it and even limits it in a striking fashion in the interests of his theology of justification.

In all, the conclusion that Paul most clearly refers to Jesus-tradition in the context of ethical paraenesis is again confirmed from the other side by the observation that he does not adduce such Jesus-tradition in support of his central Christological and soteriological statements. This confirms the view that Paul's soteriological Christology is essentially independent of the early church's pre-Synoptic Jesus-tradition.

IV

It is incontestable that, despite all our study of the Pauline texts, the possibility cannot be ruled out that sometime—for instance through early Hellenistic Jewish Christianity, but assuredly it could just as well be through Peter and other disciples of Jesus—Paul may have learnt far more of the Jesus-tradition than he reveals to us. Yet then our study of the text would show that there is a difference between 'learning' and an active 'making use' of such tradition. This can to some extent be explained further by referring, firstly, to the peculiar nature of the connection of Paul with Jesus in the transmission of tradition, and, secondly, to one factor that emerges from the field of psychological learning theory.

On the first point: if we ignore for the moment any later contacts with disciples of Jesus like Peter, then originally Paul was in immediate contact with the tradition handed down by that group which he at first persecuted and then, conquered by the *Kyrios*, joined, that is, with the Hellenistic Jewish movement in early Christianity. This movement more clearly questioned the basis of Judaism than did the group around Peter (or indeed than the Jerusalem church which later took its cue above all from James); their words and actions allowed only a relative importance to remain attached to the Torah and Temple, and, as time passed, they regarded former Gentiles as full members in the church who possessed the same rights there as converted Jews (Acts 11.20–6). This group certainly had contact from the start with Jesus-tradition (in a more or less fixed form). But for them those sayings and other traditions which revealed an implicit criticism of the Torah or the Temple would probably have been especially important. So many of the apophthegms which show Jesus in conflict with the norms of Judaism may have taken shape and then have been handed on within this circle.[54] Paul gives no sign of

---

54. 'Taken shape' does not necessarily mean 'were invented', as the form-

knowing such stories. But certainly not only sayings like the 'double commandment' discussed immediately above, in which the Torah is summarized, but also and just as well the tradition lying behind Rom 14.14*a* which holds that Jesus did away with the idea of impurity (Mark 7.15) could well stem from the same line of tradition. Sayings of Jesus of such a kind, which questioned Jewish values either wholesale or in detail, may well have been taken up with special interest and transmitted in early Hellenistic Jewish Christianity. That could, for instance, explain why Paul is so vividly aware of precisely that saying of Jesus which declares divorce to be contrary to the will of God, as is shown in 1 Cor 7.10–11. For this saying too—at least according to its context in Mark 10.2–9—is indeed in explicit contrast with a specific 'commandment' of the Torah which makes divorce legal (Deut 24.1ff); at the same time we have seen that this saying of Jesus is found in Mark 10.11–12 in a form which reveals a Hellenizing application of it, and Paul apparently knew it in this form.

Naturally this early Christian group will have possessed much traditional material which took more the form of 'wisdom' sayings of Jesus concerning how to live aright according to God's will. Yet if one considers the use which Paul made of such material, then he seems to show less interest in the fact that Jesus was its author than he did in the instances mentioned above; rather he is simply concerned with their content which is self-explanatory and authoritative—since and inasmuch as the contents of such material did not involve matters that were at variance with Jewish tradition.

---

critics are frequently charged with saying. But it is still worth noting how at a relatively late stage in the tradition we can still see that the motif of breaking the sabbath has been added to the stories of healing as a secondary development: this occurs in the interpretation that carries on the narrative of John 5.2–9*a* in 5.9*b*–16 and that of 9.1–7(–12) in 9.14.—It is true that U. B. Müller, 'Zur Rezeption gesetzeskritischer Jesustradition im frühen Christentum', in *NTS* 27 (1980–1) 158–85, sees the setting of Jesus-tradition that is critical of the Law as having its home amongst missionaries carrying on a Gentile mission from Galilee, not amongst the Hellenistic Jewish group that goes back to Stephen. Yet cf. now too the important article on the subject by J. D. G. Dunn, 'Mark 2.1–3.6: a Bridge between Jesus and Paul on the Question of the Law', in *NTS* 30 (1984) 395–415; according to him we can detect in the pre-Markan unit Mark 2.15–3.5 the stance of an (older) Jewish-Christian group, which has not yet decided on out and out criticism of the Torah, while in 2.1–12 a pericope has been added through which 2.15ff undergoes a further stage of interpretation; in general Dunn assumes that the Antiochene church—which Paul joined—was influenced by traditions of this sort which were critical of the Law and from which the Law-free Gentile mission then developed.

It seems to me to follow from these observations and considerations that the Hellenistic Jewish part of the early church and then, in continuity with it, Paul had a use for and actively 'cultivated' such material from the Jesus-tradition as could help to justify their Law-free gospel which was open to the Gentiles. Apart from that, any sayings which were relevant to the 'apostolic existence' of their missionaries were also, of course, important within this line of tradition. To this category belong—to judge from the evidence of Paul—the 'word of the Lord' in 1 Cor 9.14 as well as the motifs drawn from the benedictions pronounced upon the hungry and the persecuted, to which Paul apparently alludes in 1 Cor 4.11–13; here he is aware of the relationship to Christ of such descriptions of the apostles' existence (1 Cor 4.10). That then means that the selection from the stock of Jesus-tradition possibly known to him which Paul actively 'cultivated' mostly concerned, in one way or another, the foundations and the basic insights of his preaching and theology (but not his central Christological and soteriological statements—see above p. 63) or else his apostolic existence.

Here we come naturally to the consideration from psychological learning theory of which I gave notice above.[55] In itself it is a self-evident insight that, out of the mass of pieces of information which any one individual encounters, he or she will note and become aware of those which have a bearing upon some question already raised by that individual, or upon a problem of which that person is already conscious, or upon particular experiences in the life of the one who receives these pieces of information. That will be the motivation which above all decides, out of all the information that is on offer, what will be chosen, 'internalized' and then also passed on.

Paul—in contrast to Peter and others (and also James the 'brother of the Lord'!)—did not know Jesus. So we cannot suppose that his personality had impressed itself upon him as one can without difficulty postulate was the case with the disciples of Jesus, a fact which also easily explains their extensive recollections of him.[56] The first—indirect—

55. In his new book *Psychologische Aspekte paulinischer Theologie* (FRLANT 131, Göttingen: Vandenhoeck & Ruprecht, 1983; ET: Philadelphia: Fortress & Edinburgh: Clark, 1987) G. Theißen does not consider the question 'What did Paul know of Jesus—and what picture did he have of Jesus?'; but I could well imagine that investigating this through a psychological approach would be fruitful.

56. Thus we avoid recourse to the hypothesis that Jesus himself deliberately shaped the future Jesus-tradition and impressed it like a schoolmaster upon his disciples—a hypothesis which *may* perhaps be correct at any rate for a limited basic stock of sayings and other material (like parables).

contact which Paul had with Jesus took place by way of the preaching of his disciples after Easter. To this Jew, devoted to the Torah and belonging to the Pharisaic movement, the idea that Jesus of Nazareth, who was already dead and indeed had even been executed, was (or had been?) the Messiah would have appeared more absurd than worthy of persecution. According to Acts 5.34–9 the Pharisee Gamaliel too—Acts 22.3 claims that he had taught Paul—was of the opinion that one could best let this business die its own death. But when appeal was made to this dead person to justify relativizing in some way the importance of the Torah and the Temple and subsequently opening up membership in the people of God to Gentiles as well, that is to those who were impure, without requiring of them circumcision and allegiance to Judaism, then Paul— like the authorities in Jerusalem—felt that it was necessary for him to act. It is well-known that the sudden appearance of 'Saul' in Acts 8.1, following the story of the stoning of Stephen (7.57), and his persecuting activities in Jerusalem (8.3) and his being supplied with full authority from the High Priest for similar actions in Damascus (9.1–2) all raise historical problems of various types which cannot be discussed here. But, be that as it may, it may be significant that Paul's activities as a persecutor, which are adequately attested by him himself, are connected particularly with the group around Stephen and the relativizing of the importance of the Torah and the Temple which they represented (Acts 6.13–14). Here the Pharisee Paul—like his Jewish opponents in Jerusalem at a later stage (Acts 21.27ff; 23.12–25)—saw the foundations of Judaism under attack; here he saw what others were later to hold against him: a message of apostasy from Jerusalem, in other words, from God; here his reaction was to seek to 'exterminate' them (πορθεῖν, Gal 1.13, 23), inspired by his zeal for God (Gal 1.14; Phil 3.6). So this was how Paul first came into contact with Jesus—namely through those who preached of him; that the message which they preached also appealed to one who had been cursed by God in the sight of all (Deut 27.26; cf. Gal 3.13) was naturally an especial stumbling-block (1 Cor 1.23) to Paul the devout Pharisee. But then as a result of his experience at Damascus it was precisely these scales of value that were turned upside down (Gal 1.15– 16); what he had formerly regarded as blasphemous he now recognized to be God's will, and he immediately put himself at the disposal of that will with the same zeal, as an ἀπόστολος Ἰησοῦ Χριστοῦ, an 'apostle of Jesus Christ'. Yet the starting-point for his understanding of Jesus remained unchanged, at least as regards the categories in which he understood him, although of course the values attached to them were changed. So at first he had no need, either, to consult anyone (Gal 1.16b); he needed no 'authoritative interpretation of what he (Paul) had seen and heard on the

Damascus road' in order to know what the content of his new commission was.[57] And if three years later he was in fact interested in meeting Peter, this was apparently because circumstances had arisen in the meantime which compelled him to seek out someone who could confirm to him that he was justified in appealing to the Lord Jesus as authority for the course he was following (see pp. 64–6 above). One would love to extend the scope of what he learnt about Jesus on this occasion from Peter; what he remembered was what was important and decisive for him within the context of the questions that concerned him, namely with regard to his preaching of the gospel to the Gentiles. And within the limits of the Jesus-tradition known to us that may above all have been those sayings which provided a starting-point for a critique and a new interpretation of the Torah.

V

Paul never disclosed in his extant letters how he, the apostle of Jesus Christ, understood the work of the 'earthly' Jesus (to use our categories) in his preaching and actions; it was only his passion and crucifixion for which he offered a theological interpretation. There is no hint that he—unlike ourselves who cannot avoid it—ever recognized the 'Lord Jesus Christ', whose apostle he knew that he was called to be, and the 'earthly Jesus' as belonging to different categories.[58] Moreover, as I have said, we cannot be sure whether he himself wrote those passages, in which we detect echoes of the Jesus-tradition, in the consciousness that he was referring to sayings of Jesus. If we could put our questions to him using our categories and could thereby draw his attention to those parallels in the tradition, he would perhaps reply as follows:

The work of the 'earthly Jesus', as you call him, is in my view above all that of a teacher of a new Torah with full authority (=a 'messianic' one?),[59] of a preacher

---

57. J. D. G. Dunn, 'The Relationship between Paul and Jerusalem according to Galatians 1 and 2', in *NTS* 28 (1982) 461–78, here 462–3; on this article see above in Excursus 2.

58. On 2 Cor 5.16 in this respect see above in n. 22. A largely convincing interpretation of this verse has very recently been put forward by O. Betz: 'Fleischliche und "geistliche" Christuserkenntnis nach 2.Korinther 5,16', in *TBei* 14 (1983) 167–79: knowing Christ 'according to the flesh' does not concern the problem of the 'historical' Jesus, but refers to the unbelieving view that the crucified Jesus was rejected by God, a view that Paul himself had once shared (cf. Isa 53.3 and 4b; also Gal 3.13). The article of J. W. Fraser, 'Knowledge' (n. 1.2), points in the same direction, although no reference is made to the background in Isa 53 which is so important for Betz.

of the real, true will of God for our 'service of righteousness' (cf. Rom 6.18ff and Rom 12). It was particularly important for me to have it confirmed by Peter that Jesus took his new teaching of the Torah so far as to criticize many passages in the 'old' Torah as contrary to the will of God; thus he also created the possibility of carrying the preaching of God's will without preconditions beyond the bounds of Judaism—even if he used to do so himself only occasionally (cf. Mark 7.24–30; Luke 7.2–10 and 13.29 par.). But what you think that you have discerned to be the 'heart' of the preaching of the 'earthly' Jesus, his way of speaking of the βασιλεία τοῦ θεοῦ, that I have either not heard aright or I have not understood it aright. The real heart of the message of Christ, as God disclosed it to me by revealing God's Son to me (Gal 1.16), is, in my opinion—and here I am conscious of being led by God and by the Holy Spirit of God (Gal 1.11–12; cf. also 1 Cor 7.40b)—, neither the preaching of the 'new Torah' as such nor the anticipation of the βασιλεία τοῦ θεοῦ (as I understand this expression), but the preaching of God's grace to all people, Jews *and* Gentiles (Rom 1.16c), since *all* people—Jews and Gentiles alike—are in need of this grace of God (Rom 1.18–3.20 and also 11.30–2). And it is certainly important for me also to learn from you that, in your view, in this centre of the gospel of Christ my message ultimately agrees with the preaching of my Lord Jesus Christ, despite all differences in the terms used. True, I was sure of that anyway—not on the basis of any demonstrable continuity in the line of tradition, but for the reason that it was this very message which I originally persecuted in my persecution of that 'radical' group of Jesus' messengers, but whose truth God then proved to me.

Peter Stuhlmacher closes his exposition in the article which I have quoted a number of times with the following sentence (emphasized in italics): 'In Romans too Paul regards himself as the apostle of Jesus Christ, whose gospel of justification in the light of Easter corresponds to Jesus' own message of the kingdom of God and is to be interpreted in continuity with the Jesus-tradition' (250). As my remarks above show, I can thoroughly agree with this conclusion, if I understand the last words of this quotation rather differently from Stuhlmacher himself. At any rate I am convinced that it is in no way a necessary condition for holding there to be an agreement in substance between the preaching of Paul and the message of Jesus that one presupposes and hopes to demonstrate as unbroken, direct and complete a chain of tradition as possible between Jesus and Paul. Even if the 'links in the tradition' assumed by Stuhlmacher and others could be proved as comprehensively and as surely as possible, that would still leave the question of agreement in substance to be investigated: handing on tradition is in itself still no guarantee of a real continuity in substance! But one can still uphold the view that Paul's gospel agrees in substance with Jesus' message if the

59. Cf. the thesis of the work of R. Riesner (in n. 3 above) 499 (following M. Hengel).

connections with the tradition—which are of course still necessary—exist in a far more indirect form or (to use images from the sphere of optics) with groupings, refractions and reflections of rays and also partial loss of rays and on the other hand with input from other sources. Yet this latter process is more probable historically and seems to be suggested by what we have observed in the Pauline texts.[60]

60. As a postscript I should refer to the paper of F. Neirynck, 'Paul and the Sayings of Jesus', in (ed.) A. Vanhoye, *L'apôtre Paul: personnalité, style et conception du ministère*, BETL 73, Leuven: University & Peeters, 1986, 265–321, which was delivered at the *Colloquium Biblicum Lovaniense* in Leuven on 29th August 1984. Neirynck examines in great detail the parallels between those parts of Romans and 1 Corinthians which I have also mentioned and the Jesus-tradition, and comes to conclusions which broadly agree with what I have assumed to be the case here (esp. in the case of 1 Cor 11.23–5), or are even more sceptical with regard to the assumption that Paul actually used Jesus-tradition. On the theme of this essay the following may also be compared: E. P. Sanders, 'Jesus' (n. 1.2), and now the *Festschrift* for F. W. Beare (n. 1.2) with a whole series of relevant essays, and W. Schmithals, *Einleitung* (n. 27) 99–110.

4

TRUE APOSTOLIC KNOWLEDGE OF CHRIST: EXEGETICAL REFLECTIONS ON 2 CORINTHIANS 5.14ff.

Christian Wolff

Even those who worked strenuously against Paul in the Corinthian church could not gainsay the power which his letters possessed to persuade their readers. Thus they sought to limit the influence of Paul's writings as far as possible. So Paul quotes in 2 Cor 10.10 the words of his opponents: '(His) letters, (so) it is said, (are) indeed weighty and powerful, but his personal presence is weak and his speech contemptible'. Yet 80 to 100 years later the author of 2 Pet (3.15–16) could now remark that in the letters 'of our beloved brother Paul...some things are hard to understand'. One can understand how this difference in evaluation could arise. Paul's letters presuppose situations with which the apostle and his church were fully familiar and therefore did not need further description; allusions sufficed.[1] But when these letters were read at a later point of time and in other churches, their readers were unaware of the original situation and much was thus δυσνόητος, 'hard to understand'. This problem had already, as I said, arisen 80 to 100 years after Paul's ministry, and today too there are, despite refined exegetical methods, a considerable number of Paul's statements whose meaning is unclear or disputed. One of these passages is 2 Cor 5.16.[2] This verse exercises a really magical fascination upon exegetes, for Paul here speaks of his earlier relationship to Christ:

---

1. Cf. also E. Fascher, *Der erste Brief des Paulus an die Korinther 1: Einführung und Auslegung der Kapitel 1–7* (THKNT 7.1, Berlin: Evangelische Verlagsanstalt, 1980²) 21, where he remarks that the letters 'as "conversations cut in two" contain allusions that are immediately intelligible to those who receive them, but which much later readers can only very hesitantly interpret'.

2. W. Schmithals, *Die Gnosis in Korinth* (FRLANT 66, Göttingen: Vandenhoeck & Ruprecht, 1969³; ET: Nashville & New York: Abingdon, 1971) 286 describes 5.16 as 'probably the hardest *crux interpretum* of II Corinthians, which is not poor in such *cruces*' (quoted from ET 302).

'Therefore from now on *we* know no one (else) according to the flesh. If we also knew Christ according to the flesh, yet we now know (him thus) no longer.' A brief survey of the study of this verse[3] will show the different possible ways in which this verse may be understood.

In the older exegetical discussion the question was frequently posed, whether Paul had known Jesus in person. Representatives of such diverse position as the likes of J. Weiß and P. Feine were in agreement that this question should be answered in the affirmative. J. Weiß[4] concluded his consideration of this question thus: 'I must insist that the words themselves [he means 2 Cor 5.16] allow of no other interpretation than that Paul had seen and known Jesus in person.' This was during Jesus' last days in Jerusalem; Paul was 'somehow present' during Jesus' passion. Paul, however, emphasizes that he accords no more importance to this, in stark contrast to his opponents, who, he supposed, boasted that they had known Jesus personally. P. Feine[5] combined 2 Cor 5.16 with Acts 7.58; 22.3; 26.4ff and inferred that Paul during his schooling in Phariseeism had spent his entire youth in Jerusalem; his hatred of the first Christians was to be explained by the fact that 'already during Jesus' lifetime' he had 'been troubled by his behaviour and his teaching'. Paul had therefore been present during the proceedings before the Sanhedrin and even at Jesus' crucifixion.—Yet such an interpretation of 2 Cor 5.16 could not prevail. For Paul nowhere else mentions his earlier hostility to Jesus which arose from *personal contact* with Jesus. On the other hand, he repeatedly mentions that he persecuted the *Christian church* (1 Cor 15.9; Gal 1.13, 23; Phil 3.6), and this he regards as proof that his conversion and call are to be traced to God's action *in grace*. Had Paul formerly known and rejected Jesus in person, then such a background would have been a far more impressive witness to the grace which the apostle had experienced; but of this Paul breathes not a word.

Another solution is to interpret 2 Cor 5.16 as a hypothetical real or as an unreal condition:[6] 'Assuming that we had...'. But the very

---

3.   Cf. here the detailed survey in J. W. Fraser, 'Knowledge' (n. 1.2), esp. 293–7 and 301–7.

4.   *Paulus* (n. 2.43) 2–30 (the quotation is from p. 29).

5.   *Der Apostel Paulus: das Ringen um das geschichtliche Verständnis des Paulus* (BFCT 2.12, Gütersloh: Bertelsmann, 1927) 413–37 (the quotation is from p. 432).

6.   So C. F. G. Heinrici, *Der zweite Brief an die Korinther* (MeyerK 6, Göttingen: Vandenhoeck & Ruprecht, 1890[7]) 174 (referring to the earlier views of Erasmus and H. Grotius); H. Lietzmann–W. G. Kümmel, *An die Korinther I/II* (HNT 9, Tübingen: Mohr, 1949[4]) 125; Bultmann, *2 Kor* (n. 1.3) 157; D. Georgi,

expression 'hypothetical real condition' is inappropriate; for hypothetical statements express a possibility, and it is well known that this is expressed in Greek by εἰ, 'if', with the optative. And if the reference is to an unfulfilled condition in the past, then we would expect the aorist indicative (instead of the perfect).[7] Nor does the context—in contrast to Gal 5.11—suggest a hypothetical way of speaking.

Many exegetes have taken the 'we' in 5.16 to refer, not to Paul, but more widely. So H. Windisch[8] thinks that Paul included himself in what did not apply to himself, but 'which really only *certain prominent representatives* had experienced'. In his polemic against his opponents Paul denied the value of such links with the earthly Jesus. E.–B. Allo[9] gives a more precise and exact meaning to the collegiality implied in the 'we' in that from amongst the ranks of Paul's co-workers Barnabas, Silas and John Mark would have known Jesus during his earthly activity, but after Easter and Pentecost the importance of the earthly Jesus would have diminished for them, and more attention would have been paid to the redemptive work of Christ; that is what Paul is referring to.—Yet it must be objected that such a spurious use of 'we', in which Paul would have included himself in a statement that did not apply to him at all, is in itself unlikely, but also is the unlikelier because of the first half of the verse, where Paul cannot be excluded from the emphatic 'we'. Apart from that, there is no conclusive evidence for the personal links of Paul's co-workers with the earthly Jesus.

This approach of H. Windisch and E.–B. Allo raises by implication the matter of Paul's relation to the Jesus-*tradition*. Previously this question had been broached more clearly by W. Bousset.[10] He drew attention to the possibility 'that Paul is here referring to an indirect knowledge of the earthly Jesus *via* the church and means that he too

---

Die Gegner des Paulus im 2. Korintherbrief (WMANT 11, Neukirchen–Vluyn: Neukirchener, 1964) 256–7; E. Dinkler, 'Die Verkündigung als eschatologisch-sakramentales Geschehen', in *Die Zeit Jesu (Festschrift* for H. Schlier, Freiburg-i-B., etc: Herder, 1970) 169–89, esp. 174 n. 17; U. Schnelle, *Gerechtigkeit und Christusgegenwart: vorpaulinische und paulinische Tauftheologie* (GTA 24, Göttingen: Vandenhoeck & Ruprecht, 1983) 183 n. 131.

7. Cf. BDR §360 n. 4.

8. *Der zweite Korintherbrief* (repr. ed. G. Strecker, MeyerK, Göttingen: Vandenhoeck & Ruprecht, 1970[9]) 187.

9. *Saint Paul: seconde épître aux Corinthiens* (Paris: Gabalda, 1956[2]) 179–82: Excursus 11—'Ce que signifie "Ne plus connaître le Christ selon la chair (V,16b)"'.

10. *Der zweite Brief an die Korinther* (SNT 2, Göttingen: Vandenhoeck & Ruprecht, 1917[3]) 195.

once set store by acquiring knowledge of the earthly Jesus through eyewitnesses' accounts'. Now, however, he wants 'to know no more of him. It is enough for him to be sure that he is preaching his gospel as the exalted Lord would wish.'—Such an interpretation of 2 Cor 5.16 then occurs in various forms in the debate over the basic theological significance of the earthly or—as one now put it—the 'historical' Jesus; the phrase Χριστὸς κατὰ σάρκα, 'Christ according to the flesh', which is derived from our verse became an important one in this context as a description of the historical Jesus; so R. Bultmann said in what was really a programmatic statement:[11] 'The Χριστὸς κατὰ σάρκα is no concern of ours. How things looked in the heart of Jesus I do not know and do not want to know.' On the strength of 2 Cor 5.16, for instance, one found in Paul an ally in such a view; for the verse was now taken to mean that Paul was here expressing a clear disinterest in the historical Jesus or the Jesus-tradition.[12] We will come back to that in our detailed exegesis.

M. E. Thrall[13] has taken a different line: in v 16 Paul is referring to an earlier stage of his preaching; formerly he concentrated more in his preaching in Corinth on the risen and glorified Christ, as the second Adam, and that was more what the Corinthians had expected. But now he was putting that right. But the apostle's reference back to the past in 1 Cor 2.2 tells against such an interpretation: 'But I decided to know nothing amongst you except Jesus Christ, and him as crucified.'

On the other hand, there are very many exegetes,[14] who take our verse to refer to an earlier knowledge of Jesus on the part of Paul, a

11. 'Zur Frage der Christologie', in id., *Glauben* 1 (n. 2.64; ET: *Faith and Understanding*, London: SCM, 1969, 116–44) 85–113 (the quotation is from p. 101=ET 132, quoted here).

12. Cf. particularly R. Bultmann, 'Bedeutung' (n. 2.64) esp. 202ff; ET here 235ff.

13. 'Christ Crucified or Second Adam? A Christological Debate between Paul and the Corinthians', in (ed.) B. Lindars, S. S. Smalley, *Christ and Spirit in the New Testament* (*Festschrift* for C. F. D. Moule, Cambridge Univ., 1973) 143–56, esp. 153ff.

14. Cf. P. Bachmann, *Der zweite Brief des Paulus an die Korinther* (Kommentar zum Neuen Testament 8, Leipzig: Deichert, 1909) 260; A. Schlatter, *Paulus der Bote Jesu* (Stuttgart: Calwer, 1962³) 562; K. Prümm, *Diakonia Pneumatos* 1 (Rom, etc: Herder, 1967) 338–9; C. K. Barrett, *A Commentary on the Second Epistle to the Corinthians* (Black's NT Comms, London: Black, 1982) 171; A. Oepke, 'Irrwege in der neueren Paulusforschung', in *TLZ* 77 (1952) 449–58, esp. 454; O. Michel, '"Erkennen dem Fleisch nach" (II. Kor. 5,16)', in *EvT* 14 (1954) 22–9, esp. 26; J. B. Soucek, '"Wir kennen Christus nicht mehr dem Fleisch nach"', in *EvT* 19 (1959) 300–14, esp. 312; J. Blank, *Paulus und Jesus* (n. 1.2) 317ff.

knowledge that he had *before* his conversion; but this is a knowledge that is no personal acquaintance with Jesus, but a *conclusion* that he reached concerning what he had learnt of Jesus before he became a Christian, and which he then radically corrected as a result of his conversion experience.

Finally we should note a radical attempt at a solution, proposed by W. Schmithals:[15] 2 Cor 5.16 is not by Paul's hand, but is a conclusion from v 17 written as a gloss in the margin of the original letter by a Gnostic; a later copyist then set this *before* v 17. The main argument which he gives for this hypothesis is that v 16 does not fit the context and is un-Pauline in its contents. This line of argument as well as the mass of different interpretations of 2 Cor 5.16 compel us to undertake anew the exegesis of this text.

Let us first trace the sequence of thought that leads up to 5.16. Its chief characteristic is an argument with people 'who pride themselves on their outward appearance (πρόσωπον), but not on their heart' (v 12b). This is Paul's description of his opponents who complacently appeal to fascinating external features (3.1; 11.18; 12.1) in support of their apostleship (11.3, 23), but who in their hearts, in their thinking, feelings and wills, which are disclosed to God (Rom 8.27; 1 Thess 2.4; 1 Sam 16.7), are not shaped by the Spirit of God (Rom 5.5).[16] In contrast Paul's life is not centred on himself,[17] but (v 13) on God and on the church. At the same time these statements of Paul's are a check upon an over-evaluation of ecstatic experiences:[18] they concern a person's relation to God and are entirely directed towards God; if they become something to impress others, or if such experiences are used to demonstrate one's special position, then that does not promote the church's spiritual growth (but rather its being treated as immature, indeed its suppression; cf. 11.20). On the other hand when the mind is given full scope, as is the case in Paul's preaching of the gospel and his writing of his letters, that is spiritually profitable for the church (cf. similarly 1 Cor 14.2–4, 18–19). In v 14 Paul justifies his orientation solely towards God and the church by a reference

15. *Gnosis* (n. 2) 286–99; in basic agreement is E. Güttgemanns, *Apostel* (n. 3.29) 288–98.

16. E. Güttgemanns, ibid. 282–3 n. 3, rightly emphasizes that 'the καρδία of Christians is to be understood as the "place" of the πνεῦμα'.

17. On the contrasting behaviour of his opponents cf. 10.12.

18. The aorist form ἐξέστημεν (the verb only occurs here in the Pauline corpus) is striking; it refers to earlier experiences. Does Paul regard them as a thing of the past?

to the 'love of Christ'.[19] It is, as the use of συνέχειν, 'constrain, impel' (cf. Phil 1.23), shows, 'the dominant principle, the decisive norm and the driving power of the apostle's activities'.[20] Through the love of Christ Paul has come to the conviction that Christ died representatively that death which the human race had incurred through their sin;[21] in his death all are thus included, so that the basis of a new existence is thus granted to them which is free from all self-seeking. Paul sets great store by this argument, as v 15 shows. This sentence is probably also part of the apostle's judgment (κρίναντας, 'judging', v 14) and thus goes with v 14*b*, as is suggested by the juxtaposing of the third person singular (referring to Christ) with the third person plural (contrast the 'we'-style referring to Paul in vv 11–14*a* and again in v 16). Now (v 15) we have a description of the nature of the new existence based on Jesus' representative death and realized in faith (note the difference between πάντες, 'all', and οἱ ζῶντες, 'the living': Christ's act of love is valid for all, but its consequences are only realized by those who live a new life as a result of it).[22] No longer are we in control[23] of this new life; rather we are free from ourselves and belong entirely to him[24] who has taken our place (Rom 7.4*b*; also 14.7–8) and who through his resurrection was really the first to bring this new human existence into being (significantly

19. *Τοῦ Χριστοῦ* is a subjective genitive; for the second half of the verse and 15*a* are dealing with Christ's death, which is regarded as a proof of his love (Gal 2.20; also Rom 8.34–5).

20. J. Blank, *Paulus und Jesus* (n. 1.2) 314. The plural κρίναντας refers to Paul; cf. v 13.

21. Cf. also F. Froitzheim, *Christologie und Eschatologie bei Paulus* (FB 35, Würzburg: Echter, 1979) 41: 'On the cross of Christ God definitively passed sentence and that sentence is "death" for all. All the world was open before God in the crucified body of Christ (cf. Rom 7.4) and received their just sentence'; and 43: 'the death that Christ died...is nothing but the eschatological death which is the consequence and the wrathful judgment of God upon sin and thus the destruction of all people in so far as they are sinners; Christ's death was thus at the same time the death of all humanity.'

22. Cf. E. Dinkler, 'Verkündigung' (n. 6) 172; also W. Thüsing, *Per Christum in Deum: Studien zum Verhältnis von Christozentrik und Theozentrik in den paulinischen Hauptbriefen* (NTAbh Neue Folge 1, Münster: Aschendorff, 1969²) 103. Contrast Blank, *Paulus und Jesus* (n. 1.2) 316.

23. The dative refers to the possessor; cf. BDR §188.3.

24. Behind this argument perhaps lies the idea of *redemptio ab hostibus*: the one freed belongs to the one who has paid the ransom (cf. 1 Cor 6.19–20; 7.23); see here W. Elert, 'Redemptio ab hostibus', in *TLZ* 72 (1947) 265–70.

ὑπέρ, 'on behalf of', refers to the statement about dying *and* to that about resurrection; cf. also Rom 6.4, 10–11; 1 Cor 15.17).[25] This brings us to the much-discussed verse 16 which we must now consider in more detail. The introductory ὥστε, 'so', shows that now the consequences are being drawn from the saving work of the loving Christ, a work that 'controls' the apostle (v 14). For Paul the consequences are these:[26] the new life derived from Christ and directed towards him includes a refusal to know people κατὰ σάρκα, 'according to the flesh'. The term οὐδένα, 'no one', is inclusive and thus corresponds to the πάντες of v 15, but yet the statement refers particularly to all believers including Paul himself (cf. v 15*b*!). Because of its position the prepositional phrase κατὰ σάρκα must refer to οἴδαμεν, 'we know'; when Paul combines it with a verb he does so to express the self-willed, sinful orientation of one's life; one plans (1.17), struggles (10.3) and boasts in oneself (11.18) 'according to the flesh'. Thus οἴδαμεν contains an element of judgment, understanding (cf. κρίναντας, 'judging', v 14). For Paul, who emphatically distances himself from his opponents by the word ἡμεῖς, 'we', such a self-sufficient evaluation of the human person and of himself is inappropriate, for the good reason that he no longer lives for himself and by his own resources, but belongs totally to Christ (v 15); thus he judges everything in the light of Christ and his loving self-offering (cf., e.g., Gal 6.14–15). If, then, the apostle's opponents pride themselves on external and demonstrable advantages which they enjoy (v 12*b*), and if they reject Paul because he does not fit the criteria which they have themselves picked, then they merely show that they have not been grasped by the saving work of Christ at all.

In the second half of the verse Paul gives the reasons for the impossibility of a knowledge according to the flesh; the basis of his

25. Cf. also Thüsing, *Per Christum* (n. 22) 104: we should live 'for him in whom, as the risen one, this love lives on—, who was raised from the dead in order to draw us into his life and thereby into his love'.

26. We should regard the first person plural as referring to Paul; cf. vv 11–14. So too Bachmann, *2 Kor* (n. 14) 257; A. Plummer, *A Critical and Exegetical Commentary on the Second Epistle of St Paul to the Corinthians* (ICC, Edinburgh: Clark, 1915) 176–9; Schlatter, *Paulus* (n. 14) 559–64; Prümm, *Diakonia* (n. 14) 336; Blank, *Paulus und Jesus* (n. 1.2) 313. O. Betz, 'Christus-erkenntnis' (n. 3.57) esp. 174, takes the plural to be an apostolic one: 'all apostles and former disciples of Jesus have experienced a change in their perception of the cross'. Bultmann, *2 Kor* (n. 1.3) 155, and Dinkler, 'Verkündigung' (n. 6) 174, take it to refer to all believers; so too J.-F. Collange, *Énigmes de la deuxième Épître de Paul aux Corinthiens* (SNTSMS 18, Cambridge Univ., 1972) 257–8 and 263.

argument is the radical change which he himself had experienced.[27] The formulation of the conditional clause with εἰ καί, 'if indeed', expresses a fact. Κατὰ σάρκα is, as in v 16*a*, to be taken with the verb; it is therefore speaking of an evaluation[28] of Christ from purely human, self-sufficient perspectives, and the contrasting νῦν, 'now', a '*nunc soteriologicum*',[29] like the ἀπὸ τοῦ νῦν, 'from now on', in v 16*a*, shows that such an evaluation took place *before* the time of salvation became a reality for Paul.[30] In other words, Paul is here speaking of an evaluation which he held before his conversion and call to be an apostle. The use of the title 'Christ'[31] shows that this estimate referred above all to what Paul had heard of Jesus' death and of his being raised from the dead. Then he had regarded Jesus' crucifixion as meaning that he was a trouble-maker with messianic claims who had failed and was accursed by God (Deut. 21.23; Gal 3.13); it could not be expected that God would put him in the right in any way whatever. But 'now', after his conversion, this knowledge 'in the manner of the flesh'[32] has been shown to be a false one.

Thus κατὰ σάρκα in v 16*b* qualifies ἐγνώκαμεν, 'we have known',[33]

27. S. Kim, *The Origin of Paul's Gospel* (WUNT 2.4, Tübingen: Mohr, 1981) 13ff, rightly detects in 5.16 an allusion to Paul's conversion; similarly Blank, *Paulus und Jesus* (n. 1.2) 322. Cf. also O. Betz, ibid. 170 with n. 22 and pp. 173–4—Paul was particularly influenced by Isa 53.3–4: '"Knowing Christ according to the flesh" (v 16) corresponds to the mistaken opinion that the Servant of God is punished by God' (173); correspondingly Betz interprets judging according to the flesh as a failure to understand the scriptures (177).

28. The switch from εἰδέναι to γινώσκειν is purely stylistic, and indicates no difference in meaning; cf. 1 Cor 2.11–12 and Gal 4.8–9.

29. Prümm, *Diakonia* (n. 14) 338; cf. also Blank, *Paulus und Jesus* (n. 1.2) 317: 'The ἀπὸ τοῦ νῦν denotes *a point of time that once occurred, but at the same time this is an event that qualifies the present.*'

30. This is a further reason for rejecting the view of Thrall, 'Christ' (n. 13).

31. Cf. also W. Kramer, *Christos, Kyrios, Gottessohn: Untersuchungen zu Gebrauch und Bedeutung der christologischen Bezeichnungen bei Paulus und den vorpaulinischen Gemeinden* (ATANT 44, Zürich & Stuttgart: Zwingli, 1963; ET: SBT 50, London: SCM, 1966) 133: '*Christ* is the person in whom the saving events took place' (ET 135).

32. We have to supply κατὰ σάρκα after γινώσκομεν, cf. Schlatter, *Paulus* (n. 14) 561: 'That Paul understood this here is certain since an unqualified "We know Christ no more" would be an impossible statement for him...'.

33. So already F. C. Baur, *Vorlesungen über neutestamentliche Theologie* (Leipzig: Fues, 1864) 131 (cited by Moule, 'Jesus' [1970, n. 1.2] 17) and the authors cited in n. 14, as well as A. Sand, *Der Begriff 'Fleisch' in den paulinischen Hauptbriefen* (Biblische Untersuchungen 2, Regensburg: Pustet,

and not Χριστόν, 'Christ'.[34] This is, as should already be plain, suggested by the word-order (if Paul uses the phrase to qualify a noun, he places it after the noun: Rom 4.1; 9.3, 5; 1 Cor 1.26; 10.18), by the parallelism with v 16a, and also just as much by the context; for the issue is the apostle's existence, not statements about the nature of Christ.[35] It is true that R.

Bultmann argues that 'this decision means nothing for the sense of the total context, for a "Christ regarded in the manner of the flesh" is just what a "Christ after the flesh" is';[36] or 'to know people as they are met with in the world means also to know them in worldly fashion.'[37] But this interpretation puts all Paul's varied use of κατὰ σάρκα on the same level; for in connection with a substantive[38] the phrase is neutral, meaning that which is natural, or happens to occur, or one's physical lineage or ties, and this is not perhaps irrelevant even for Paul *as a Christian*. That can be seen, firstly, from his basic statement of his principles for his missionary work in 1 Cor 9.20–23: 'I became to the Jews as a Jew, that I might win Jews. ...To those without the Law I became as one without the Law..., that I might win those without the Law. I became to the weak as one who is weak, that I might win the weak.' On the other hand Paul can very well understand 'the existence (*Vorfindlichkeit*) of a person in the world' from a *spiritual* perspective too. That we can see from Romans 4, where Abraham, 'our forefather according to the flesh' (4.1), is portrayed as a type of the person justified by faith; we can see it too from Rom 9.3–4, where the apostle's συγγενεῖς κατὰ σάρκα are described as the 'Israelites',[39] 'to whom belong the sonship and the glory and the covenants and the Law-giving and the worship and the promises'. Finally, Rom 9.5 shows that Paul even as a Christian was very much interested in Jesus' existence in the world: that the Christ is descended from Israel

1967) 177; Moule, ibid. 17–18; Fraser, 'Knowledge' (n. 1.2) 298; Collange, *Énigmes* (n. 26) 260–1.

34. So already John Chrysostom, *Homilies on 2 Corinthians* 11.2; Bousset, *2 Kor* (n. 10); Bultmann, *2 Kor* (n. 1.3); Dinkler, 'Verkündigung' (n. 6) 174 n. 14; Georgi, *Gegner* (n. 6) 291–2.

35. Cf. also Sand, *Begriff* (n. 33) 177.

36. *Theologie* (n. 2.86) 239, quoted as in ET 239.

37. *2 Kor* (n. 1.3) 155–6, quoted as in ET 154; *Glauben* 1 (n. 2.64) 185, 207, 211, 244, 259.

38. Cf., e.g., Bultmann, *Theologie* (n. 2.86) 237 (ET 237)!

39. This term had for Hellenistic Judaism and for Paul an emphatically religious content; it was used of the elect people of God and its faith-history; cf. K. G. Kuhn in *TWNT* 3, 368.35ff; W. Gutbrod, ibid. 374.9ff; D. Georgi, *Gegner* (n. 6) 51–60; J. Wanke in *EWNT* 1, 892–4.

κατὰ σάρκα counts as *the* decisive testimony to the election of the Jewish people,[40] which will find its fulfilment in the coming salvation of Israel (11.26–7).[41]

Our decision about the position and the meaning of κατὰ σάρκα in v 16*b* also means that it is not the case that Paul was answering the charge that he was no valid apostle because he had not known Jesus personally.[42] Nor, however, is he attacking a particular image of Jesus held by his opponents. D. Georgi, it is true, regards v 16 as polemic against a Christology that glorified the earthly Jesus as a θεῖος ἀνήρ, a 'divine man'.[43] Quite apart from the fact that this interpretation takes κατὰ σάρκα with Χριστόν, I can find no support for such a reconstruction of the Christology of Paul's opponents in 2 Corinthians. Georgi in fact refers to 11.4, where Paul gives us to understand that his adversaries are preaching 'another Jesus'. But here we have to remember that, when Paul uses the name 'Jesus', he is focussing primarily on the historical event of the crucifixion (cf. 4.10, also 4.5; Gal 6.17; 1 Thess 4.14*a*; it is this Jesus who will rescue from wrath in 1 Thess 1.10; towards him faith is directed in Rom 3.25–6). Thus 11.4 is merely saying that Paul's opponents are preaching the event of the cross in another way to that of Paul. They believed that Paul, with his weakness and lowliness, could not be a true apostle, and that they themselves were attested (12.1, 11–12) as servants of Christ (11.23) through ecstatic experiences and miracles; from this we can but infer that the cross of Christ did not have the central importance for them as it did for Paul; to such a view the Corinthians were decidedly sympathetic, as we can see from 1 Cor 1.18ff. We certainly cannot try to recover a form of the preaching of Jesus or of the cross that was characteristic of Paul's opponents;[44] at any rate Paul does not go into any detail here. But the whole demeanour of his adversaries and their self-esteem had convinced him that the crucified one was not of significance for them.

It is true that one can detect a polemical undertone in v 16*b*, but of a

---

40. Cf. here Wilckens, *Röm* (n. 3.11) 2, 188.

41. On the relationship between Rom 9.1–5 and 11.25ff cf. P. von der Osten-Sacken, *Grundzüge einer Theologie im christlich-jüdischen Gespräch* (München: Kaiser, 1982) 39–41.

42. So Lietzmann–Kümmel, *1–2 Kor* (n. 6) 125 and 211; H. Windisch, *2 Kor* (n. 8) 188; J. Héring, *La seconde épître de Saint Paul aux Corinthiens* (CNT 8, Neuchâtel & Paris: Delachaux & Niestlé, 1958) 52.

43. *Gegner* (n. 6) 254–7 and 290ff.

44. Cf., e.g., the attempts to reconstruct it in Allo, *2 Cor* (n. 9); Héring, *2 Cor* (n. 42) 85; Schmithals, *Gnosis* (n. 2) 126–7. Contrast Bultmann, *2 Kor* (n. 1.3) 204.

quite different kind: Paul questions whether his opponents possessed a true knowledge of Christ (compare the emphatic ἡμεῖς, 'we', in v 16*a*); they indeed boast of such a knowledge (11.6), and hold it against Paul that his preaching of the gospel is inadequate and 'veiled' (4.3). But they judge themselves and Paul according to their own, typically human criteria; thus they show that their knowledge of *Christ* too is only a 'fleshly' one, and that thus all that matters about Christ for them is what confirms their estimate of themselves, and so they live for themselves (v 15*b*!).[45]

How does Paul's argument continue after v 16? V 17 contains a further consequence of Christ's saving work (vv 14–15) and is closely connected with the first consequence drawn in v 16 in so far as a positive statement now follows the negative one (v 16): through being (a being that is conferred in baptism) in the realm of the salvation brought by Christ and of his lordship (ἐν Χριστῷ εἶναι, 'being in Christ', corresponds to 'being mastered' by the love of Christ—v 14) a person is drawn into the eschatological creation[46] that begins with the crucified and resurrected one (cf. on this the earlier 1 Cor 8.6; already in 2 Cor 4.6 Paul had portrayed his own conversion as a creative act of God), and that person's judgments correspond to this. As a 'new creation' the believer (τις, 'anyone') walks in newness of life (Rom 6.4), and his or her life is no longer centred on the σάρξ, 'flesh' (v 16; cf. Gal 6.14–15), but on God's Spirit (πνεῦμα). The idea of the πνεῦμα is suggested here both by the antithesis to the 'fleshly' knowledge of v 16 (cf. Rom 8.4–6, 13; Gal 6.8) and by the ἐν Χριστῷ ('in Christ') phrase;[47] for being in Christ 'presupposes Christ's working through his Spirit'.[48] Taken with v 16*a* that means that the Spirit through which Christ discloses his saving work (1 Cor 2.10–12) allows the believer to appear in the light of the love of

---

45. Cf. Schlatter, *Paulus* (n. 14) 650: 'But it is possible that even when people deck themselves with spiritual pretensions and lofty insights they are thinking of nothing but themselves.'

46. Cf. here esp. P .Stuhlmacher, 'Erwägungen zum ontologischen Charakter der καινὴ κτίσις bei Paulus', in *EvT* 27 (1967) 1–35.

47. It is true that the Spirit is not expressly mentioned; cf. O. Betz, 'Christuserkennnis' (n. 3.57) 178: 'Perhaps Paul deliberately omitted the reference to the Spirit here. For the Corinthian pneumatics also boasted of a knowledge bestowed by the Spirit, which made them proud (1 Cor 8.1), while Paul came to them with the gentleness and kindness of Christ (2 Cor 10.1).'

48. Thüsing, *Per Christum* (n. 22) 65; see also O. Merk, *Handeln aus Glauben: die Motivierungen der paulinischen Ethik* (Marburger Theologische Studien 5, Marburg: Elwert, 1968) 17–19, esp. 19: 'New creation exists where God's eschatological gift of the Spirit is found.'

Christ.[49] At the same time the connection between v 16*b* and v 17 implies that in Paul's eyes the 'fleshly' knowledge of Christ has been overcome by the spiritual; that Spirit which causes Christ's saving work to be understood has also disclosed to the apostle the true understanding of what has been handed down to him concerning his death and his resurrection. V 16 and v 17 thus contain an indirect reference to the spiritual hermeneutics by which Paul interprets the early Christian Jesus-tradition.

In a new, Spirit-formed existence of this sort Old Testament prophecies of salvation were fulfilled, as Paul shows when he refers back to Isa 43.18–19: 'Take no thought for the former thing and do not *take account* of that which is old (τὰ ἀρχαῖα μὴ συλλογίζεσθε); see, I am making a new thing (ἰδοὺ ποιῶ καινά)'. The reference to the fulfilment of this prophecy of salvation underlines the impossibility of boasting in external things or continuing to judge 'in a fleshly way'; whoever does that is still entirely in the grip of the old which is past.

V 18 sums up the saving event and its consequences (i.e. vv 14–17) with reference to its original cause. Time does not permit us to offer an extensive treatment of the much-discussed problem whether and how far Paul made use of traditional early Christian material in his statements about reconciliation in vv 18–21.[50] To my mind the fact that we find talk of reconciliation solely in the Pauline corpus justifies us in assuming that here we have a specifically *Pauline* theologoumenon.[51] At any rate it is noteworthy that the apostle links the 'new creation' so closely with reconciliation when he says in v 18*a* that that is all based on God's reconciling activity. Paul perhaps found such a connection between 'new creation' and 'reconciliation' already in the Jewish understanding of the forgiveness of sins—in particular at the New Year and on the Day of Atonement—: according to this a person was made a new creature, a בְּרִיָה חֲדָשָׁה, no longer burdened with the sins of the past.[52] In Paul's eyes, of

49. Chapters 10–13 (esp. 11.13–15) show very plainly that this can also lead to a radical break with 'false brothers' (11.26).

50. Cf. here the survey of research in R. Bieringer, 'Die Versöhnung zwischen Rechtfertigung und Sühne', Licentiate dissertation, Leuven, 1983.

51. Cf. also Kim, *Origin* (n. 27) 311–12; Barrett, *2 Cor* (n. 14) 163.

52. Cf. here E. Sjöberg, 'Wiedergeburt und Neuschöpfung im palästinischen Judentum', in *ST* 4 (1951–2) 44–85, esp. 57–9 and the summary on 59: 'Those who returned to God were fashioned by God to a new creature, in that their sins were forgiven, so that they could begin a new life, without being burdened by their previous sins. This is usually the aspect which is being taken up when forgiveness is compared with new creation.' Barrett, ibid. 173–4, rejects such a

course, God's work of reconciliation has been accomplished once for all through the crucifixion and the resurrection of Christ, and the connection between new creation and reconciliation is important because it preserves the statement concerning the καινὴ κτίσις, 'new creation', from a misunderstanding that could easily arise in Corinth: we owe this new creation solely to Christ's self-offering for us; for that reason an enthusiastic feeling of superiority cannot be a mark of the new creation. The new light that falls on humanity is rather that of our being reconciled finally by God with God. Paul formulates this very personally once more: the two 'we' forms in this verse refer again to himself; that is clear in the second half of the verse and there is nothing which compels us to understand the first half differently, for καταλλάξαντος ἡμᾶς, 'having reconciled us', and δόντος ἡμῖν, 'having given to us', are plainly parallel. That means that in the first half of the verse Paul applies to himself a fact that is universally valid (without of course 'commandeering' it for himself); he is looking back to the saving event and to its application to him individually at his conversion and calling. Then, when God revealed the crucified Christ as the risen one to him, the persecutor of the church and thereby God's enemy, and enrolled him in the service (διακονία; cf. 3.7–8) of proclamation, he experienced personally God's reconciling grace. This experience of reconciliation shaped Paul's apostolic existence; in other words, reconciliation is for him the foundation of the true apostolic knowledge of Christ and thus at the same time the foundation of a correct evaluation of all that belongs to an apostle; apostles must be judged by how far they are true to the διακονία τῆς καταλλαγῆς, 'the service of reconciliation'.

In v 19*a* Paul derives his own experience of reconciliation and his apostolic message of reconciliation from the universal (κόσμος='world of human beings'; cf. v 14) reconciling act of God which consists in the blotting out of the guilt of sin.[53] This became a reality for Paul personally at his conversion. Therefore the apostle then once again emphasizes his commissioning by God. The switch from the present participle λογιζόμενος, 'reckoning', to the aorist participle θέμενος, 'having placed', shows that the two participles are not co-ordinates but that θέμενος is to be treated as a finite verb.[54] God's universal work of reconciliation and the apostolic message of reconciliation are thus distinct

connection and paraphrases: 'there is a new act of creation'.

53. Παράπτωμα is synonymous with ἁμαρτία; cf. the summary in Bultmann, *2 Kor* (n. 1.3) 163–4 (ET 162).

54. Cf. here Barrett, *2 Cor* (n. 14) 178; F. Büchsel in *TWNT* 1, 257 n. 3; O. Hofius, '"Gott hat unter uns aufgerichtet das Wort von der Versöhnung" (2 Kor 5,19)', in *ZNW* 71 (1980) 3–20, esp. 6–7; BDR §468.1.

from one another, and that as the once for all act of God in Christ's cross on the one hand and the realization of this in the present in the apostolic preaching on the other. Here the aorist sense of the participle θέμενος points to a once for all, finished event, namely—as with the δόντος in v 18—the apostle's call. Ἐν ἡμῖν, 'in us', refers, as in v 18b, to the *apostle*;[55] when he was called the message of God's reconciling act (cf. 1 Cor 1.18) was *laid* on the apostle's heart.[56] We can compare here the Old Testament phrase τιθέναι τοὺς λόγους ἐν τῷ στόματι, 2 Sam 14.3, 19 LXX; 2 Esdr 8.17 (lit. 'to set words in the mouth'). Paul does not mention the 'mouth', but writes 'in us' and thereby shows that the message entrusted to him has grasped his entire inward being (cf. likewise Isa 63.11, ὁ θεὶς ἐν αὐτοῖς τὸ πνεῦμα τὸ ἅγιον, 'the one who has set the Holy Spirit in them').

In v 20 Paul deduces from his commissioning to the task of proclaiming God's universal reconciling act that he exercises the function of an ambassador; the use of the verb πρεσβεύειν, 'serve as an ambassador' (only elsewhere in the New Testament in Eph 6.30), emphasizes the official character of this activity of his: 'The ambassador legally represents the political authority which sends him.'[57] Christ is named as the one giving the commission;[58] he, as the one through whom

55. So too Heinrici, *2 Kor* (n. 6) 183: 'The doctrine of reconciliation is treated as something deposited in the preacher's heart to be communicated to others'; Bachmann, *2 Kor* (n. 14) 268: 'deposited in us'; Plummer, *2 Cor* (n. 26) 165; Allo, *2 Cor* (n. 9) 169 and 171; Schlatter, *Paulus* (n. 14) 566; Prümm, *Diakonia* (n. 14) 342 and 344–5; M. Wolter, *Rechtfertigung und zukünftiges Heil: Untersuchungen zu Römer 5,1–11* (BZNW 43, Berlin & New York: de Gruyter, 1978) 83; Barrett, ibid. 177–8.

56. Hofius, '"Gott"' (n. 54), uses Ps 77.5 LXX to interpret v 19c: in both cases it is a matter of 'establishing' God's word in the community and of commissioning for preaching; Paul deliberately offers a contrast to God's self-revelation at Sinai.—But the phrase νόμον τιθέναι ο r τίθεσθαι is a regular expression in classical Greek and Hellenistic Judaism, where it means 'to give a law' (cf. Rom 9.7); see the evidence in W. Pape, *Griechisch-deutsches Handwörterbuch* 2 (Braunschweig: Vieweg, 1880³) 1110–1 s.v. τίθημι 2c; W. Bauer, *Griechisch-deutsches Wörterbuch zu den Schriften des Neuen Testaments und der übrigen urchristlichen Literatur* (Berlin: de Gruyter, 1958⁵) 1615 s.v. 1b. Τίθεσθαι τὸν λόγον can hardly be regarded as a parallel to this usage.

57. G. Bornkamm in *TWNT* 6, 680.4 (quoted from *TDNT* 6, 681). In the eastern part of the Roman Empire the verb and its cognates are used of the imperial legates; cf. A. Deißmann, *Licht vom Osten: das Neue Testament und die neuentdeckten Texte der hellenistisch-römischen Welt* (Tübingen: Mohr, 1923⁴) 320.

58. This function is often expressed by ὑπέρ; cf. Bornkamm, ibid. 681.2–6;

God accomplished the work of salvation, appeared to Paul and called him
to preach the gospel (1 Cor 9.1; Gal 1.15; 1 Cor 15.8–10), so that he
speaks through his apostle (cf. 2 Cor 13.3; Rom 15.18). In all this Paul is
convinced (ὡς, 'in the conviction that', with a participle)[59] that God is
making the divine voice heard (cf. 1 Thess 2.13),[60] and that as an appeal.
Παρακαλεῖν here (cf. also 1 Thess 2.3) means 'the wooing proclamation of
salvation in the apostolic preaching'.[61] This character which it has of
seeking to win people over is underlined further by the use of δεόμεθα,
'we beseech' (cf. here 5.11!). On the authority[62] of the one who has
brought salvation Paul begs that they should now let God's reconciling
work be realized and recognized. His appeal aims therefore at the ὑπακοὴ
πίστεως, the 'obedience of faith' (Rom. 1.5). Here the aorist form of the
imperative refers to God's initial conversion of a person, and the passive
underlines once again that reconciliation is accomplished *entirely by
God*. N. Walter rightly comments on v 20: 'Here Paul proclaims the God
who sends messengers to move amongst us human beings with what is
nothing short of a pleading request to "Be reconciled with God!"...How
could it not appear ridiculous (μωρόν) to Hellenistic σοφία ("wisdom") that
the one God should move amongst human beings pleading for reconciliation?!'[63] This is precisely what Paul wants to stress here: whoever
has the true knowledge of Christ and is truly an apostle of God's act of
reconciliation is also entirely immersed in the reconciling self-abasement
of God;[64] such an apostle becomes 'a slave of all' to win people for this
loving God (1 Cor 9.19); such an apostle can do nothing else but seek to
win people over and plead with them. The dignity and the lowliness of
the apostle are thus inseparably bound up together in v 20: the apostle is

Lietzmann(–Kümmel), *1–2 Kor* (n. 6) 127, is too vague: 'in Christ's name'.

59. Cf. BDR §425.3 with n. 3.

60. Cf. Schlatter, *Paulus* (n. 14) 567: 'Because God is the one who acts in all
that Christ does the word spoken on behalf of Christ is God's own word; God
speaks through Paul.'

61. O. Schmitz in *TWNT* 5, 792.24 (in spaced type; quoted here from *TDNT*
5, 795); cf. too its use in the sense of 'invite'—cf. Bauer, *Wörterbuch* (n. 56)
1223 s.v. 1*b*.

62. Ὑπὲρ Χριστοῦ is to be interpreted in the same way on both occasions in v
20; cf. Bornkamm in *TWNT* 6, 682.25–34.

63. 'Christusglaube' (n. 3.30) esp. 440 and 441.

64. Cf. T. Holtz, 'Der Apostel des Christus', in (ed.) H. Falcke, *Als Boten des
gekreuzigten Herrn* (*Festschrift* for W. Krusche, Berlin: Evangelische Verlagsanstalt, 1982) 101–16, esp. 113: 'True messengers...are themselves a piece of their
true message. Paul did not only have to give a word to the world; he gave it
himself as well.'

one sent by God and Jesus Christ, invested with the fullest authority, but sent by that God who in Jesus Christ trod the way of suffering and death in order to save the world. One can readily see the contrast with the self-understanding of Paul's opponents with their one-sided emphasis on their glory; their programme was to impress and evangelize through brilliant rhetoric (10.10; 11.6) and remarkable deeds (12.11–12); the simple but persistent ways of Paul they could only regard as mere 'persuasion' (5.11).

V 21 is most easily seen as still using the language of the apostle's missionary message of reconciliation, and in particular following on from v 20c, καταλλάγητε τῷ θεῷ, 'be reconciled with God'.[65] For the subject of the sentence ('God') is to be inferred from the appeal 'Be reconciled with God', and the 'we' now—in contrast to the previous and the following use of the first person plural—refers not to the apostle only but to humanity in general. This sentence describes the *event* of reconciliation which forms the basis for the appeal of v 20c. When v 21 speaks of Christ's not knowing sin, then γινώσκειν means a being versed in, acquainted with, very much in the sense of the Old Testament ידע.[66] The sense is then that Christ never practised sin; he did not fall victim to the power of sin. So Paul endorses (cf. also Gal 3.14; Rom 8.3) the widespread early Christian idea of Christ's sinlessness (John 7.18; 8.46; 1 John 3.5; 1 Pet 2.22; Heb 4.15; 7.26; Matt 3.13–15); that presupposes a knowledge of a corresponding conduct on the part of the earthly Jesus. It must be noted that Paul does not say 'God made him a sin*ner* for us', but 'made him *sin*'. This way of putting it draws attention to Jesus' sinlessness, and the 'for us' shows that it is *our* subjection to the power of sin which Christ suffered, and which was, as it were, concentrated upon him; Christ took the place of humanity in the grip of the power of sin and thus of death; so it is not his own sin and he is also no sinner. The purpose of the divine action is justification. Strikingly Paul does not say 'so that we might be justified' or 'so that we might be shown to be righteous' (Rom 5.19), although this is what he means. The expression 'so that we might become God's righteousness' is to be regarded as a positive parallel to the statement that 'God made Christ *to be sin* for us'; as Christ was given up by God to the power of sin in whose grip *we* are, so we experience 'in' *him* God's righteousness (cf. 1 Cor 1.30), i.e. God's saving power which takes effect in us when we give ourselves over to a living fellowship with the crucified and risen Christ. The use of γίνομαι,

---

65. So too Bachmann, *2 Kor* (n. 14) 270; Windisch, *2 Kor* (n. 8) 196; Allo, *2 Cor* (n. 9) 172.

66. Cf. W. Schottroff in *TWAT* 1, 690.

'become', shows that a basic alteration of the person is involved, the emergence of a new condition that God has brought about;[67] the link with v 17 that is formed by the ἐν αὐτῷ, 'in him', once again makes clear that justification, as liberation from the power of sin, means a new creation.[68]

6.1–2 then shows that the missionary appeal of the apostle continues in his appeal directed towards the church that he has already evangelized. It has already given its basic assent to the apostolic call to accept the act of reconciliation; to it now comes the appeal to continue to act consistently with that, and not to have received God's grace in vain; the Old Testament quotation emphasizes the urgency of this appeal. It is only as those who really live on the basis of God's reconciliation that they are in a position rightly to appreciate Paul's apostolic service and to reject the claims of his opponents. Only in that way can the Corinthians understand, as the catalogue of afflictions (*Peristasenkatalog*) of vv 4–10 is meant to show, that it is precisely in his enduring all humiliations that Paul shows himself as a servant of that God who through Christ became reconciled with those who were enemies of God.

In conclusion, then, we may say that the section 2 Cor 5.14–6.2 is, like most passages in 2 Corinthians, to be understood throughout against the background of Paul's quarrel with those opponents who contested his apostleship in Corinth. Over against their claim to validate themselves as servants of Christ by their amazing qualities Paul brings to bear the essential nature of the apostolic knowledge of Christ: its content is God's reconciling work in the representative death of Christ and in his resurrection; this alone is the reason why the believer, amidst all the afflictions of the age that is passing away, belongs to God's new, eschatological creation. Such knowledge of Christ provides the standard by which Christians measure themselves and their fellow Christians. Arrogance is totally misplaced and only shows that those who are so disposed have no true knowledge of Christ and are no messengers of reconciliation. Paul furthers these arguments by referring to his call. Here v 16*b* is of central importance and is to be regarded neither as hypothetical nor as a later addition. Rather, Paul is here emphasizing that through his call all his former standards are destroyed, those by which he judged and condemned what he heard of Jesus' death and being raised from the dead; the death of the crucified one under a curse and his

---

67. Cf. Bauer, *Wörterbuch* (n. 56) 316 s.v. I.4.

68. Cf. here too W. Thüsing, 'Rechtfertigungsgedanke und Christologie in den Korintherbriefen', in (ed.) J. Gnilka, *Neues Testament und Kirche* (*Festschrift* for R. Schnackenburg, Freiburg-i-B., etc.: Herder, 1974) 301–34, esp. 310ff.

resurrection were now disclosed to the apostle as God's work, reconciling and bestowing new life; the message concerning this was then so implanted in his innermost self that it shaped his entire being. From then on he judged his fellow human beings, and in particular his fellow Christians, from the perspective of God's act of love; he saw himself as one who, even in his insignificant and weak, and at the same time persevering, existence, was the authoritative bringer of the divine message of reconciliation and the envoy of the crucified and risen Christ; thus he writes of himself in 6.10: '(we are) as poor, but who make many rich (through the preaching of the gospel); as those who have nothing and yet possess all (reconciliation with God).' With this attitude Paul is a messenger of Christ, of whom he writes in 8.9: 'he became poor for your sake, although he was rich, so that through his poverty you might become rich.'

5

PAUL AND JESUS: THE PROBLEM OF CONTINUITY

Alexander J. M. Wedderburn

The question of the relationship between Paul and Jesus has exercised scholars for the past century and a half, although J. Blank has argued that it is only since the beginning of this century that we can really speak of the scholarly treatment of the questions of 'Paul and Jesus' or 'Jesus and Paul'.[1] The attempts to answer this question of the relationship between the two have been both many and various, but we can perhaps discern three major areas of interest:[2]

(1) There is the question of the meaning of 2 Cor 5.16, which Bultmann sought to interpret as indicating Paul's disinterest in a 'Christ according to the flesh',[3] but which most now agree to be repudiating a flesh-dominated or flesh-oriented knowledge of any person, including Christ. So H. Weder has recently argued that this verse does not mean that Paul's new 'way of knowledge "according to the Spirit" is not interested in the knowledge of Jesus "*in* the flesh". On the contrary, it is Jesus "in the flesh" who is known anew, and that not "according to the flesh" but "according to the Spirit".'[4]

---

1. *Paulus und Jesus* (n. 2.1) 66; cf. G. Bornkamm, *Paulus* (Urban Bücher 119, Stuttgart, etc.: Kohlhammer, 1969) 234; V. P. Furnish, however, traces the modern debate back to F. C. Baur—see chap. 2 above, esp. p. 17.

2. A fuller list can be found in D. C. Allison, 'Epistles' (n. 3.4) here p. 1; cf. too O. Kuss, *Paulus: die Rolle des Apostels in der theologischen Entwicklung der Urkirche* (Auslegung und Verkündigung 3, Regensburg: Pustet, 1971) 440–1, for a different threefold division of the questions.

3. Cf. his 'Bedeutung' (n. 2.64) esp. ET p. 241; also id., *Theology* (n. 2.86) 238–9, and most recently his comm. *ad loc.* (n. 1.3).

4. *Das Kreuz Jesu bei Paulus: ein Versuch, über den Geschichtsbezug des christlichen Glaubens nachzudenken* (FRLANT 125, Göttingen: Vandenhoeck &

(2) A second major problem is the paucity of references to Jesus' teaching in Paul's letters. Had Paul made *no* express mention of Jesus' teaching we could perhaps have argued that he did not know this teaching; but three times he refers to what is recognizably part of the Synoptic tradition (1 Cor 7.10; 9.14; 11.23). Since he therefore seems to know at least part of that tradition[5] it becomes more plausible that he elsewhere alludes to other sayings of Jesus contained in that tradition. Yet, even if one adopts a generous estimate of the number of allusions to that teaching in Paul's letters, the fact that they are almost all *allusions*, not explicit quotations, remains a problem, particularly when one considers the readiness of Paul's contemporaries or near-contemporaries, be they Jewish rabbis or Hellenistic philosophers, to lard their teaching with appeals to the sayings, and to incidents in the lives, of their teachers and heroes.

This problem then remains and may, in my judgment, require for a solution some such hypothesis as the suggestion that the teaching of Jesus was largely, at that time and in Paul's eyes, 'in enemy hands' in the sense that it was being used in a legalistic way by his Judaizing opponents: Jesus' teaching was being treated by them in much the same way as Matthew or, perhaps more likely, his Jewish Christian predecessors regarded it, as a demand for a continued and indeed yet more rigorous faithfulness to the Jewish Law in some form or other; in fact Matthew may have modified earlier Jewish Christian traditions which did not subordinate the entire Law to the principle of the twin commands to love (22.34–40) as he did.[6] But in that case the problem arises why Paul used Jesus' teaching explicitly at all, and one would have to suggest that what little use that he does make of it was either forced upon him by his opponents' use of it to attack him (e.g. 1 Cor 9.14), or stems from such scanty elements of that teaching as had by his time already been wrested from the hands of the Judaizers and reinterpreted to justify the Pauline mission and to be used in its service. Express quotation of the majority of the traditions of Jesus' teaching in circulation in his day might have seemed to endorse a view of the Christian gospel which imposed on

---

Ruprecht, 1981) 232; cf. also Moule, 'Jesus' (n. 4.33), esp. 17–18.

5.   His knowledge of it is argued for by P. Stuhlmacher, 'Jesustradition' (n. 3.4); which part he knew is the question handled by Allison, 'Epistles' (n. 3.4).

6.   Thus H. Hübner, *Das Gesetz in der synoptischen Tradition: Studien zur These einer progressiven Qumranisierung und Judaisierung innerhalb der synoptischen Tradition* (Witten: Luther, 1973) sees in Matt 5.18; 23.2–3 'judaistische' traditions used by the Evangelist and hopes that the use of the former as the key to interpreting Matt is a thing of the past (206); cf. U. Luz, 'Die Erfüllung des Gesetzes bei Matthäus (Mt 5,17–20)', in *ZTK* 75 (1978) 398–435, here 399, 405–8, 417.

converts a law that was neither 'the law of the Spirit of life' (Rom 8.2) nor the 'law of Christ' (Gal 6.2), but a righteousness according to Jewish law which exceeded that of the scribes and Pharisees (Matt 5.20). U. Luz argues that

> Matthew seems to presuppose the validity of the whole Law for the church in this age, including in principle the validity of all its regulations. This cannot be reconciled with Paul's view that Gentile Christians were free from the requirements of circumcision and obedience to the Law.

Matthew may not be an exponent of righteousness by works, he suggests, and probably represents a Jewish Christian church that is turning to evangelize Gentiles, but has not thought through the resultant problem of the Law and is in some respects 'pre-Pauline' in its thinking on this.[7] My suggestion is simply that there were predecessors to Matthew whose thought made even fewer concessions to the Gentile mission and who were chronologically 'pre-Pauline' as well.[8]

In addition to this hypothesis, and related to it, is the further suggestion that Paul may well have felt that to appeal too often to the authority of this body of teaching might well call in question his own independence and authority in relation to the leaders of the Jerusalem church who could, after all, speak more authoritatively of the content of this body of tradition by drawing upon their own first-hand knowledge of it. It is perhaps significant that when Paul's authority and independence are most under threat, e.g. in Galatians and 2 Cor 10–13, even allusions to Jesus' teaching are for the most part very hard to detect.[9] These two explanations for Paul's lack of reference to that teaching may be at best hypothetical, but some explanation of this phenomenon is called for.

(3) But my main concern here is with a different, but not unrelated problem, that of the continuity between the message of Jesus and that of Paul. This issue can perhaps be grasped most clearly in the denial of continuity implied in William Wrede's labelling of Paul as the 'second

---

7.   Cf. Luz, ibid. 434–5.

8.   To that extent to speak of a progressive 'Judaizing' or even 'Rethoraisierung' (Hübner, *Gesetz* [n. 6] 238) of the Synoptic tradition would be an oversimplification: a 'Judaized' version could have existed from the start and indeed may well have been the original form of the tradition within the early church.

9.   Yet the indefatigable Resch (*Paulinismus* [n. 2.29] 64–72) found many there too; plausible are perhaps 2 Cor 10.1 (or both Matt 11.29 and this passage reflect Hellenistic ethical teaching—cf. Barrett, *2 Cor* [n. 4.14] 246); 13.1; Gal 1.4 (cf. 2.20; or the Synoptic tradition has been influenced by this Pauline—or more general early Christian—theologoumenon); 4.6; 5.14, 21; 6.17.

founder of Christianity'.[10] It is true that Wrede's formulation of the thesis has had to be qualified, principally by the realization that Paul was not so much of a pioneer as this description suggests, but was in many respects indebted to other Christians before him and contemporary with him.[11] Yet the datum upon which Wrede based this description, the apparent discontinuity between the messages of the two men, remained, and still remains, a problem. It is related, too, to the two other problems which I have just mentioned, since the dearth of references to Jesus' teaching helps to create the impression of discontinuity, and a lack of interest in the earthly Jesus could be either the product or the cause of such discontinuity. But since we have seen that the absence of explicit references to Jesus' teaching may be for reasons that might be termed 'tactical' and that the key text for Paul's supposed lack of interest in the earthly Jesus probably does not mean that at all, the problem of discontinuity becomes, if anything, even more acute. Is there continuity and wherein does it lie?

Bultmann, looking at this question of the continuity between the teaching of Paul and that of Jesus, suggested that 'the concept of the "righteousness of God", of "justification" (δικαιοσύνη θεοῦ)...corresponds to the "kingdom of God"'.[12] This was developed in Eberhard Jüngel's monograph *Paulus und Jesus*, which embodied his 1962 Tübingen dissertation on the relation of Paul's doctrine of justification by faith to Jesus' teaching.[13] Rom 14.17 was, in his eyes, evidence that 'Paul has replaced the concept of the βασιλεία ["kingdom"] by that of δικαιοσύνη ["righteousness"]', although he failed adequately to explain why only 'righteousness' was the Pauline counterpart to 'kingdom'; why not also 'joy' and 'peace' mentioned alongside it in that verse? Thus Jüngel compared 'what was given expression in Jesus' preaching and Paul's doctrine of justification respectively': Jesus proclaimed by his message of the eschatological kingdom of God God's nearness to history, thereby opposing the old word of the Law with a new word; for Paul the revelation of God's eschatological righteousness ends the era of the

10. *Paulus* (nn. 1.1, 3.34) 69. Kümmel, 'Jesus' (nn. 1.5, 3.2) 164–6, shows the dominance of this portrayal in Jewish studies.

11. Furnish in chapter 2 above, p. 32, traces this modification to W. Heitmüller, 'Problem' (n. 2.51) 330=135–6 (the intervening influence of 'Hellenistic Christianity'), yet already this insight seems clear in A. von Harnack, *History of Dogma* (London & Edinburgh: Williams & Norgate, 1897; ET of Freiburg-i-B.: Mohr, 1898) 89, and *Christianity* (n. 2.27) 177.

12. 'Bedeutung' (n. 2.64), here quoted from ET 232.

13. See n. 2.1.

bondage of the human race to the Law; in both forms of proclamation God's eschatological 'Yes' offered us a new being. Both were 'language-events which followed one another as events in a language-history' (263). The correspondence between these two terms and this attempt to trace a continuity between Jesus' message and Paul's rest upon a number of assumptions:

(1) Jüngel regards 'justification by faith' as central to Paul's thought; despite its prominence only in Galatians and Romans (and also in Phil 3) and despite the objections of Wrede and Schweitzer[14] this assumption seems to me in large measure valid; as Blank rightly observes, 'Paul's "doctrine of justification" and the closely related teaching on the Law are based upon his personal experience of turning from Pharisaism to his apostleship and do so in a way which is true of hardly any other complex of his theological ideas';[15] he sees the Hellenists' critique of the Law, which he regards as derived from that of Jesus, as the most important link between Jesus and the pre-Christian Paul and as an extremely influential factor in his theology subsequently (244, 247). We may agree that the controversy over justification and righteousness lays bare the experiential foundation of Paul's whole life and work as a Christian, as his testimony in Phil 3.7–11 discloses.

(2) Less certain is Jüngel's contention that the theme of God's righteousness in Rom 1.16ff runs parallel to that of the cross of Christ in 1 Cor 1.18–31 and that therefore 'in 1 Cor 1.18ff too the doctrine of justification controls the theology of Paul's argument' (31). What may be nearer the truth is that the same fundamental experience underlies both his polemic against the Jews and Judaizers in terms of righteousness, and his polemic against the supposedly wise Corinthians in terms of the truly wise folly of the cross of Christ. It is not clear why primacy should be given to the one form of polemic over the other,[16] and there are other ways too in which Paul can give expression to the same fundamental

---

14. Wrede, *Paulus* (nn. 1.1, 3.34) 72ff; Schweitzer, *Mysticism* (n. 2.65) 220–6; cf. also more recently G. Strecker, 'Befreiung und Rechtfertigung. Zur Stellung der Rechtfertigungslehre in der Theologie des Paulus', in (ed.) J. Friedrich, W. Pöhlmann, P. Stuhlmacher, *Rechtfertigung* (*Festschrift* for E. Käsemann, Tübingen: Mohr & Göttingen: Vandenhoeck & Ruprecht, 1976) 479–508, repr. in id., *Eschaton und Historie: Aufsätze* (Göttingen: Vandenhoeck & Ruprecht, 1979) 229–59. See too the discussion of the views of F. Watson in chapter 6 below, pp. 124–6.

15. *Paulus und Jesus* (n. 2.1) 227. On the matter of the 'Hellenists' critique of the Law' and its relation to the teaching of Jesus see now Räisänen, '"Hellenists"' (n. 1.4) and my own attempt to trace the nature of the 'link' in chapter 6 below.

16. Cf. J. M. Robinson, 'Hermeneutic' (n. 2.89) 348.

experience and conviction, for instance by speaking of God's love and
above all God's grace.

(3) Still more questionable is Jüngel's belief that the phrase 'God's
righteousness' has a single meaning in Paul's writings: it is a righteousness from God (genitive of the author) as God pronounces us righteous
before God's self.[17] That belief is controversial.[18] 'God's righteousness' is a singularly elusive and elastic phrase, at least to our ways of
thinking. Not only does it refer to God's character (Rom 3.5, 25–6), but
even within a single verse like Rom 10.3 the meaning seems to shift: Paul
there contrasts God's righteousness and Israel's own righteousness,
which suggests that the former, like the latter, is also something one can
have, the 'righteousness (that comes) from God' of Phil 3.9; that fits
Jüngel's interpretation of the phrase, but Paul then goes on to accuse
Israel of not submitting to God's righteousness in their ignorance of it.
Rightly, Käsemann sees this latter reference as telling in favour of his
interpretation of 'God's righteousness' as a power,[19] but he does not
allow for the possibility that the meaning of the phrase may have shifted
somewhat within the verse. Then in v 4 Christ's being the τέλος of the
Law is 'for the righteousness' of all believers; here again righteousness
seems to be something which comes to one and which one then has. In
Paul's eyes one can apparently even 'become' that righteousness (2 Cor
5.21), in Christ who has become righteousness from God for us (1 Cor
1.30). Thus in these passages 'God's righteousness' seems to denote
both that which we have or are *and* the activity of God which either
gives us that righteousness or makes us into it *and*, in the passages
mentioned first, that in God's nature which causes God to act in this way.
That the one expression embraces all three uses may perhaps be
explained by arguing that this characteristic of God is unintelligible apart

17. *Paulus* (n. 2.1) 45, 48; cf. R. Bultmann, 'Δικαιοσύνη θεοῦ', in *JBL* 83
(1964) 12–16, here 12, also his *Theology* (n. 2.86) 1, 284–5 (yet he does not
provide a uniform interpretation of the phrase—see p. 288 on Rom 3.3–6; in the
article he expressly rejects the idea that the same meaning is found throughout—
this sense is simply the dominant one); Strecker, 'Befreiung' (n. 14) 258.

18. Cf., e.g., E. Käsemann, '"The Righteousness of God" in Paul', in *New
Testament Questions of Today* (London: SCM, 1969; ET of *Exegetische
Versuche und Besinnungen* 2, Göttingen: Vandenhoeck & Ruprecht, 1965²,
181–93=ZTK 58, 1961, 367–78) 168–82, esp. 168 n.; J. M. Robinson,
'Hermeneutic' (n. 2.89) 349; see also M. T. Brauch's appendix, 'Perspectives on
"God's Righteousness" in Recent German Discussion', in E. P. Sanders, *Paul
and Palestinian Judaism: a Comparison of Patterns of Religion* (London: SCM,
1977) 523–42.

19. Ibid. 173; cf. his *An die Römer* (HNT 8a, Tübingen: Mohr, 1974²) 269.

from appropriate activity which expresses it and that, since God does not act righteously in isolation, that activity must have its outworking in our world; for 'righteousness' involves a relationship and 'declaring righteous' is for Paul an activity which does not simply observe what is already the case, but rather creates a state of affairs embodying that relationship.[20] Thus Paul can say, perhaps quoting a traditional formulation,[21] that Jesus 'was raised for our justification' (Rom 4.25); as his resurrection created for Jesus a new life, indeed a new relationship to God (Rom 6.10), so too for those whom he represents; and the effecting of this new life and new relationship Paul describes as justification (δικαίωσις).

This oscillation between the activity of God and the results of that activity is also a feature of Jesus' use of the phrase 'the kingdom of God' and it is this feature, I suggest, which may point us towards a way of tracing one element of continuity between Jesus' thought and Paul's that lies at a deeper level than the seemingly rather arbitrary equation of the two terms suggested by Jüngel. For while at times in this century students of Jesus' usage have seemingly been almost dazzled by the insight that 'kingdom of God' refers to God's activity of ruling,[22] which was a healthy corrective to some interpretations of the phrase, it should not be lost sight of that Jesus *also* speaks of God's kingdom as if it were a thing to be received or a place to be entered (e.g. Mark 10.15 par.).[23] This

---

20. Just as the opposite, 'condemn', in a passage like Rom 8.3 has not only a 'declaratory' sense of passing sentence, but also a 'performative' sense, of executing that sentence; it is the latter which the Law could not do; cf. C. E. B. Cranfield, *The Epistle to the Romans* 1 (ICC, Edinburgh: Clark, 1975) 382–3, citing F. Büchsel in *TDNT* 3, 951. On 'God's righteousness' see further A. J. M. Wedderburn, *The Reasons for Romans* (Studies of the New Testament and Its World, Edinburgh: Clark, 1988) 108–23.

21. But cf. Wilckens, *Röm* (n. 3.11) 1, 279–30

22. Cf. N. Perrin, *The Kingdom of God in the Teaching of Jesus* (London: SCM, 1963) 24, on Dalman's work; J. Jeremias, *New Testament Theology* 1: *The Proclamation of Jesus* (London: SCM, 1971; ET of Gütersloh: Mohn, 1971) 98. I call it a 'healthy corrective' also because a text like Luke 17.20–1 seems to warn us against a similar objectifying of God's kingdom.

23. Or, in the words of B. F. Meyer, *The Aims of Jesus* (London: SCM, 1979) 131, an '"order of things" to which men could be admitted and from which they might be excluded', citing G. Dalman, *The Words of Jesus Considered in the Light of Post-Biblical Jewish Writings and the Aramaic Language* (Edinburgh: Clark, 1902; ET of Leipzig: Hinrichs, 1898) 106–21. Cf. also E. P. Sanders, *Jesus and Judaism* (London: SCM, 1985) chapters 4 and 8. But see now the persuasive aricle of J. Marcus, 'Entering into the Kingly Power of God', in *JBL* 107 (1988) 663–75.

possibility that the phrase might refer either to God's activity or to the
result of it or to the place of it is perhaps at least partly what led Norman
Perrin to insist that 'kingdom of God' was a 'symbol', not a conception;
it was a 'tensive symbol', both in apocalyptic Judaism and in Jesus'
teaching,[24] in that no one referent (or conception) exhausts the meaning
of the term.[25] Similarly, this has more recently led James Breech to
argue that Jesus saw God's kingdom as a power, for only a power is
'polymorphous' enough to allow it to be spoken of in so many different
ways.[26]

But 'kingdom of God' could be used to refer not just to God's activity
or the result of that activity or its location, but also to God in person. In
other words it was yet another of the many phrases that might be used to
refer obliquely to the divine person.[27] So when Jesus spoke of the
kingdom's nearness he spoke of the nearness of God's person—as king;
after all the central and the creative element in Jesus' message was not
some new concept of the kingdom, but a new and distinctive perception
of God, of God's nature and of the divine will for the people of God.[28]
This God he proclaimed as near, and near perhaps as much relationally as
temporally:[29] in his ministry and words God draws near and addresses

24. *Jesus and the Language of the Kingdom: Symbol and Metaphor in New
Testament Interpretation* (London: SCM & Philadelphia: Fortress, 1976) 33,
197; he uses 'symbol' as distinct from 'sign', using the terminology of P. Ricoeur,
The Symbolism of Evil (New York: Harper & Row, 1967 & Boston: Beacon,
1969), in which the former has 'a set of meanings that can neither be exhausted
nor adequately expressed by any one referent'; P. Wheelwright, *Metaphor and
Reality* (Bloomington: Indiana Univ., 1962) similarly distinguishes 'steno-
symbols' from 'tensive symbols' (esp. 94–8).

25. Perrin, ibid. 31, 33.

26. J. Breech, *The Silence of Jesus: the Authentic Voice of the Historical Man*
(Philadelphia: Fortress, 1983) 45.

27. Cf. Jeremias, *Theology* (n. 22) 102 (Dalman, *Words* [n. 23] 101, notes that
in the Targumim 'kingdom of God' was used 'to avoid the thought that God in
person should appear on earth'). Besides the Targumim one can also point to the
parallelism of, e.g., 1QM 12.7f: 'you...in the glory of your kingdom...the King of
glory'. For further bibliography cf. n. 6.60 below.

28. Cf. Jüngel, *Paulus* (n. 2.1) 196–7 (§6); Meyer, *Aims* (n. 23) 162; J.
Riches, *Jesus and the Transformation of Judaism* (London: Darton, Longman &
Todd, 1980) 99, 106, 170. Breech, *Silence* (n. 26) 53, puts it rather the other way
round: the Lord's Prayer is addressed to the power to which Jesus elsewhere
refers as God's kingdom (cf. 62); this does not seem to do justice to Jesus' choice
of 'Abba' as a mode of address to God, a mode of address that befits a person but
hardly anything so impersonal as a 'power'.

women and men. The loving, creative, healing power of God's rule was tangible and visible in Jesus' ministry for those who were ready to see it,[30] and in that ministry God gave the divine self to them.[31] To press the question when Jesus expected God's kingdom to come may distract us from the message that God and the rule of God were near, indeed in the very midst of Jesus' hearers (Luke 17.21)—incognito and unrecognized for the most part, but real and tangible to those who let themselves be healed by him and taught by him. To ask when something else would come reveals that his hearers were blind to what was under their noses and before their eyes, where God was already at work in person.

In the same way, too, Ernst Käsemann has insisted that, when Paul speaks of 'God's righteousness' as something given to us by God, the gift is inseparable from the giver.[32] For, were it separable, it would not be God's righteousness; 'righteousness' as the state which we enjoy, as a parallel term to 'salvation' (Rom 10.10), consists in peace with God, fellowship with God and nearness to God, as well as all that flows derivatively from that relationship, both to us and to God's world; it is something that comes to us from outside of ourselves, but it is not something which God creates apart from the divine presence, but something which God creates precisely in drawing an alienated world into that presence (2 Cor 5.19, 21). Paul can certainly also use other language to speak of this self-giving of God, as when he speaks of God's transforming presence as love or Spirit (e.g. Rom 5.5),[33] but he also uses

---

29. Cf. Jüngel's critique of the categories in which the problem of the kingdom of God as present or future is usually discussed—e.g. ibid. 154, 173, 181, 288–9; in this he is followed by H. Weder, *Die Gleichnisse Jesu als Metaphern: traditions- und redaktionsgeschichtliche Analysen und Interpretationen* (FRLANT 120, Göttingen: Vandenhoeck & Ruprecht, 1978) e.g. 282.

30. On 'God's kingdom' as power cf. Jüngel, ibid. 169, 187–8, 196.

31. Riches, *Jesus* (n. 28) 153–4, argues that what God gives to those who will receive it is 'his own gracious and merciful presence' with them; on God's kingdom as a gift cf. also Meyer, *Aims* (n. 23) 132.

32. *Questions* (n. 18) 174; *Paulinische Perspektiven* (Tübingen: Mohr, 1969) 145.

33. G. Herold, *Zorn und Gerechtigkeit Gottes bei Paulus: eine Untersuchung zu Röm. 1,16–18* (Europäische Hochschulschriften Reihe 23: Theologie 14, Bern & Frankfurt: Lang, 1973) 172–3, stresses the close relationship of πνεῦμα and δικαιοσύνη: the one can replace the other (cf. 2 Cor 3.8–9; Gal 3.5–6) and both refer both to God's nature and to God's gift which claims those to whom it is given; he compares P. Stuhlmacher, *Gerechtigkeit Gottes bei Paulus* (FRLANT 87, Göttingen: Vandenhoeck & Ruprecht, 1966²) 222—'The Spirit is the renewing power of God's righteousness'—and H. W. Heidland in *TDNT* 4, 292

the basically forensic language of 'righteousness'; then, however, he transforms the normal sense which such language would have for Jewish ears by the subtle use of genitives, adjectives and prepositional phrases in order to redefine the sense of 'righteousness' which he intends.[34] Yet again, as with Jesus' language of the 'kingdom of God', at the centre is the intervention of the God who is righteous, who in faithfulness and self-consistency carries through the divine purposes towards all creatures, and heals the broken relationship between the world and its Creator. For both Jesus and Paul, too, there spring from that divine intervention and healing the ethical implications which both of them embody in their instructions for fitting conduct. In both cases that which had hitherto been regarded as the normative declaration of God's will, namely the Jewish Law, was at the same time both endorsed and qualified: endorsed as containing within it a true perception of God's nature and will; qualified in that aspects of it were declared to be superseded or misleading, leading those who heard it away from God's ways or blinding them to the new, fuller manifestation of God's will and purposes. In other words, for both it could sometimes amount to setting scripture against scripture.[35]

So 'God's kingdom' and 'God's righteousness' can both be ways of referring to God which concentrate on two different aspects of the divine nature and activity; and yet, though different, these aspects are not too widely separated, for righteousness was expected to characterize the king's rule and it was his business to establish righteousness in his land.[36] And this was equally true of God.[37] But the teaching and style

---

(=*TWNT* 4, 294).

34. To this extent the 'transformation of language' to which Riches refers (*Jesus* [n. 28]) and the techniques which Paul employs to achieve it are more obvious than in Jesus' teaching: e.g. qualifying genit. and adj. (Rom 10.3), genitives (Rom 3.27; 8.2), adjectives and prepositional phrases (Phil 3.9).

35. Thus, in my opinion, at least in Mark 10.2–12 (see further H. Braun, *Spätjüdisch-häretischer und frühchristlicher Radikalismus: Jesus von Nazareth und die essenische Qumransekte* [BHT 24, Tübingen: Mohr, 1957] 2, 6 and n. 1, 15); Rom 10.5–8; Gal 3.11–12. The first of these texts may not entail more than a downgrading of parts of the Law, as 'concessions' (A. E. Harvey, *Jesus and the Constraints of History*, London: Duckworth, 1982, 48, appealing to D. Daube, 'Concessions to Sinfulness in Jewish Law', in *JJS* 10, 1959, 1–13, and K. Berger, *Gesetzesauslegung* [n. 3.12], who traces parallels to the view of commandments being enacted because of 'hardness of heart'—pp. 16ff—and apocalyptic and Hellenistic Jewish concepts of 'law' which largely limited its content to belief in one God and various social commandments and virtues—esp. pp. 38ff), but may nevertheless, within the context of Jesus' ministry, imply a more radical critique; the Pauline texts seem to go further: parts of the Law encourage a wrong, even fatal (Rom 7.10), misplaced confidence in it and misuse of it.

of Jesus' life and ministry did not, to many of his contemporaries, seem to conform to the righteousness and the kingship of God,[38] and John Riches has suggested that this implicit rejection by Jesus of the common view of God as one who rewards those already righteous and punishes the unrighteous fuelled Paul's reflection on God's righteousness.[39] Paul's own departure from previously accepted views occasioned his qualifications of the term 'righteousness' referred to above, but it also sprang from a view of God which burst open the legal framework within which the Creator's dealings with all creatures had all too often been confined; we should not then expect him to confine or even concentrate his reflection within that framework, however much he could qualify it. Just as Jesus acted with a freedom in God's name that ran counter to the expectations of many of his religious contemporaries, so too Paul, although prepared to use the language of 'righteousness', qualified by the insistence that it was on the basis of grace and not on that of anything owing to us, and that it was even open to the ungodly (Rom 4.4–5), yet found a whole range of other terms which were more obviously suited to express his vision of God's true nature: grace, love, reconciliation and the like. These define his language of 'God's righteousness', just as God's fatherliness defined Jesus' talk of God as king.

For we have seen that these two phrases, 'God's kingdom' and 'God's righteousness', point to a shared vision of God's activity in which the often rather forbidding and menacing ideas of God as king and of the righteous one were transformed by their being invested with predominantly positive and salvific connotations. For Jesus this king showed himself in healing (Luke 11.20) and dealt with his subjects as a father with his wayward children. For Paul God's righteousness is equivalent to God's saving activity (Rom 10.10).[40]

Both terms, however, embrace in their range of meanings not only the activity of God but also the effects of this saving activity, be it a kingdom to be received or entered or a righteousness in human lives that has God as its author and source. But this is also true of other terms which Paul

---

36. 2 Sam 8.15=1 Chr 18.14; 1 Kgs 10.9=2 Chr 9.8; Ps 72.1–3; Prov 16.12; 25.5; Qoh 5.8–9; Isa 9.7; 32.1ff; Jer 22.2–3, 15; 33.15; Ezek 45.9, etc.

37. Ps 9.7–8; 96.13; 97.2; 98.9; 99.4, etc.

38. Cf. L. E. Keck, *A Future for the Historical Jesus: the Place of Jesus in Preaching and Theology* (London: SCM, 1972) 223: 'from Jesus' style, no less than from his words, one infers the conception of God's kingdom of which it is the reflex'.

39. *Jesus* (n. 28) 146; cf. Meyer, *Aims* (n. 23) 160.

40. Cf. G. Schrenk in *TDNT* 2, 195.

uses of God's saving activity: I find it, for instance, hard to understand Rom 5.5 unless it is saying that God's love is both that love which leads God to save us and at the same time a power which grips us and moulds us and creates in us a love that reflects God's own love.[41] Grace, too, is used both of God's gracious approach to us (e.g. Rom 3.24; 5.20; 1 Cor 15.10) and of something which we receive (Rom 1.5; 5.17; 12.3, 6; 15.5; 1 Cor 1.4; 3.10, etc.) and in which we exist (e.g. Rom 5.2; contrast Gal 5.4). Thus it would seem to me to be mistaken to concentrate on 'God's righteousness' as the connecting link between Paul's thought and Jesus' teaching. It is rather more helpful to ask after the source of this recurring idea in Paul's letters, the idea of something in God's self which reaches out and draws us into such conformity with God that a single term can be used of what God is, what God does and what God fashions in us and in the world. Such a use of language may not be wholly without parallel, but it is sufficiently distinctive to cause us to ask what provoked it. Partly it may stem from the conviction, of both Jesus and Paul, that God takes the initiative and that our salvation is God's doing and not ours. But, true as it is, that observation is not enough to explain this usage.

So I would also like to suggest tentatively that this linguistic phenomenon stems from the impression left by Jesus of one who was both at one with God and near to, at the side of his fellow human beings: he manifested both God's presence and rule and at the same time the realization of that rule amongst God's creatures in his filial obedience to his Father's will. Thus there was on the one hand the overwhelming impression created in Jesus' followers of an incomparable unanimity and singleness of activity between Jesus and his heavenly Father, a unanimity and oneness of action which in turn he invited his followers to share as they shared his personal and intimate manner of addressing God as 'Abba'. For Jesus' ministry was a living out on earth of his Father's ministry; as God willed and acted, so he willed and acted; as God reigned, so he reigned—paradoxically, and in an all too unkingly fashion. God's power and activity were so channelled through Jesus that in him they were fully present; the Fourth Evangelist's testimony here is apt, that he who received Jesus received the one who sent him (John 13.20).[42] This view of Jesus would only have been reinforced for his followers by their belief that God had acknowledged him by raising him from the dead. Yet

---

41. Cf. Käsemann, *Röm* (n. 19) 126: ' a divine power that grasps us', but surely the Spirit does not just assure us of that love, but, as he also sees, 'grasps us in the centre of our personality and makes us entirely...its own', as a loving power and a power that is love.

42. On Jesus as God's representative and agent cf. Harvey, *Jesus* (n. 35) chapter 7.

on the other hand what he did he did not only as God's representative, but also on behalf of his fellow human beings. While he spoke to them on God's behalf, he acted towards God on their behalf and represented them before God, from the time of his penitent baptism at the hands of John the Baptist onwards. To take one example: the gracious approach of Jesus to outcasts was God's gracious approach to them, but also, as he took his place alongside them, despised and rejected, he shared in their utter dependence on God's gracious initiative and approach. In short, in him the activity of God's grace and the reception of God's grace coalesced. It is the latter aspect that Paul develops into his view of Christ as the Adam of the end-time, humanity renewed in God's image (Rom 5.12–21; 1 Cor 15.20–2, 45–9).

At the same time the action of God as a self-giving was most dramatically exemplified in his life, so that here we may perhaps see the impetus towards that insight whose influence on Paul's thought Käsemann has stressed, as was noted above, namely that God's gift and its Giver are inseparable, for with that gift God gives us the divine presence. Jesus was for Paul one who gave himself for us (Gal 1.4; 2.20). But for Paul too, as for much, if not all, of early Christianity, God and Christ had also given themselves as the Spirit to them in their experience: the Spirit which indwelt them was Christ in them (Rom 8.9–10), and collectively and individually they were God's temple in which God dwelt as Spirit (1 Cor 3.16; 6.19). Without that dimension to their experience, in addition to those more external factors in their experience which we shall consider further in the next chapter, Jesus' self-giving, and indeed salvation itself, would have remained something external to them; with it it also became something gripping and transforming them from within (Rom 5.5).

But as well as drawing attention to this underlying conviction which governs Jesus' use of 'God's kingdom' and Paul's teaching on 'God's righteousness' we must also consider the problem of why Paul makes such little use of the former term, except in 1 Corinthians.[43] That is, apart from trying to trace continuity we must also try to face up to and understand the discontinuity between Jesus' message and Paul's. It is not enough simply to say that Paul's audience would not have understood the form of Jesus' message.[44] Nor is the suggestion all that convincing that the associations of 'kingdom' were different in Galilee and in the Hellenistic cities, although there were undoubtedly further possibilities

43. Rom 14.17; 1 Cor 4.20; 6.9–10; 15.50; Gal 5.21; cf 1 Thess 2.12; 2 Thess 1.5. See also Haufe, 'Reich' (n. 3.34).

44. The approach adopted by Bruce, *Paul* (n. 1.2) 17; indeed the term was probably used in the Gentile mission—probably by Paul himself (cf. Gal 5.21).

for interpreting the idea in the latter.[45] What is more likely to be true is
that one could get away with references to a 'kingdom' and, by implication, another 'king' more easily in rural areas, being less under the
immediate supervision of pro-Roman authorities. It was not that the term
was understood differently; rather attitudes to what the term stood for
were different. (Just as the announcement, 'the police are here', would
convey the same sense at a Conservative Party conference and amongst a
group of young coloured people in an inner city ghetto, but the statement
would arouse rather different emotions and reactions.) Generally Paul
may have found it safer politically to avoid references to God's kingdom
in his preaching, but the possibility of an enthusiastic misunderstanding
of the announcement of God's reign at Corinth, which perhaps lies
behind 1 Cor 4.8,[46] may have provided him with another very good
reason for caution in using this language. For it seems likely that either he
or some other Christian preacher had used the term in Corinth and that it
had given rise to misunderstanding there; it is likely that the
announcement of Christ's present reign, perhaps coupled with heady
ecstatic experiences of Spirit-possession, had led to a misplaced
confidence which Paul had ironically to rebuke in 1 Cor 4.8,[47] and this
perhaps accounts for the relative frequency of references to God's
kingdom in that letter; for Paul had both to stress that that reign in its
fullness still lay in the future, and that participation in it involved both
moral and physical transformation.

Thus, although the use of the language of God's kingdom was not
unintelligible to Paul's hearers, and although it would undoubtedly have
supplied him with a terminology that was broader in its compass and
possibly even richer in its appeal to Old Testament imagery than the
language which he characteristically used, we can perhaps see that it may
have been expedient for him to find other ways of expressing his

---

45. But see Riches, *Jesus* (n. 28) 40. What did exist in the cities of the Graeco-
Roman world was popular philosophical speculation on who was the true king
(see A.J.M. Wedderburn, 'The Problem of the Denial of the Resurrection in I
Corinthians XV', in *NovT* 23, 1981, 229–41, here 233–6 on 1 Cor 4.8 and its
possible background; also now my *Baptism and Resurrection: Studies in Pauline
Theology against Its Graeco-Roman Background*, WUNT 44, Tübingen: Mohr,
1987, 25–6); but this re-interpretation of kingship existed alongside and in
addition to the political connotations which also existed in Galilee (cf. Acts 17.7)

46. See my 'Problem' as in the previous note, and my *Baptism* (ibid.) 24–7.

47. C. M. Tuckett, '1 Corinthians and Q', in *JBL* 102 (1983) 607–19, has
shown that the likes of J. M. Robinson and H.-W. Kuhn were probably wrong to
trace many of the Corinthians' views to their use of 'Q', but grants that a text like
1 Cor 4.8 (or 13.2) is good evidence of their use of Jesus-tradition.

message. Had he used this language more, then it is possible that the shift in temporal perspective which many have invoked as an, or even the, decisive explanation for the difference between his message and that of Jesus[48] would have become clearer, for nowhere does the adjustment that has taken place in the period after Christ's resurrection and exaltation become plainer than in 1 Cor 15.23–8 where Christ's present kingdom is inserted before the coming of God's. There the pressure of a particular need to clarify what was already accomplished and what was was still to come caused Paul to use this vocabulary; it is not seemingly a need that arises elsewhere in his letters.

There were, however, also at least sometimes good reasons apparent for Paul's choice of alternative terms to express his convictions. Sometimes they were experiential reasons: God's intervention in his life to turn him from a persecutor of the church into a herald of the Christian gospel doubtless made the language of 'grace' and of God's love and reconciling work peculiarly relevant to his own experience (cf. Gal 1.15; 2.20). His stress on the Spirit of God arose from the common experience of first-century Christians, including Paul (cf. 1 Cor 14.18) of the overpowering presence in their midst of often ecstatic phenomena of Spirit-possession, phenomena which do not seem to have been nearly so prominent in the earthly ministry of Jesus.[49] Looking back, too, on his pre-Christian life Paul saw it as characterized by a quest for 'righteousness'.[50] Now he found his message challenged as promoting 'unrighteousness', by its (a) making God out to be unrighteous in forsaking the promises made to Israel, God's own people, and (b) encouraging unrighteousness in Paul's converts. Confronting both these challenges in Romans[51] Paul naturally presents 'God's righteousness' as a key theme of the letter (1.17), God's righteousness both in the sense of the character and nature of God and of the actions of God and in the sense of what was created in those who turned to God in response to the divine approach and offer.

Thus we can say that continuity and discontinuity between the messages of Jesus and Paul are based upon both continuity and discontinuity of religious experience, in the broadest sense of the term

---

48. E.g. Bultmann, 'Significance' (n. 2.64) 233–5; Jüngel, *Paulus* (n. 2.1) 272; Kümmel, 'Jesus' (nn. 1.5, 3.2) 180–1; cf. also Kuss, *Paulus* (n. 2) 446–7.

49. Cf. Kümmel, ibid. 180.

50. Cf. Phil 3.6 (also Rom 9.31; 10.3). Sanders, *Paul* (n. 18) 205, reminds us that for Judaism 'being righteous is not the goal of a religious quest'; hence this is properly regarded as Paul's verdict on his life in Judaism which he reached retrospectively.

51. (a) Rom 3.1–8 (esp. 5); chapters 9–11; (b) 3.8; 6.1. See now my *Reasons* as cited in n. 20 above.

'experience' which embraces both external and internal factors; at the same time, looking solely at external factors, some differences between the situation of Jesus and the situation in which his followers, including Paul, had to preach their message account for some of the differences in their respective messages, but it is important to try to identify which differences these were and how they may have influenced the various versions of the Christian proclamation.

So, as far as religious experience is concerned, I have tried to argue that the way in which Jesus viewed and exercised his ministry, and the impact made by that ministry upon his followers, as recorded in Christian tradition, left its mark upon the whole way in which Paul conceived of and spoke of the way that God reaches out to and transforms us. But equally the time after Jesus' death and resurrection was marked by the physical absence of Jesus coupled with a new experience of the Spirit of God and of Jesus, as well as of situations in which some of his followers believed that they saw analogies to the conditions of Jesus' ministry.[52] So, too, the way in which Jesus' ministry ended and what his followers believed to be its sequel created a new situation, and called for a different orientation of their thought. That aspect of the new situation did not as such necessitate new terminology; indeed I have suggested that one of the clearest expressions of that new situation uses language closer to that of Jesus in his ministry than most of Paul's utterances (1 Cor 15.23–8). It is rather the new and different situations in which Jesus' followers later and subsequently found themselves that called for new language and ways of expressing their message, either negatively to avoid misunderstanding or misinterpretation, or positively to express their convictions better and more adequately. But their experiences, although different in some ways, were yet in continuity with those of the followers of the earthly Jesus and of Jesus himself, or at least it was felt by leaders like Paul that they ought to be: they ought not to be allowed to become, for instance, the intoxicating experiences of an impersonal spiritual force that could be divorced from the loving and self-giving figure of Jesus of Nazareth;[53] the Spirit remained for him the Spirit of Jesus (Rom 8.9).

That is a divorce which Christian theology cannot allow either if it is to deserve that epithet 'Christian'; it, too, in new situations, has to find a language giving expression to an experience which, though different, is still recognizably continuous with the experience of Jesus and his original followers; while the Spirit of Jesus may lead it into new apprehensions of truth, the Spirit which leads it must remain that of Jesus. Continuity with

---

52. See chapter 6.

53. Cf. my *Baptism* (n. 45) 266–8.

him remains the touchstone by which all past statements of Christian theology, including Paul's, must be judged, and is the challenge confronting all present affirmations of Christian faith and its practice.

6

PAUL AND JESUS: SIMILARITY AND CONTINUITY

Alexander J. M. Wedderburn

Studies like those of Dr Walter and Professor Räisänen to which reference has already been made[1] might lead one to despair of ever

---

1. See Walter in chapter 3 above; Räisänen, '"Hellenists"' (n. 1.4). Dr Walter had started with the 'minimal hypothesis' that 'Paul only knew that Jesus-tradition of which he gives evidence in his extant letters, or not significantly more' (53). He ends with the conclusion that passages where allusions to Jesus-traditions have been detected do not show whether Paul was conscious, in writing them, of referring to sayings of Jesus (78; cf. 56–9); the alternative, as he puts it with reference to Rom 14.14 a, is that Paul was basing himself upon what he knew as the Christian gospel. (Cf. H. Räisänen, 'Zur Herkunft von Mk 7,15', in [ed.] J. Delobel, *Logia: les paroles de Jésus*, BETL 59, Leuven: Peeters & Univ., 1982, 477–84=*Torah* [n. 1.4] 209–18, here 480–4.) A week later F. Neirynck was to reach broadly similar conclusions at the Biblical Colloquium in Leuven: apart from 1 Cor 7.10–11 and 9.14, 'there is no trace...in the Pauline letters of a conscious use of a saying of Jesus. Possible allusions to such sayings...also show significant differences, and a direct use of a gospel saying in the form it has been preserved in the synoptic gospels is hardly provable. ...Because of the paucity and the anonymity of the possible allusions and reminiscences and their presence in paraenetical sections...it remains doubtful whether Paul was using them as sayings of Jesus' ('Paul' [n. 3.59], here 320). The poverty of express references to Jesus' teaching by Paul is a problem, both for our understanding of the transmission of that teaching and as regards the role that Paul did or did not give it in his own instruction of, and arguments with, his churches: did he really know so little and why did he not appeal more often to the teaching of Jesus? After all he does enter into controversies over the observance of certain days (Gal 4.10; Rom 14.5–6); he has no 'command of the Lord' for the 'virgins' of 1 Cor 7.25–8 (cf. Matt 19.10–12?); his teaching in Rom 13.1–7 makes no express reference to any teaching of Jesus on the subject; when the question of what a Christian may or may not eat arises there is no clear evidence that he even knew of texts like Mk 7.15, 18–19 or Lk 10.7–8, although such a reference has been seen in 1 Cor 10.27 (F. F. Bruce, 'Paul' [n. 1.2] 329–30; Räisänen, '"Hellenists"' [n. 1.4] notes that a

tracing the links that bound the life and message of Paul to those of Jesus. The purpose of the present chapter is, however, to show that the question of such links and of the continuity between the two men is nevertheless a necessary one that cannot and should not be avoided, and moreover that it need not be quite as fruitless as might seem to be the case.

I

Professor Räisänen's task at the Trondheim meeting of the 'Paulus und Jesus' seminar had been the historical one of investigating whether the Hellenists of Acts 6 were a 'bridge' between Jesus and Paul. The title which had originally been suggested for his theme had been 'Criticism of the Law in Hellenistic Jewish Christianity between Jesus and Paul', and, although the title changed, the focus and content of the paper did not: the question of continuity was posed in terms of a shared tradition of *criticism of the Law*.[2] In the discussion of his paper I argued, and still

text like Mk 7.15 is not even used in the conflict with Peter in Gal 2.11ff; cf. his 'Jesus and the Food Laws: Reflections on Mark 7.15', *JSNT* 16 [1982] 79–100 [=*Torah* [n.1.4] 219–41], here 87–8—nor, he comments, did Peter know it in Acts 10—, and 'Herkunft' 479–80); he gives no hint that he knows of a parable like that of the workers in the vineyard (Matt 20.1–16) which might aid him in his arguments over whether one is saved by grace or because it is owed to one. (Cf. Rom 4.4; or was this parable as we know it a post-Easter formation in which the eleventh-hour workers represent Gentile converts who have entered God's people late in the day? After all, a setting in the context of Jesus' ministry might have been more intelligible if diligent workers had been contrasted with lazy or disobedient ones.) All this, Räisänen argues (257), following Müller, 'Rezeption' (n. 3.53) 159–60 (cf. 167), is evidence that the Hellenists whom Paul met did not communicate to him the Law-critical Jesus-tradition. Yet this problem need not perhaps trouble us too greatly: Walter, after all, questions the assumption that 'the continuity in substance (*Sachkontinuität*) between Jesus' ministry and that of Paul can only be assured if one can show as extensive as possible a continuity of tradition (*Traditionskontinuität*) between the two' (ibid. 42; cf. 69). Simply to reproduce traditional material is no guarantee that the content of Paul's message is in continuity with that of Jesus, and conversely the two may be in harmony (*Übereinstimmung*) even if the tradition that connects them is far more indirect and complex (69). Thus he invites us to seek this harmony or agreement at another level and by other means than that of Paul's use of traditions of Jesus' teachings.

2. '"Hellenists"' (n. 1.4) 243: 'my interest will focus solely on the question of the law'; cf. too G. Schneider, *Die Apostelgeschichte* 1 (MeyerK 5.1, Freiburg-i-B., etc.: Herder, 1980) 416. It had been the view of Walter, chapter 3, 74–5, that Paul had originally been in immediate contact with that group which he had persecuted, a group more clearly subversive of the foundations of Judaism than Peter and his fellows had been; these relativized the importance of Torah and

would wish to argue in the course of this one, that this way of posing the question was leading us astray, and that one would perhaps come to rather different answers if it was posed in terms of *neglect of, and thus at least apparent indifference to, the Law*.

Räisänen began by asking whether it is quite clear that Jesus *was* in fact so critical of the Law.[3] Are the later disputes in the church over its status for Christians intelligible if Jesus had clearly spoken for or against the Law? Rather he treats the Law as important and valuable, yet not as final or absolute. If we must seek a cause for the opposition to Jesus which led to his death, we must seek it in his attitude to the Temple: he held that the present one was to be destroyed and replaced by a new one, belonging to the new age that was at hand.

When we turn to Stephen and the Hellenists it is hard to be sure how much firm historical tradition lies behind Acts' account. Even if the charges against Stephen (which are false ones in Luke's eyes) are based on tradition, the reference to changing the Law in the *future* need mean no more than that Jesus as the Messiah would issue a new law, not annulling the Torah, but reinterpreting it. That was no capital offence. What is more likely to have provoked Stephen's death is the threat posed by him to the Temple.[4] But then Paul did not say much at all about the Temple. If Stephen's attitude to the Temple was a legacy of that of Jesus, then the criticism of the Temple as such was not so directly a criticism of the Jewish Law; it would have been different had the attack been on the ordinances of the Jewish cultus; then there would have been an implicit attack on at least part of the Jewish Law.

What was an issue for Paul, Räisänen argues, was 'the Gentile question':

If Gal 1.15f. is not mere hindsight, it was immediately clear to Paul that the encounter with Christ entailed for him a commission to proclaim the gospel

---

Temple and treated Gentiles more and more as equal members in the church with Christian Jews; they had contact with Jesus-traditions, but would above all have treasured those which implied a criticism of Torah or Temple. They and, following them, Paul would have 'cultivated' material helpful for their Law-free gospel.

3.   Appealing to Sanders, *Jesus* (n. 5.23); cf. too Harvey, *Jesus* (n. 5.35) chap. 3. Müller, 'Rezeption' (n. 3.53) seems simply to assume that Jesus criticized the Law, yet refers on 167 to Paul persecuting Christians because of their freedom from the Law which is in his eyes something different (see n. 14 below).

4.   Yet, against both Räisänen and E. P. Sanders, ibid. 301–5, it must be noted that prophesying the Temple's destruction brought Jesus b. Ananias, at an even tenser period of Jewish history, only floggings and the verdict that he was mad, not death—Jos., *Bell.* 6.5.3 §§301–5. It is, however, true that Jesus of Nazareth acted and did not just speak, and that he was accompanied by a following, rather than being a solitary figure.

among *Gentiles*. This indicates that, before the conversion experience, the Gentile question had constituted a crucial bone of contention between Paul and the Hellenists he had persecuted.[5]

The connection which Paul makes in Galatians between neglecting circumcision and persecution 'might indicate that admission of Gentiles without circumcision on the part of the Hellenists was an important reason for Paul's persecuting them'.[6] Put this way, this need mean no more than a laxity and indifference on the part of the Hellenists to the 'ritual' parts of the Law; it need not imply 'any thoroughgoing critique' of the Law.[7] Yet he sees them prepared for this laxity and indifference by the '"spiritualizing" tendencies at work in the Dispersion', which 'probably prepared them for the decision to give up those parts of the law which were most offensive to would-be converts'.[8] In this general

5. '"Hellenists"' (n. 1.4) 282 (his emphasis; cf. also 251, and C. Dietz-felbinger, *Die Berufung des Paulus als Ursprung seiner Theologie* (WMANT 58, Neukirchen–Vluyn: Neukirchener, 1985) 144–5. In *Torah* 285, Räisänen quotes with approval H. Kraft, *Die Entstehung des Christentums* (Darmstadt: Wissenschaftliche Buchgesellschaft, 1981) 260–1: the story of Philip's conversion of the Ethiopian eunuch belongs to the period before the Hellenists were driven out of Jerusalem; this would be a sign that uncircumcised God-fearers had been baptized by Hellenists at a very early stage indeed.

6. Räisänen, ibid.; cf. Sanders, *Jesus* (n. 5.23) 282; J. C. Beker, *Paul the Apostle: the Triumph of God in Life and Thought* (Edinburgh: Clark, 1980) 185, sees Paul's persecution as motivated by the Christian preaching of a crucified Messiah who must be by definition an impostor; yet if Deut 21.23 were so important for him did he consider the Pharisees crucified by Alexander Jannaeus (Jos., *Bell.* 1.4.6 §97–8; *Ant.* 13.14.2 §§380–3) as also similarly accursed because of the manner of their death? This is also a problem for a central element in the argument of Dietzfelbinger, *Berufung* (n. 5) esp. 33–9; how one came to terms with the curse thought to be implicit in crucifixion depended upon one's prior evaluation of the characters of the crucifier and the crucified, and thus the suggestion that the Messiah had been crucified would not have been intrinsically more outrageous than the fact that righteous people had been crucified (as they were); a different evaluation became possible, and necessary, because the righteousness of the claimed Messiah had been questioned on other grounds; that made possible an evaluation of his crucifixion different to the interpretation of the crucifixion of those whom the Pharisees regarded as righteous. And the likeliest ground for the rejection of Jesus' righteousness would be those aspects of his conduct (and teaching) which Paul's fellow-Pharisees had found offensive, and unrighteous, during Jesus' ministry.

7. Ibid. 286.

8. Ibid. 287; cf.300; in 288–95 he follows up a suggestion made by Professor G. Sellin in response to his Trondheim paper, that these exegetical traditions of the Diaspora left their mark at a number of places in Paul's exegesis.

picture Räisänen reiterates some of the conclusions of his *Paul and the Law*:[9] Paul found a Gentile mission already in progress (256), in which the Hellenists probably had 'a *somewhat* relaxed attitude to the observance of the ritual Torah, perhaps even a neglect of circumcision as part of missionary strategy' (254, his emphasis).[10] The rise of this circumcision-free mission was 'haphazard', with no 'decisive theological step' being taken (255).[11] Paul simply went along with this 'liberal' attitude, and only when it was challenged around 48 C.E., perhaps due to growing numbers of former Pharisees joining the church,[12] was Paul, grown accustomed to being 'internally alienated from the ritual aspects of the law' (258), compelled to defend his attitude and practice, often with *ad hoc* arguments.

Thus he concludes his article by saying that the Hellenists were not really a bridge between Jesus and Paul:

> The temple issue connects Jesus with Stephen but not with Paul. If circumcision does connect Paul with Stephen, that connection does not extend back to Jesus who was not concerned with the Gentile question.[13]

Two points need to be made here. The first is that the Hellenists must have been guilty, not just of laxity or carelessness in consorting with Gentile converts, but also of admitting these Gentiles to their fellowship as a *deliberate policy*. They would not have been so rigorously persecuted had they not persisted in their practice even when they saw the outrage that it caused their fellow Jews, and the consequent danger which their ways presented to themselves. Räisänen in his book had conceded as much when he referred to the dropping of the need for circumcision 'as

9. WUNT 29 (Tübingen: Mohr, 1983); cf. Müller, 'Rezeption' (n. 3.53) 167–8.

10. This is surely compatible with, indeed a likely corollary of, G. Strecker's contention that in the earliest phase of Paul's mission, and indeed in the early church in general, the Law was treated as an 'Adiaphoron': 'Befreiung' (n. 5.15) ; but see 231.

11. Quoting S. G. Wilson, *The Gentiles and the Gentile Mission in Luke–Acts* (SNTSMS 23, Cambridge Univ., 1973) 152, and the phrase of J. Jervell, *Luke and the People of God* (Minneapolis MI: Augsburg, 1972) 136: 'action preceded theology'; cf. his 'Jesus' (n. 1) 88.

12. A further reason might well be the rise of nationalist feelings in Judaea, making it increasingly uncomfortable, even dangerous, to appear disloyal to the traditions of Judaism; cf. R. Jewett, 'The Agitators and the Galatian Congregation', *NTS* 17 (1970–1) 198–212, esp. 205–6.

13. '"Hellenists"' (n. 1.4) 300.

part of missionary strategy' (254). 'Strategy' suggests choice, rather than simply naive unawareness of what they were doing. Yet still Räisänen's point remains valid, that the choice which they made was not then the negative one, to criticize the Law, but a positive one, to admit Gentiles without insisting on obedience to the fullness of the Law. It was, in other words, a matter of neglect of, or indifference to, the Law, not out of laziness or ignorance, but as a deliberate decision. But again I would stress that it is a matter of the *non-observance of the Law rather than explicit criticism of it at this stage*.[14] That their position implied a criticism is a later perspective on their conduct. In fact, whatever the historical value of Acts' account of the origins of the Gentile mission, this is where the emphasis is placed, particularly in the story of the conversion of Cornelius and his friends in Acts 10–11: in the light of God's guidance and above all the evidence of the presence in Cornelius and his friends of the spirit of God, Peter, and subsequently the Jerusalem church, decide to admit Gentiles; they cannot gainsay their claim to be a part of God's people. It is only subsequently that the question arises as to how far they must keep the Law. However, even if the step thus taken was not 'theological', in the sense of being backed up by careful theoretical reflection, but rather practical, it was a step; they did not just 'drift' into admitting Gentiles.[15]

If, then, as I believe was probably the case, it was chiefly the 'Hellenists' who were affected by the persecution which broke out in Acts 8.1, and the 'Hebrews', as well as the apostles, were unaffected,

---

14. I.e. 'gesetzesfrei' rather than 'gesetzeskritisch', to use Müller's distinction: 'Rezeption' (n. 3.53) 158 n. 1a; yet how consistent is he in observing it? He seems rather just to shift his focus from the latter to the former in the course of the article. But the question then arises why, if they possessed 'Law-critical' Jesus-tradition (cf. 183), they only practised freedom from the Law and did not go further and criticize it. Moreover where are these 'Law-critical' traditions if the ones investigated for evidence of them point merely to freedom from the Law (cf. 184)? Dietzfelbinger, *Berufung* (n. 5), and A. Suhl, *Paulus und seine Briefe: ein Beitrag zur paulinischen Chronologie* (SNT 11, Gütersloh: Mohn, 1975) 30–5, also regards the Hellenists as critical of the Law, and W. Schrage, '"Ekklesia" und "Synagoge"', *ZTK* 60 (1963) 178–202, here 197–200, slides from a 'Law-free Gentile mission' to criticism of the Law; but a neglect of the Law would be enough to explain their preference for ἐκκλησία rather than συναγωγή (Schrage's point). For A. Hultgren, 'Paul's Pre-Christian Persecutions of the Church: Their Purpose, Locale and Nature', *JBL* 95 (1976) 97–111, the earliest Hellenists did not 'set themselves against the law', and he distinguishes this from a later stage when 'a Christianity free from the law' came into being at Antioch (98–9). But how sound is Acts' picture of the development here?

15. Cf. my 'Paul and the Law', *SJT* 38 (1985) 613–22, here 621.

then the cause, the offence lay with the former group and not with the latter.[16] This is intelligible in Jerusalem too, and not just in centres of the Diaspora like Damascus,[17] for in worship and in social intercourse Greek-speaking Jews of the synagogue mentioned in Acts 6.9 would be more likely to come into contact with visiting or resident non-Jews than would their fellows who habitually used a Semitic tongue. If the issue that sparked off the persecution was one of contact with Gentiles, then it is the former group who would have been affected first. The 'Hebrews' would thus have been largely shielded by their language from the questions of how much share in the new Christian message and community non-Jews might have and on what terms, whereas these problems would have been more likely to present themselves to their Greek-speaking fellow-Christians. They would presumably have been presented in the form of Gentiles interested in this new Jewish grouping and seeking to join it in its worship and its meetings; if table-fellowship

16. Cf. A. Weiser, *Die Apostelgeschichte* (Ökumenischer Taschenbuchkomm. zum NT 5.1, Gütersloh: Mohn & Würzburg: Echter, 1981) 168. That surely is enough to show that the explanation of the persecution as provoked by the proclamation of Jesus as Messiah is inadequate despite the arguments of Dietzfelbinger, *Berufung* (n. 5) 40–1, to explain this; the same difficulty confronts Hultgren's account—'Persecutions' (n. 14), and that of Strecker, 'Befreiung' (n. 11), esp. 234; cf. Sanders, *Jesus* (n. 5.23) 283; Schrage and Suhl as in n. 14.

17. Thus I question whether it is only 'wandering missionaries' who would be likely to meet Gentiles as suggested by Räisänen, '"Hellenists"' (n. 1.4) 284; those who remained in their place might well find Gentiles making their way to them.

At the same time it should be noted that Jerusalem was a more dangerous place in which to extend such a welcome to Gentiles or to speak against the Temple, for Jerusalem's prestige as well as the well-being and the livelihood of many of its inhabitants were bound up with the status of the Temple and the Jewish religion; the inhabitants of Jerusalem might well feel threatened by the Hellenists' actions and message in the same way as Christian preaching endangered the livelihood of those of Ephesus according to Acts 19.23–40 and presumably also many of those of Bithynia according to Pliny, *Ep*.10.96.10.

But Räisänen, ibid. 249, is inclined to doubt whether persecution took place in Jerusalem; and yet, if Stephen was killed for speaking against the Temple (e.g. 275), then the likeliest place for this to happen was in Jerusalem; thus Räisänen grants (250) that at least Stephen was killed in Jerusalem; is it so unlikely that Paul was in Jerusalem at the time and sympathized with those who took this action against Stephen, even if his role at this point was a minor one? (See too n. 30 below.) But is it not then rather unsatisfactory to say that the Hellenists then left Jerusalem because it was 'increasingly inconvenient' (Räisänen, ibid.) to continue their activities there? Is it not far more convincing if these activities were liable at any point to provoke a fate like Stephen's? That surely implies that Stephen was not so 'singular' (Räisänen 286).

played a central role in that worship then questions of ritual purity would naturally arise. The implication of the argument thus far is that it was, at least tacitly, decided that ritual purity should not be insisted upon. The question then arises, what led them to consider this policy a possible and legitimate one for them to adopt. May it not be that *the example of Jesus' attitude and behaviour towards the despised outsiders of his world led them to adopt a similar welcoming attitude and behaviour towards the despised outsiders of their own, more cosmopolitan world?*

The second consideration is more serious and was raised particularly by Dr Francis Watson in his book *Paul, Judaism and the Gentiles*.[18] Here he presents a very different picture of the development of the Gentile mission in which he argues that Paul's mission to Gentiles only began relatively late in his ministry after the failure of his (and others') ministry to Jews, and he questions the very existence of the Hellenist group in the church at all.

He starts from the premise that the origins of Paul's statements about the Law are to be found in the origins of the Gentile mission (23). He adopts a highly sceptical attitude towards Acts' account of the latter: he doubts 'whether the Cornelius narrative is of any historical value' (24). What many hold to be an alternative explanation of the origins of the Gentile mission, the activity of the Hellenists, is equally doubtful: it must be questioned whether 'there ever were two groups in the Jerusalem church, the Hellenists and the Hebrews' (26). The attribution of the Gentile mission in 11.20–1 to members of the former group driven out of Jerusalem by persecution reveals Luke's 'tendency to emphasize the centrality of Jerusalem at every point' (ibid.); *pace* Acts Paul cannot have persecuted Christians in Jerusalem, for that cannot be reconciled with Gal 1.22–23. The Hellenists of Acts 6 are for Luke Diaspora Jews now residing in Jerusalem; their joining the church is described in Acts 2, but that account 'is manifestly unhistorical' (25).

Our primary source, Paul's letters, presents a different picture, in which Paul began his Christian career as a missionary to Jews, and 'Paul (and others) first preached to Gentiles as a response to the failure of their preaching among the Jews' (31).[19] They 'did not require full submission to the law from their Gentile converts' (33), implying perhaps 'a relaxed attitude towards the law on the part of the Antiochene Jewish Christians, rather than a complete renunciation of the law' (ibid.), while Gentile Christians there were exempted from Jewish food-laws, sabbaths and festivals as well as circumcision. This relaxation was in order to make it easier for Gentiles to become Christians, and increased the success of the Gentile mission by removing those aspects of the Jewish faith which were most

18. *Paul, Judaism and the Gentiles: a Sociological Approach* (SNTSMS 56, Cambridge Univ., 1986) chap. 2, 'The Origins of Paul's View of the Law'.

19. But cf. now the arguments of Dietzfelbinger, *Berufung* [n. 5] 142–4, that Paul took up his ministry to the Gentiles immediately following his Damascus road experience.

offensive to Gentiles (cf. 1 Cor 9.19–21; 10.32–3); originally this was 'not a matter of theological principle but of practical expediency' (36). This however separated the church from the synagogue.

2 Cor 11.24 for Watson refers to the earlier period when Paul was under the discipline of the synagogue, but it could as easily be interpreted against the background of Acts' account of the Gentile missionary Paul preaching in the synagogues of the Dispersion until driven out. Would his earlier message of a Christianity subservient to the Law, such as Watson postulates, have merited such chastisement? 1 Cor 9.20–21 in his eyes refers not to a constant switching from obedience to the Law to a Gentile way of life and back again, but to being as a Jew and then subsequently becoming as one outside the Law. But to insist as he does on the aorist ἐγενόμην as opposed to the present, so that v 21 refers to Paul's 'irrevocable break with the Jewish way of life when he began to think of himself as "apostle to the Gentiles"' (29), is difficult since the aorist verb is understood from v 20; does it then in v 20 refer to an 'irrevocable break'? Obviously not, since there was no question of Paul 'becoming' a Jew earlier. Or is 'Jew' to be understood in the pregnant sense of a 'Jewish Christian missionary to the Jews'? But then he goes on to say that he became as one under the Law to win those under the Law, 'although not being myself under the Law', when Watson's thesis should entail that in fact he did still then reckon himself to be 'under the Law'. Gal 1.16, he argues, reflects Paul's thinking about his conversion about seventeen years later, and one should not therefore read his calling to preach to the Gentiles back into it.[20] Gal 5.11 ('still'), he thinks, implies that Paul had once preached circumcision and 'κηρύσσειν is a technical term for Christian proclamation' (30), but this word *could* refer to Paul's previous career as a Pharisee; even if 'preach' is 'a technical term for Christian proclamation', Paul is quite capable of using terms appropriate in a Christian context to describe Judaism: e.g. 1 Cor 10.2.

Despite granting extensive editorial work by Luke, Räisänen[21] upholds the view that the Hellenists existed and were persecuted by Paul and established a 'liberal' church in Antioch; otherwise one would have to duplicate them with yet other like-minded Christians. It is unlikely that Stephen's arrest and death is Luke's invention (ibid. 260).

Watson's reconstruction presents a major challenge to Räisänen's thesis. The Hellenists have not only ceased to be a bridge between Jesus and Paul but have ceased to exist, and so cannot be a bridge between anything (and Räisänen still wants to make them a bridge, 'between Jesus' apocalyptic proclamation of a new temple and later writers critical of the temple cult as such (Mark, Hebrews, Letter of Barnabas)', and 'between Hellenistic Judaism of the Dispersion and the Palestinian Jesus movement').[22] Yet is Acts self-consistent enough for its contents to be

20. This point is taken up by Räisänen, *Torah* (n. 1) 251 n. 2: *could* Paul have thus reinterpreted his original commission in the polemical context of Galatians where his claims were liable to be repudiated? (He cites Kim, *Origin* [n. 4.27] 59.) He tells us little of those seventeen years of Jewish mission because he is now engaged in mission to Gentiles.

21. '"Hellenists"' (n. 1.4) 244–52.

attributable in so wholesale a fashion to the creativity of its author? If he were a novelist writing what is largely fiction with scanty sources and even scantier regard for questions of historical accuracy, then he would be a rather poor novelist. Is it not at least as plausible to regard him as seeking to be a historian, after the fashions of that day, but succeeding perhaps in only being a second-rate one, imperfectly understanding his sources and sometimes exercising insufficient scrupulosity in his handling of them? That is not to deny his theological motivation, but simply to deny that in those days historiography and writing with a theological purpose were necessarily mutually exclusive alternatives.[23] Moreover Watson's thesis raises considerable problems, the chief of which is the question why Paul then persecuted Christians, as he himself acknowledges that he did. It is one thing for the Jerusalem hierarchy to proceed against the early church; in proclaiming Jesus as Messiah the latter were by implication accusing those authorities of sinning against God in conniving at Jesus' arrest and death. It is another thing when the persecution is carried out by a Pharisee who, as far as we can judge (despite Acts 26.10), was probably not part of the Jerusalem establishment; Gal 1.22 would be difficult were that the case. The Jewish Christians presumably witnessed to Jews in much the same terms both before and after this persecution. There is little sign of persecution of James and the Jerusalem church except by the Jewish leadership, be it Herod Agrippa I (Acts 12.1–5) or the high priest Ananus (Jos., *Ant.* 20.9.1 §§200–3). Räisänen's account, in which he is inclined to think that already the status of the Temple and the need for Gentiles to be circumcised were at issue when Stephen died, at least has the considerable merit of explaining what at least some early Christians said and did which roused the ire of Paul and others.

I myself am more inclined than Räisänen to think that these two issues were more closely connected than has hitherto been apparent. In Acts 21.27–30 certain Asian Jews stir up feeling against Paul by suggesting that he has defiled the Temple by introducing Greeks into it. If there is any historical truth in the account then it raises the question why it should be thought and believed that Paul had done this. Was it simply an inference from Paul's Law-free gospel or from his reputation as one who encouraged apostasy from Judaism (21.21)? Or was it that they had reason to believe that one who preached to the Gentiles on such terms as he did might also seek to bring them into the Temple, justifying this

---

22. Räisänen's conclusions (ibid. 301).

23. Cf. M. Hengel, *Acts and the History of Earliest Christianity* (London: SCM, 1979) esp. chap. 5.

action by according them an equal status with Jews in God's people? Did suspicion fall all too easily upon Paul because this had already been suggested, if not actually perpetrated, by his predecessors in the Gentile mission? In other words, *was Stephen guilty, not so much of speaking against the Temple as such, as of speaking against Jewish restriction of its use to their own nation?* Without claiming that the quotation of Isa 56.7 in Mark 11.17 represents an authentic saying of Jesus,[24] we may yet ask whether or not

24. Cf. Harvey, *Jesus* (n. 5.35) 132; Sanders, *Jesus* (n. 5.23) 66–7, 221; M. Trautmann, *Zeichenhafte Handlungen Jesu: ein Beitrag zur Frage nach dem geschichtlichen Jesu* (FB 37, Würzburg: Echter, 1980) 87–90; Walter, chapter 3, p. 57 n. 12 and lit. cited there. It may be that the attribution of this quotation to Jesus is occasioned by earlier Hellenist use of it rather than that Jesus' use of it led the Hellenists to take it up. The thrust of this chapter will indeed be that it was Jesus' conduct and openness towards outsiders in general that encouraged this attitude on the part of the Hellenist Christians rather than reflection upon any proof text. In the same way the sort of conviction expressed by Paul in Rom 14.14 may have influenced the formulation of Mark 7 rather than vice versa; cf. H.-J. Klauck, *Allegorie und Allegorese in synoptischen Gleichnistexten* (NTAbh Neue Folge 13, Münster: Aschendorff, 1978) 269; Räisänen, 'Jesus' (n. 1) 88–90, and 'Herkunft' (n. 1) 480–4. But cf. M. J. Borg, *Conflict, Holiness and Politics in the Teachings of Jesus* (Studies in the Bible and Early Christianity 5, New York & Toronto: Mellon, 1984) 171–7.

It seems striking that, despite widespread agreement on the historicity and the symbolic nature of this action by Jesus, there is less agreement on what was symbolized by it; there is far more agreement that the interpretations suggested by the scriptural verses cited as explanations are secondary. Nor does it seem to be a readily intelligible way of symbolizing the destruction of the Temple (*pace* Sanders, ibid.), unless one also follows Trautmann in seeing here the original setting of a prophecy of the Temple's destruction as suggested by John 2.19 (ibid. 122–7) and perhaps not even then; as an attack on the Temple cult it could more readily be understood, but does not seem to have been so understood by those Christians who remained devoted to the Temple during the following decades (*pace* Trautmann, ibid. 120–1, 129); if its purpose was the clearing away of encumbrances and distractions to the worship of God, a symbolic act of 'Temple reform and renewal...associated with the inauguration of a new era, and...as preparatory to the Messianic Age' (R. H. Hiers, 'Purification of the Temple: Preparation for the Kingdom of God', *JBL* 90 (1971) 82–90, here 86), then its spirit would be caught quite appositely by the quotation of Isa 56.7 (cf. F. Hahn, *Mission in the New Testament*, SBT 47, London: SCM, 1965, 38 n. 2), but more by the 'house of prayer' (but not 'prayer' as opposed to sacrifice) than the 'for all the nations' (and possibly also by the allusion to Zech 14.21 detected by some behind John 2.16—cf. Hiers, ibid. 86–7; B. Lindars, *New Testament Apologetics: the Doctrinal Significance of the Old Testament* (London: SCM, 1961) 70). Or was it not so much symbolic of Temple reform, but 'a prophetic act symbolizing God's imminent judgmental destruction, not just of the building, but of the Temple system', as is now suggested by R. A. Horsley, *Jesus and the Spiral of*

this Old Testament verse may not have early on been the subject of reflection in the early church; if so it could have led to the conviction that the Gentiles had a place in the Temple, and that the Temple was meant for them too. That is to take the words of Isaiah as a promise and an offer;[25] it does not follow that this is how it was interpreted by the Evangelists who used it to interpret the cleansing of the Temple, still less by Jesus. We cannot, of course, prove that the Hellenists were influenced by this verse, or even that such an attitude *vis-à-vis* the Gentiles and the Temple lay at the root of their persecution. But such a hypothesis allows us to see the basis of the charges of speaking against the Temple and the Law (Acts 6.13) as being far more homogeneous than might otherwise be the case: *they had welcomed uncircumcised Gentiles into their gatherings; they had suggested that they might also rightfully share with them in the worship of the Temple* (but had only suggested it rather than acting upon the suggestion, for in that case there would have been more executions to record); *in both these ways they had broken down the distinctions that marked off Jews from non-Jews.* It does, however, mean that the amplification of the former charge by the explanation that Stephen had said that Jesus would destroy the Temple (6.14) goes off on another tack, a false tack even, and one which receives no support from the following speech, even if one sees that speech as highly critical of the Temple as an institution, an interpretation of the speech which is open to considerable doubt;[26] it does not predict that Jesus will destroy the

Violence: Popular Jewish Resistance in Roman Palestine (San Francisco: Harper & Row, 1987) 300, or rather, as is now perhaps more plausibly suggested by R. Bauckham, 'Jesus' Demonstration in the Temple', in (ed.) B. Lindars, *Law and Religion: Essays on the Place of the Law in Israel and Early Christianity by Members of the Ehrhardt Seminar of Manchester University* (Cambridge: Clarke, 1988) 72–89, a protest against the exploitation of the poor by the Temple hierarchy?

25. See Pesch, *Markusevangelium* (n. 3.19) 199; cf. Lindars, ibid. 107: 'Jesus is staking a claim...for the inclusion of the Gentiles in its [the Temple's] worship'; also W. D. Davies, *The Gospel and the Land: Early Christianity and Jewish Territorial Doctrine* (Berkeley, etc: Univ. of California, 1974) 351 n. 46: that Jesus' action took place in the Court of the Gentiles shows that Jesus was 'concerned with the right of, and the hopes of Judaism for, the Gentiles as with the Temple itself. Jesus acted both to judge the community that had slighted the rights of Gentiles in its supreme sanctuary and to point forward to a better, larger community.' But, while the early church was interested in the place of the Gentiles, was Jesus?

26. Räisänen, '"Hellenists"' (n. 1.4) 275, argues that Stephen's speech generally is more positive about the Temple than is widely supposed, or at least abstains from the sort of critique that 17.25 might lead us to expect.

Temple. This explanation of Stephen's offence also means that the future tense, 'will change' in 6.14 is likewise misleading:[27] the implications of Stephen's beliefs (and actions) as argued in this paper was that the status of the Law had *already* been changed by the coming of Jesus.

Tentatively, then, I would want to suggest that *the Temple and the Law*, the twin pillars of Jewish self-consciousness and national identity, 'life and death symbols' to the Jewish people,[28] *had both been threatened by the Jewish-Christian Hellenists' readiness to accommodate Gentiles within God's people, and to admit them to the full privileges of membership in it*, and they had done this in a period when Jewish sensibilities had already been rendered tender, to say the least, by the insensitivity of Pontius Pilate's rule.[29] Moreover, one cannot dismiss the martyrdom of Stephen as an isolated incident, and say that he just happened to say the wrong thing in a provocative way at the wrong time, for clearly the persecution, once started, continued, involving, as we have seen, Paul himself, even if not in Jerusalem.[30] Others besides Stephen were implicated and were thought to pose a serious enough threat to occasion the spread of persecution even beyond the bounds of Jewish territory to a neighbouring city like Damascus.

---

27. Müller, 'Rezeption' (n. 3.53) 164, fails to note this future tense: 'the charge traces the Law-critical attitude of the "Hellenists" back to the preaching of Jesus (Acts 6.14)'. Räisänen, ibid. 266, rightly doubts whether a prediction that the Messiah would give a new interpretation of the Law or even change it *in the future* would be sufficient grounds for killing the one who predicted it.

28. Cf. Borg, *Conflict* (n. 24) 56.

29. Cf. Borg, ibid. 42–4; E. Schürer, *The History of the Jewish People in the Age of Jesus Christ (175 B.C.–A.D. 135)* 1 (Edinburgh: Clark, 1973[2]) 383–7; E. M. Smallwood, *The Jews under Roman Rule: from Pompey to Diocletian* (SJLA 20, Leiden: Brill, 1976) 160–74. On most chronologies the persecution of Stephen would still fall under Pilate's rule.

30. The clash between Gal 1.22 and Acts is perhaps best resolved by postulating that Acts has exaggerated Paul's persecuting role in Jerusalem; it may not even have amounted to that of a 'cloakroom attendant' to those stoning Stephen (Acts 7.58); cf. Dietzfelbinger, *Berufung* (n. 5) 21–2. But it seems unnecessary to deny that he had been in Jerusalem; it is intrinsically plausible that he would have attended the synagogue there frequented by those from Cilicia (6.9), where opposition to Stephen first arose. On the other hand Beker's account in *Paul* (n. 6) 185 seems to imply that Paul alone was chiefly responsible for stirring up opposition to the Hellenists; Gal 1.22 is then very difficult.

II

The conclusions of the previous section cannot but remain highly hypothetical and controversial. The sort of suggestions made there, however, are nevertheless worth making, even necessary to make, if we are trying to explain historically the rise of the various movements and traditions within earliest Christianity. For parallel phenomena within traditions about Jesus and the various traditions of the early church strongly suggest a causal connection between them; similarities between religious movements that are far removed from one another in time and geographical location, and lack any known historical connection with one another, may be explained as coincidences or the products of some factor common to humanity and the human spirit. But it is another matter when the similarities occur shortly after one another, and when, in this case, the one set of similarities occurs within a movement that claims to be a continuation of the other, i.e. within the Christian church that looks back to Jesus as its originator and cause. Then *we are more or less compelled to posit some sort of causal link between the two, even if the link or links remain hidden from our view.* Such a supposition becomes even more necessary if, as Sanders argues,[31] Paul was unaware of the precedents in Jesus' actions for his Law-free gospel. Such a coincidence is surely only explicable if Paul copies intermediaries who in their turn follow Jesus' example. The Hellenists *may* not be the 'bridge', but a 'bridge' there must be, even if it has been submerged without trace beneath the onrushing stream of past history.

But *are* there similarities between the teaching and ministry of Jesus and the teaching and ministry of his apostle, Paul? We have seen in Räisänen's article how the attempt to find such a similarity in their attitude to the Jewish Law proved abortive. But his earlier book had suggested that Paul's attitude to the Law was a later rationalization of an earlier indifference to the Law, or at least to its ritual requirements (254), a rationalization undertaken when this indifference came under challenge from other Christians. That raises the question of how they could have felt free to be thus indifferent. What were their warrants for their conduct or, as Räisänen puts it, their 'strategy'?

Professor Nils Dahl, in an important article on justification,[32] pointed out that, whereas Jesus rarely, if ever, spoke of justification, we have the

---

31. *Jesus* (n. 5.23) 283.

32. 'The Doctrine of Justification: Its Social Function and Implications' in *Studies in Paul: Theology for the Early Christian Mission* (Minneapolis: Augsburg, 1977) 95–120, here 115.

record of 'his beatitudes of the poor, his miraculous help to the disturbed and his solidarity with outcasts'; this was a 'justification of the ungodly'. Thus

what Paul stated systematically, Jesus had already lived, in his attitudes and in his activities. The correspondence between them becomes clearer when we realize that Paul does not present the doctrine of justification as a dogmatic abstraction. As Jesus' work destroyed the significance of the distinction between sinners and the righteous in Israel, so Paul's fidelity to the truth of the gospel had to forbid discriminating within the church between Jews and Gentiles.

In other words *both Jesus and Paul were in their lives and ministries characterized by what might be called an openness to the outsider, and that in the name of their God.* Whereas, within the context of his ministry, Jesus was primarily confronted with outsiders from within the nation of Israel,[33] Paul came into contact with outsiders of another sort, those nations whom he had hitherto believed to be outside the saving plan of God, or who at the most played a marginal role within it, at least within the confines of this present age. Both Jesus and Paul welcomed those outsiders with whom they each came into contact and received them into fellowship with themselves, without prior conditions, and thus into the fellowship of God's renewed people. The views of Räisänen, quoted above, would suggest that Paul learnt these habits of openness and of an unconditional welcome into the fellowship of God's saved people from the Hellenists whom he had once persecuted; he may well have persecuted them for this very reason, for such conduct threatened to undermine the distinctive status of Israel, to subvert the very *raison d'être* of his people.

The Hellenists, it may very naturally be suggested, *had learnt these habits from Jesus.* Some of them, being Diaspora Jews, were perhaps already used to a greater degree of openness to non-Jews through having lived amongst them and having had to achieve a certain *modus vivendi* with them. But that was by no means true of all of them: for others this same exposure to the non-Jewish world led to a contempt for, and abhorrence of, the pagan world around and a fierce loyalty to their own traditions and customs. It would, then be surprising neither if some of them, confronted with the problem whether or not to welcome non-Jews into their Christian gatherings, seized upon the example of Jesus towards the outcasts in his own environment,[34] nor if others of their fellows, who

---

33. It was only with difficulty that the early church could find scattered instances of Jesus' contact with non-Jews, and his restriction of his activity largely to rural Galilee meant that his contact with Gentiles would be severely limited.

34. Müller, 'Rezeption' (n. 3.53) 165-6, rightly questions how far the

had not the same reverence for Jesus, regarded their un-Jewish conduct as treachery. *The same openness which had occasioned resentment against Jesus was now taken a step further, and resentment gave way to outright hostility and violent opposition.* This example of Jesus has recently been explored by E. P. Sanders in his *Jesus and Judaism*, where chap. 6 deals with the subject of 'The Sinners'.

Using the 'criterion of dissimilarity' he argues that 'a high tolerance for sinners' was not, as far as we know, characteristic of the early church, nor, we may add, of many streams of contemporary Judaism, but seems to have been a 'distinctive note' of Jesus' teaching about God's reign (174). These 'sinners' were, however, not just the common people but rather 'those who sinned wilfully and heinously and who did not repent' (177). Lumped together with the 'sinners' are tax-collectors (or perhaps we should rather call them 'toll-collectors')[35] since the latter were traitors, for, Sanders argues, they collaborated with Rome (178).[36] However O. Michel's explanation perhaps more

Hellenists appealed to particular sayings of Jesus in their Law-critical (or Law-free?) stance. But is it not easier to see how they could be influenced by Jesus-tradition without resort to particular teaching if what they were following was not primarily the words of Jesus but his actions (not towards the 'people of the land' [so 166], but more especially towards 'sinners')? He argues, too, that the prominence of 'sinners' in Mk 2.15–17 (n.b. esp. 2.16) is evidence that this story of Jesus' table-fellowship with tax-collectors has its setting amidst the later church's arguments over 'table-fellowship with (former) Gentiles' (169); one can, however, perhaps leave out the 'former': the problem is those who remain Gentiles, even after becoming Christians; cf. Dunn, 'Mark 2.1–3.6' (n. 3.53) 404–5.

35. Cf. I. Abrahams, 'Publicans and Sinners', in *Studies in Pharisaism and the Gospels: First Series* (Cambridge Univ., 1917) 54–61, here 55: 'persons of immoral life, men of proved dishonesty or followers of suspected and degrading occupations'; cf. J. Jeremias, 'Zöllner und Sünder', in *ZNW* 30 (1931) 293–300, here 295. J. R. Donahue, 'Tax Collectors and Sinners: an Attempt at Identification', in *CBQ* 33 (1971) 39–61, e.g. 45, 50: the τελῶναι of the Gospels are toll-collectors, who were, if anything, even more unpopular because of their rapacity and dishonesty (53, citing L. Goldschmid, 'Les impôts et droits de douane en Judée sous les Romains', in *REJ* 34 [1897] 192–217, esp. 215–7).

36. Cf. N. Perrin, *Rediscovering the Teaching of Jesus* (London: SCM, 1967) 93. Yet does that hold good if those operating in Galilee were in fact working for Herod Antipas?—see esp. Donahue, ibid. 45–7, 51, 53; cf. A. N. Sherwin-White, *Roman Society and Roman Law in the New Testament* (Oxford: Clarendon, 1963) 125–6: 'Except at Jerusalem and perhaps Jericho the tax-farmers must be collecting either for the Tetrarch or for the municipality. But it is very questionable whether there were any municipal taxes in Jewish lands except at the very few cities which had been given Hellenistic city organization by the Herods'; also H.

accurately reflects contemporary attitudes and their basis: 'In Judaism...tax-farmers were regarded as people who tried to get money dishonestly'.[37] It may thus be significant and possibly historically accurate (rather than just a piece of Lukan theology) that John the Baptist's injunction to toll-collectors says nothing about dealings with Gentiles, but only about demanding more than their due (Luke 3.12–13). Dishonesty imperilled them more than their dealings with Gentiles.

M. J. Borg has attempted to offer a more precise definition of the possible meanings of the term 'sinner':[38]
(a) those practising one of seven trades which deprived them *de jure* of all civil rights, and thus rendered them 'as a Gentile' (gamblers with dice, usurers, organizers of games of chance, dealers in produce of the sabbatical year (*m. Sanh.* 3.3=*m. Roš. Haš.* 1.8) are ineligible as witnesses; *b. Sanh.* 25*b* adds shepherds, tax-collectors and publicani.[39] *M. Roš. Haš.* 1.8 adds 'and slaves' which Jeremias interprets as Gentile slaves;[40] is this the basis of Borg's phrase 'as a Gentile'? (See also *b. 'Erub.* 36*b* where 'foreigner' can be interpreted to mean 'tax-collector') or those involved in one of that wider group of trades thought to be immoral and depriving them of those rights *de facto* (transport workers, herdsmen, shopkeepers, physicians, butchers, goldsmiths, flaxcombers, etc.: *b. Qidd.* 82*a*; cf. *m. Qidd.* 4.14—one reason given is 'their craft is the craft of robbers';[41]

Hoehner, *Herod Antipas* (SNTSMS 17, Cambridge Univ., 1972) 73–9; Schürer, *History* 1 (n. 29) 375. It is, nevertheless, true that Antipas was a non-Jew and regarded as a foreigner, and that he owed his position to the Romans; Borg argues that tax-collectors, even if not directly serving the Romans, had 'daily commercial intercourse with Gentile inhabitants and traders' (*Conflict* [n. 24] 85), and this would be even more true of toll-collectors; they were thus no better than non-Jews themselves (cf. Matt 18.17 which reflects this Jewish attitude to toll-collectors).

37. In *TDNT* 8, 101 (although he also adds the reason that they had many contacts with Gentiles; that may be implied by the ref. to Gentiles in *m. Tohar.* 7.6: there they seem to be regarded as even more unclean than thieves: 'If taxgatherers entered a house [all that is within it] becomes unclean; even if a gentile was with them they may be believed if they say ("We did not enter"; but they may not be believed if they say) "We entered but we touched naught". If thieves enter a house, only that part is unclean that was trodden by the feet of the thieves' (tr. H. Danby, *The Mishnah* [Oxford Univ., 1933] 726—he notes that some texts omit the words in rounded brackets; cf. *m. Ned.* 3.4; *m. B. Qam.* 10.1–2; *b. Šebu.* 39*a*; *Der. Er. Rab.* 2.11; Donahue, ibid. 50–3; Hoehner, ibid. 78; Schürer, ibid. 376 and n. 108); cf. Jeremias, *Theology* (n. 5.22) 109, 111.

38. *Conflict* (n. 21) 84

39. Cf. J. Jeremias, *Jerusalem in the Time of Jesus: an Investigation into Economic and Social Conditions during the New Testament Period* (London: SCM, 1969) 304–5, 310, and 'Zöllner', esp. 299—the list of *b. Sanh.* 25*b* is linked by the common theme of cheating.

40. *Jerusalem* 311.

(b) those guilty of flagrant immorality;

(c) those who did not observe the Torah according to the Pharisaic understanding of it (the majority of Israel); this is an understanding of the term which Sanders rightly questions;[42]

(d) Gentiles—cf. Gal 2.15; Mk 14.41 in its immediate context seems to apply to Jews (v 43), but out of this context might refer to Gentiles.[43]

Borg does not choose between (a), (b) or (c); to consort with the third group and to eat with them might have been incompatible with being a strict Pharisee; the offence would certainly have been far greater if members of the first two groups had been amongst the company which Jesus kept, and in fact the Gospels tell of him as the companion of members of those groups (frequently with tax-collectors or toll-collectors, one of the seven trades in Borg's group (a); also with a sinful woman—his group (b): Lk 7.36–50; cf. Matt 21.31–2; the wife of Herod's steward might well be classed with these too—Lk 8.3; cf. also John 4.18; 8.1–11).

Since this article was first published there has appeared the important study of Horsley,[44] in which chapter 8 is particularly relevant to the present thesis. Rightly he dismisses the suggestion that the τελῶναι were viewed as collaborators or as Gentiles (212–13), but his attempt to play down the significance of references to Jesus' association with them is less convincing (213–17), except as a caution against assuming that such people made up a large proportion of Jesus' following. Horsley grants that 'a few toll collectors may well have responded to Jesus' preaching of the kingdom' (216–17), but that 'few' would have been sufficient to give substance to the charge echoed in Matt 11.18–19/Luke 7.33–4. (However he later goes on to support the suggestion of W. O. Walker that this reference to τελῶναι is a misunderstanding of the Aramaic טְלַיָּא, meaning, he suggests, 'playboy'—220–1.) He also grants that it is likely that 'disreputable and marginal people were attracted to Jesus' movement' (221). Numerically 'toll collectors and sinners' may not have formed a large proportion of Jesus' following, but in the eyes of Jesus' critics they are likely to have loomed

41. Tr. H. Danby (n. 37).

42. *Jesus* (n. 3) 176–7 (cf. 385–6 n. 15); he challenges the view of Jeremias, that the people of the land were identifiable with 'sinners': *Theology* (n. 5.22) 108–13; cf. also 'Zöllner' 294—but there it is clear that 'sinners' in the Gospels are sinners in the eyes of the people and not just of the Pharisees. However it is true that the very phrase, 'the people of the land', has a deprecatory ring about it if it echoes not only the OT designation of the common people of Israel but also the phrase, 'the peoples of the land(s)' found in Ezra and Nehemiah and used there of non-Jews living in Palestine; for reff. see Schürer, *History* (n. 29) 2 (1979²) 398 n. 59. How close this attitude could come to regarding them as 'sinners' is perhaps indicated by John 7.49, where on the one hand it is said that the crowd do not know the Law (and so presumably cannot sin deliberately) but at the same time are 'accursed'.

43. Cf. also K. H. Rengstorf, *TDNT* 1, 325–6. (Cf. n. 33 above on the paucity of reff. to Jesus' contact with Gentiles.)

44. *Jesus* (n. 24).

proportionally larger. That their company included such persons may also have been symbolic of, and important for, Jesus' and the first disciples' understanding of their condition and of the basis of their relationship with God: Luke 18.9–14. And it is not enough to treat these and other references with all possible scepticism; it is the historical critic's task to show too how such a charge arose against Jesus and why his followers perpetuated this picture of Jesus.

It was not, however, simply that Jesus offered forgiveness to penitent sinners, Sanders insists; that would not have been offensive to Jews of his time.[45] Rather, he suggests, what may have distressed them was that Jesus 'offered forgiveness (inclusion in the kingdom) *before* requiring reformation' (204, his emphasis). This is not just 'unconditional forgiveness' in the sense that Jesus forgives but expects a subsequent repentance and reparation; rather he offered them a place in God's kingdom while they remained sinners, i.e. without requiring repentance and restitution at all, and promised them this place symbolically by his eating at table with them. Heeding him and his call to follow was enough. That, however, in my judgment, raises the question whether no moral demands for a reformed life were implicit in following Jesus; perhaps we must say that they remained too implicit and not sufficiently explicit for Jesus' critics; at any rate that same feature was to be seen as a defect in Paul's gospel and laid him open to criticism (Rom 6.1, 15).

For Paul at least, Gentiles too were by definition 'sinners' (Gal 2.15), and there is no doubt that his fellow-Jews would have endorsed that verdict; as Sanders notes, however, that would not prevent them from hoping that some at least of them might eventually see the light and come in contrition to worship the Jewish God.[46] There would thus be little or no argument[47] over the legitimacy of a Gentile mission as such, even if Jesus himself had in fact done relatively little expressly to encourage such a strategy; what aroused bitter controversy among Christian and non-Christian Jews was the question of the 'terms and conditions' of such a mission. 'But the overwhelming impression is that Jesus started a movement which *came to see the Gentile mission as a logical extension of this*' (220, his emphasis).

Two comments should be made on this: (1) 'logical' should not be interpreted in too cerebral terms; the sort of *Sitz im Leben* postulated above (pp. 123–4), in which Greek-speaking Jewish Christians are

---

45. Cf. Abrahams, 'Publicans' (n. 35) 58.

46. Cf. Sanders, *Jesus* (n. 5.23) 217–18; cf. 214 on *Sib. Or.* 3.489–808.

47. Sanders, ibid. 220, points to Matt 10.5–6 as possible evidence of opposition to a Gentile mission at some stage, even if it is for Matthew countermanded, at least for the post-resurrection era, by 28.19–20.

approached by Greek-speaking non-Jews who wish to take part in their Christian meetings, allows for the possibility that the original decision was taken at a far more emotional level, a sort of 'gut' reaction to the request of these non-Jews; they may have felt instinctively the fitness of a policy of openness, may have felt it to be of a piece, in continuity with that openness which they had observed or had heard about in the case of Jesus' dealings with those who approached him. In other words, they would have argued that if Jesus was a 'friend...of sinners' (Matt 11.19/Luke 7.34) then he was also a friend of Gentiles who were also classed among 'sinners'.

(2) It may be suggested that the same feeling extended for some of them not just to 'Gentile mission' or rather the welcoming of Gentiles into their fellowship,[48] but to the terms upon which Gentiles were to be admitted: they were to be welcomed unconditionally, with no prior demands of ritual purity.

That early followers of Jesus, already open to the Gentile world by their ability to speak and understand its language, should act thus when approached is in the spirit of Jesus' dealings with sinners; when they reflected upon what they were doing they might well have considered that Jesus acted similarly towards those in his world who were the next worse thing to Gentiles, sinners, and in particular toll-collectors hated primarily for their greed and perhaps also because they were tainted by their contacts with, and service of, the non-Jewish world.

III

How the Hellenists defended and explained their attitude and behaviour we cannot know. Paul's defence is, we have seen (p. 121), likely to be a later development, as his missionary practice was challenged and subverted in Galatia. In that defence words of the root δικαιο- rise to

---

48. 'Mission' may be the wrong term to use here of this stage, if it implies an active going out in pursuit of converts; as with the expansion of many cults and religions in the ancient world it was at this stage as much a matter of holding one's meetings and rites and letting outsiders come in. In the earliest days what public preaching there was was likely to have been directed to the first disciples' fellow-Jews, just as the message of Jesus had been; with regard to the Gentiles the decision initially was not one whether to go out and bring them in, but whether to accept them when they came and asked to be admitted; the former decision may indeed not have been made expressly until the Jerusalem meeting of Gal 2.1–10 and what is perhaps its likely sequel, the decision of the Antioch church to carry the gospel to Cyprus and southern Asia Minor—Acts 13.1–3.); for some of the assumptions about chronology behind this see my 'Some Recent Pauline Chronologies', *ExpTim* 92 (1980–1) 103–8, esp. 106–7; cf. also F. Hahn, *Mission* (n. 24) 82.

prominence, and this is even more true of his Letter to the Romans. In his defence in Galatians he may well be adopting terminology of his opponents and critics' choosing, just as so many of the Old Testament texts with which he argues are likely to have played a part already in their arguments;[49] indeed that terminology is connected in Gen 15.6 (cf. Gal 3.6) with the figure of Abraham to whom his opponents probably appealed. In Romans this terminology is, I noted, yet more prominent, and I would see the theme of chaps 1–11 as being the defence of Paul's gospel against the charge that it was shameful (1.16), in that it impugned God's righteousness of character by suggesting that God had abandoned the promises and pledges made to the covenant people (cf. 3.1; 11.1), that God acquitted the ungodly or unrighteous, and in that it encouraged those unrighteous to persist in their unrighteousness (3.8; 6.1, 15). To this charge Paul must reply by redefining the righteousness of God (esp. 3.21–3, 26) and by stressing that human righteousness is bestowed upon the ungodly (4.5; cf. 5.6, 8) and those who are 'dead' (4.19).[50]

If this form of defence is developed late and is conditioned by this polemical context, then we should not expect to find it elaborated earlier. That raises the *question how this missionary practice was earlier expressed and expounded*—at least implicitly, if we are to allow for a degree of spontaneity and instinctive response in that practice. To pose that question may offer a healthy corrective to those attempts to link Paul's theology with that of Jesus by means of the language of justification.[51] That was ill-advised, not because the language of justification was peripheral, but because it was a relatively late development in a

---

49. See most recently J. L. Martyn, 'A Law-Observant Mission to Gentiles: the Background of Galatians', *SJT* 38 (1985) 307–24, here 318–23; also C. K. Barrett, 'The Allegory of Abraham, Sarah, and Hagar in the Argument of Galatians', in (ed.) J. Friedrich, W. Pöhlmann, P. Stuhlmacher, *Rechtfertigung* (*Festschrift* for E. Käsemann, Tübingen: Mohr & Göttingen: Vandenhoeck & Ruprecht, 1976) 1–16, here 6–10.

50. There is much that I find congenial here in the argument of S. K. Williams, 'The "Righteousness of God" in Romans', *JBL* 99 (1980) 241–90: 'Paul is at pains to show that God has not abandoned his Law, his people or his historical plan; nor does his grace mean that he tolerates sin' (248). I would suggest that, had he done any of these, his righteousness would be open to question. Williams is right to see the question of God's fidelity to the divine promises as central in Rom (e.g. 268, 289), but perhaps he has failed to do justice to the 'elasticity' of meaning of 'God's righteousness' to which I refer in the previous chapter, esp. 104: it embraces both God's nature and what this nature causes God to do and the results of that activity.

51. See particularly R. Bultmann, E. Jüngel, and even N. Walter's formulation of the problem in chapter 3 above, p. 51; cf. chapter 5, pp. 102–5.

particular polemical context; it nevertheless gave expression to *a* central, but perhaps not *the* central, feature of Paul's gospel, which had earlier been otherwise expressed or had been implicit in his preaching of the gospel, indeed since his conversion. We can perhaps infer one way in which the conviction of the unconditional openness of salvation to all found its place in Paul's earliest preaching by observing Paul's argument in Gal 3.1–5, although Paul's initial preaching in Galatia comes relatively late in his ministry as far as we can tell: there Paul argues that the Galatians' initial receiving of the Spirit, and the attendant manifestations of its power (v 5), were proof enough of their salvation, and that without 'works of the Law'. That they could be assured of that by the gift of the Spirit makes sense if that Spirit is seen as having enabled them too to cry 'Abba' as adopted children of God (4.5–7). The appeal to their receiving the Spirit is in this respect similar to the argument put on Peter's lips in Acts 15.8–9: Gentiles' receiving the gift of the Spirit convinced him, and subsequently the Jerusalem church, that God had accepted them (cf. 10.47; 11.17–18). Is there any reason to doubt that this pattern of argument is as old as non-proselyte Gentiles' receiving of the spirit of God in a manner that could not be gainsaid?

Prior, then, to the defence of his gospel in terms of God's righteousness and justification, it may be suggested that *Paul and the Hellenists before him based themselves upon the experiential truth that God had seemingly given the divine presence as Spirit to the Gentiles as well as to the Jews, unconditionally and unreservedly.*[52] That presumably presupposes that they had been ready earlier to admit those Gentiles to their gatherings at which they would be exposed to, and caught up in, those outpourings of God's spirit. When that happened they realized that God had come into those Gentiles' hearts too, as an indwelling and enabling power of love (Rom 5.5) and had taken up residence in their lives, claiming them as the divine sanctuary and consecrating them to the divine service (1 Cor 6.19–20; cf. the corporate sense of the same image in 3.16). Thus he appeals, perhaps using

52. Räisänen, "'Hellenists'" (n. 1.4) 269, argues that, although 'pneumatic experiences were probably something which *united* "Hebrews" and "Hellenists"' (and so cannot by themselves explain the latter's distinctive views), they may have had different effects, may have been given a different significance by the two groups. My thesis is rather different: the two groups evidently drew different conclusions from observing similar experiences *in the lives of non-Jews* (and because of their contacts the Hellenists would be in a far better position to observe these experiences in the first place); the importance of this Räisänen recognizes (286), and he also sees hints of this in Gal 2.8 (cf. his 'Jesus' [n. 1] 88).

traditional terminology, to the Corinthians' baptismal experience of being appropriated by Christ and possessed by God's Spirit in 1 Cor 6.11; at their baptism they, like other Gentile Christians before them, would have experienced the presence of God as Spirit and have been assured that they too had been incorporated into God's people (cf. 12.13). So too, in his earliest extant letter, 1 Thessalonians, Paul reminds his readers of their 'election' (ἐκλογή): that consisted in the gospel's coming to them 'in power and holy Spirit and great assurance' (1.4–5; cf. 1.6). The choice of the word ἐκλογή is striking: in Rom 9–11 Paul uses it of the 'election' of Jews (9.11; 11.5, 7, 28), but here he tells Gentile Christians that they too are 'elect': God has chosen them and of this they have been assured by God's power and spirit.

This seems to point to one thing: whatever impetus and example Jesus may have given to the admission of outsiders like the Gentiles to the church was subsequently confirmed experientially by the manifestation of spiritual phenomena in Gentiles admitted to the company of Jewish Christians. Interpreted as God's self-giving to them, this outpouring confirmed their status as also God's children, fellow-heirs with Jewish Christians of the divine promises. *Just as Jesus, as God's representative, had signified God's acceptance of sinners by eating with them, so now too God was signifying acceptance of Gentile sinners by pouring out the divine Spirit upon them as upon Jewish Christians.*

IV

This endowment of Gentiles with God's spirit thus had a meaning for them analogous to that which Jesus' fellowship and eating at table with sinners had for those sinners: this meant Jesus' acceptance of those sinners[53] and, Jesus being the sort of person that he was, that may have been a most significant act; as Borg comments,

given that sharing a meal symbolized acceptance in that culture, eating with a holy man with a powerful numinous presence could mediate a profound sense of acceptance and be an instrumental part of the therapeutic process whereby the internalized alienation of the outcasts was overcome and by which they would once again be able to see themselves as part of the people of God.[54]

---

53. Trautmann, *Handlungen* (n.24) 161, tellingly cites for the idea of table-fellowship as a symbol of reconciliation 2 Kgs 25.27–30; Jos., *Ant.* 19.7.1 §321; cf. Jeremias, *Theology* (n. 5.22) 115.

54. *Conflict* (n. 24) 93.

The significance of the act is therefore enhanced by the fact that the one who thus acts is one who claims to speak and act in God's name. Thus Jesus

in his table-fellowship with tax-collectors, blatant sinners, gave symbolic expression to the fact that sinners are called and invited by God, directly and without preconditions, out of their state of *Unheil* into the realm of salvation.[55]

This seems to express more adequately the significance of Jesus' actions than Jeremias' appeal to the general principle in Judaism that 'table-fellowship means fellowship before God', since they all shared in the blessing spoken by the head of the house at the start of the meal.[56] After all the toll-collectors had presumably eaten with one another previously and had said a blessing over their meals before. The difference now was the presence of Jesus with them, as one who announced that God was reigning now in his ministry, despite the expectation of his contemporaries that the coming of the reign of God would result in the judgment and exclusion of the very ones with whom Jesus was now consorting. It was this that made his action a source of hope to the 'sinners' and a source of offence to his critics.

Beyond this significance of the act of table-fellowship as meaning acceptance by Jesus now, in God's name, Borg, Sanders and Trautmann detect a further perspective to Jesus' behaviour: that which he does and offers now is a foretaste of a coming meal, the 'messianic banquet', that would be celebrated when the kingdom was consummated.[57] What they were allowed to share now promised them a share in that future too. That Jesus ate now with toll-collectors and sinners and prostitutes was a foretaste of the nature of God's reign and of the sort of company that would enjoy it (Matt 21.31b).[58]

55. Trautmann, *Handlungen* (n.24) 399; cf. 162.

56. Jeremias, *Theology* (n. 5.22) 115.

57. Sanders, *Jesus* (n. 5.23) 208–9; Trautmann, Handlungen (n.24) 161; cf. also M. Hengel, *The Charismatic Leader and His Followers* (Edinburgh: Clark, 1981; ET of *Nachfolge und Charisma: eine exegetisch-religionsgeschichtliche Studie zu Mt 8,21f. und Jesu Ruf in die Nachfolge*, BZNW 34, Berlin: Töpelmann, 1968) 67–8; Perrin, *Rediscovering* (n. 34) 106.

58. Cf. R. Bultmann, *Geschichte* (n. 3.31) 192: 'an application (of the preceding parable) whose *Ursprünglichkeit* perhaps need not be questioned'. R. Pesch, 'Das Zöllnergastmahl (Mk 2,15–17)' in (ed.) A. Descamps, A. de Halleux, *Mélanges bibliques* (*Festschrift* for B. Rigaux, Gembloux: Duculot, 1970) 63–87, here 79–80, argues that the καλέσαι of Mk 2.17 points to Jesus' role as God's eschatological messenger inviting sinners to God's great feast.

V

A further point of Borg's is perhaps worth pondering here: he observes that, whereas the Pharisees sought to avoid the contagion of impurity and unholiness, for Jesus 'holiness, not uncleanness, was understood to be contagious' (135). By that he means that Jesus overpowered and overcame infecting or contaminating forces; his touching a leper or a woman with a discharge cured that person rather than making Jesus unclean (Mark 1.40–5; 5.25–34).[59] It may be questioned here whether 'holiness' is the right way to describe that power which Jesus possessed; at best it is a misleading way. God is holy, that is true (Matt 6.9 par.), but that divine quality is not prominent in Jesus' teaching as far as we know, and certainly not in the sense of absence of pollution. What Jesus does speak of as an invading, rescuing power is God's rule, which should be regarded as a circumlocution for God as ruler, coming to save the people of God.[60] This reign, as represented in the person of Jesus, is a far more positive thing, the restoration of God's creation to the state which God wishes, purged and rescued from the evil powers besetting it, and handed back again to the beneficent power of its Maker. The 'holiness' (if one can call it that) which Jesus called for and which he embodied in his ministry was a consecration of oneself to the realization of that divine will in the world in which one found oneself.

Borg more appropriately goes on to speak of Jesus criticizing 'the quest for holiness' and, instead of speaking of Jesus as representative of a different sort of holiness, he suggests that Jesus

proposed an alternative path grounded in the nature of God as merciful, gathered a community based on that paradigm, and sought to lead his people in the way of peace, a way that flowed intrinsically from the paradigm of inclusive mercy (199).

59. He also compares the power of a Christian spouse to make a non-Christian partner holy in 1 Cor 7.12–14. Whether this sense of 'holiness' as an 'infection' is apt here is doubtful; one is surely correct to see here an echo of the language of the Jewish marriage ceremonial.

60. Cf. chapter 5, p. 106, citing Jeremias, *Theology* (n. 5.22) 102; also Borg, *Conflict* (n. 21) 254; B. D. Chilton, 'Regnum Dei Deus est', *SJT* 31 (1977–8) 261–70, *God in Strength: Jesus' Announcement of the Kingdom* (Studien zum Neuen Testament und seiner Umwelt, serie B 1, Freistadt: Plöchl, 1979) esp. 284–8, and *The Glory of Israel: the Theology and Provenience of the Isaiah Targum* (JSNTSup 23, Sheffield Academic Press, 1983) 77–81; Chilton documents further this use of the phrase to speak of God's action. Cf. also K. Koch, 'Offenbaren wird sich das Reich Gottes', *NTS* 25 (1978–9) 158–65, here 161, and n. 5.27 above.

The phrase, the 'kingdom of God', he also regards as referring to God himself as Jesus experienced him, an experience leading to

an awareness of a way other than the normative ways of the other renewal movements [in contemporary Judaism], one open to the outcasts and not dependent on holiness, but on a self-emptying and dying to self and world (261).

Trautmann likewise points to Jesus' symbolic acts as arising out of his particular vision of God's nature, a vision that transcends the views of the prophets before him.[61] His is a God who has decided irrevocably for humanity, and who accepts the totality of Israel without ethical or sacramental preconditions, forgiving the guilty and desiring to render all the people of God 'gesund und heil', and more concerned for their welfare than for their fulfilling of the divine Law. The suggestion here, then, is that *the God who reigns in Jesus' ministry is the God of Judaism, but seen in a way different from the perspective of his contemporaries.* It is the same God as his critics sought to serve, but seen anew in a fresh manner; this introduced to his service of that God a new set of priorities and a different programme of action.

It may be suggested that *for Paul also much of his thought sprang from a fresh vision of the nature of God revealed in Jesus Christ:*[62] this vision of a self-giving and loving God dominates his thought, moving him to redefine existing language to make it more apt as a vehicle for this new understanding. So, for instance, he picks up, *inter alia*, the basically forensic language of 'righteousness' and its cognates, only to qualify it with genitival constructions, adjectives and prepositional phrases to make the contrast between his own vision of how that righteousness came about and the traditional Jewish view (as he represents it). In this reformulation his central concern is God's intervention in Christ as God, in faithfulness and self-consistency, carries out the divine purposes in relation to all creatures, and heals the broken relationship between the world and its Creator. The re-interpretation and re-presentation of God which Jesus had vividly carried out above all in his parabolic teaching and in his actions Paul effected by these more prosaic linguistic means. That that world included the hitherto despised Gentiles seems to have been a conviction permeating his entire Christian ministry. God willed to draw back to their God the lost and the sinful and the ungodly (e.g. Rom 5.6, 8), and the Gentiles answered to that description as well as did the Jews. This chapter has suggested that this is a conviction which he had inherited from the Hellenists whom he had once persecuted for holding it;

61. *Handlungen* (n.24) 400–1.

62. Cf. chapter 5, esp. 106–9.

they in turn had considered it to be in harmony with the ways and attitude of Jesus, and they and Paul had seen it confirmed by the outpouring of God's spirit. For Paul too, as for Jesus, ethical implications derive subsequently from that divine initiative; for him as for Jesus the Law as an ethical norm is thus qualified and relativized, subordinated to a higher vision and a higher cause; it must not stand in the way of, or impede, God's saving purposes.

VI

The argument of the latter part of this paper has thus been that the ministry of Jesus and the ministry of his apostle Paul were both characterized by what might appropriately be described as an *openness to the outsider*; in both cases this stemmed from a conviction that they served a God who was likewise open to the outsider, offering fellowship and reconciliation freely and unreservedly to them.

If that is the case then the argument of the earlier part of this chapter suggests that this similarity between the convictions of Jesus and those of Paul is surely no coincidence. In Paul's case it is not created *ex nihilo*, but in his eyes is the authentic Christian tradition. Rather than seeing that conviction bestowed upon him in his Damascus road vision, whose cognitive content, after all, remains rather obscure, is it not preferable to argue that that authentic Christian tradition was mediated to him by those very Hellenist Christians whom he had previously persecuted? And, if we seek the reason for his persecution of them, then it lies close to hand: *they* had seen openness to the Gentiles as a natural corollary of Jesus' openness to Jewish sinners, and had welcomed them into their fellowship. To do that for the sake of convenience or financial or social gain was sinful; to do so in God's name, deliberately, and to claim that they were part of God's true people, was treachery. Or so it seemed to Paul and others, until to him at least there came the experience that convinced him that the Hellenist Christians had been right, and that he had been wrong to persecute them in God's name.

7

HUMILITY AND SELF-DENIAL IN JESUS' LIFE AND MESSAGE AND IN THE APOSTOLIC EXISTENCE OF PAUL

Christian Wolff

One can approach the cluster of problems connected with the theme 'Paul and Jesus' by posing questions with a number of different emphases. If one's interest is primarily in the history of tradition one can ask which parts of the Jesus-tradition we must assume were known by Paul.[1] If one's concerns are primarily theological then one can compare the centre of Jesus' message and that of Paul.[2] The present study seeks to complement these approaches by comparing the conduct of Jesus and Paul, and that from the perspective of renunciation for the sake of service which is characteristic of both.

I. *Deprivation*

Paul was not wealthy, but lived an itinerant life in poverty; this offended his critics in Corinth who understood apostleship very much in terms of glory. In his letters to the Corinthians Paul therefore has repeated cause to speak of his poverty and homelessness, e.g. in 1 Cor 4.11–12: 'Up to this very hour we suffer hunger and thirst, we are poorly clad..., we are homeless, we toil away, working with our own hands.' In the context of the enumeration of his troubles there the νηστεῖαι mentioned in 2 Cor 6.5 are surely not voluntary fasts, but shortages of food.[3] Similarly the third catalogue of afflictions (*Peristasenkatalog*) in 2 Corinthians mentions in

---

1. Cf. N. Walter in chapter 3.

2. So especially Jüngel, *Paulus* (n. 2.1). See also the further discussion of this by Wedderburn in chapter 5, esp. pp. 102ff.

3. So rightly V. P. Furnish, *II Corinthians* (AB 32*a*, New York: Doubleday, 1984) 344 and 355. Contrast Schlatter, *Paulus* (n. 4.14) 571.

11.27 hunger, thirst, shortage of food, and also lack of clothing (cf. also Phil 4.12: πεινᾶν καί... ὑστερεῖσθαι, 'to be hungry and...to suffer want').

In this Paul could be compared with one of the many seedy itinerant preachers of his time, and this unflattering comparison was also occasionally drawn, as we can infer from his polemical statements in 1 Thess 2.[4] But Paul understood his lowly existence otherwise: it showed him to be a true servant of Christ (2 Cor 11.23) or as a servant of that God (6.4) who had through Christ acted to bring about reconciliation (5.17–6.2), and as an apostle (1 Cor 4.9). To guard himself against any mistaken identification of himself with the wandering preachers of his time, he had earned his living through the work of his own hands during his initial preaching of the gospel (cf. 1 Cor 4.12; 9.18; 2 Cor 11.7; 1 Thess 2.9), even though it was contrary to the terms of an ordinance of the Lord (1 Cor 9.14)! For he did not wish to incur the suspicion that he evangelized for the sake of financial gain (cf. 1 Cor 9.12; 1 Thess 2.5).[5]

The κόποι, 'labours', and ἀγρυπνίαι, 'periods of sleeplessness', of 2 Cor 6.5 (cf. similarly 11.27!) are to be regarded as referring to this practice: Paul worked night after night to pay for his upkeep (cf. here 1 Thess 2.9*b*). At any rate he had no capital which he could live off. He counted himself among the 'poor, who yet make many rich', and among those 'who have nothing, and yet possess all' (2 Cor 6.10). Apparently he possessed no fixed abode either, as the term ἀστατεῖν used in 1 Cor 4.11 indicates. Perhaps the mention of ἀκαταστασίαι in 2 Cor 6.5 refers to such a condition of homelessness too.

There are obviously elements common both to these descriptions and to *Jesus'* way of life and also his demands upon his followers. All the Gospels depict Jesus as a wandering preacher. Therein he differed strikingly from John the Baptist; the latter called people to come to him in the wilderness (Mark 1.5), almost as a sign of their willingness to repent; Jesus, on the other hand, traversed Galilee and areas bordering on it (Mark 5.1: Gerasa; 7.24: the region of Tyre; 7.31: Decapolis; 8.27: Caesarea Philippi) and probably Judaea on a number of occasions (cf. Matt 23.37/Luke 13.34; John 2.13 and 23; 4.45; 5.1), in order to preach the saving reign of God to all Israel, and thus to gather the people of God

---

4. Cf. here Holtz, 'Apostel' (n. 4.64). On the comparison between Cynic itinerant philosophers and early Christian itinerant missionaries cf. G. Theißen, 'Wanderradikalismus: literatursoziologische Aspekte der Überlieferung von Worten Jesu im Urchristentum', in *ZTK* 70 (1973) 245–71, repr. in id., *Studien* (n. 3.43) 79–105, esp. 89–90 and 92–3.

5. On this problem cf. W. Pratscher, 'Der Verzicht des Paulus auf finanziellen Unterhalt durch seine Gemeinden: ein Aspekt seiner Missionsweise', in *NTS* 25 (1978–9) 284–98.

of the time of salvation.[6] This was not the rabbis' practice, but occurred only very sporadically in Palestine, if at all.[7]

With itinerancy goes homelessness. While Jesus may also have had a dwelling in Capernaum in Peter's house (Mark 1.29–31; 2.1; cf. also Matt 4.13), yet the saying about the son of man who has no home (Matt 8.20/Luke 9.58) shows his basic situation: 'The foxes have lairs and the birds of the air nests, but the son of man has nowhere to lay down his head.' There are good reasons for tracing this saying back to Jesus.[8] But even if one dates it later,[9] it nevertheless reflects an awareness of the poverty of Jesus' itinerant life, which was characterized by lack of possessions; had he had money he would always have been able to find accommodation. Correspondingly poverty is a mark of those whom Jesus chose to follow him[10] (Mark 1.16–20/Matt 4.18–22; Mark 10.21/Matt 19.21 and Luke 18.22; Mark 10.28–31/Matt 19.27–30 and Luke 18.28–30; Mark 6.8–9/Matt 10.9–10 and Luke 9.3; Luke 14.33).[11] The

6. Cf. here J. Jeremias, *Theologie* (n. 5.22) 164–74.

7. Hengel, *Nachfolge* (n. 6.57) 59, remarks that '*stabilitas loci* in a fixed school building, and an assured living were basic presuppositions for proper conduct of teaching' (quoted from ET [Edinburgh: Clark, 1981] 53–4). For discussion of this cf. Riesner, *Jesus* (n. 3.3) 355–7.

8. Cf., e.g., W. G. Kümmel, *Die Theologie des Neuen Testaments nach seinen Hauptzeugen Jesus, Paulus, Johannes* (GNT 3, Göttingen: Vandenhoeck & Ruprecht, 1969) 71–2; Goppelt, *Theologie* (n .3.5) 234; E. Gräßer, 'Nachfolge und Anfechtung bei den Synoptikern', in id., *Der Alte Bund im Neuen: exegetische Studien zur Israelfrage im Neuen Testament.*(Tübingen: Mohr, 1985) 168–82, esp. 173–80. On its interpretation see now too S. Kim, *The 'Son of Man' as the Son of God* (WUNT 30, Tübingen: Mohr, 1983) 87–8.

9. So, e.g., S. Schulz, *Q: die Spruchquelle der Evangelisten* (Zürich: TVZ, 1972) 437–9.

10. On the origins of the following of Jesus before Easter cf. Hengel, *Nachfolge* (n. 7) *passim*, and Gräßer, 'Nachfolge' (n. 8) 171: 'Easter did not produce the eschatological self-understanding of "following"; it simply modified it, and that in the light of a historical and salvation-historical situation that differed from the time of Jesus. The assumption of a sharp discontinuity between the two sides, the side of the life that Jesus lived and the side of his death and his resurrection, is not true to the historical facts.' Cf. earlier H. D. Betz, *Nachfolge und Nachahmung Jesu Christi im Neuen Testament* (BHT 37, Tübingen: Mohr, 1967) 13: 'the fact that Jesus had disciples must be supplemented by the assumption that he gave this discipleship its specific features.'

11. On the question of authenticity cf. the remarks of Theißen, 'Wanderradikalismus' (n. 4) 91: 'Jesus was the first itinerant charismatic. Those who passed on his words adopted his way of life. ...What reflects their life-style is still far from being "inauthentic" on that account. Their itinerant radicalism goes back

saying that 'Where your treasure is, there will your heart be too' (Luke
12.34/Matt 6.21; cf. similarly Matt 6.24/Luke 16.13)[12] first really comes
true for those who were called to be messengers of the approaching reign
of God. Therefore Jesus also says 'It is easier for a camel to go through
the eye of a needle than for a rich person to enter God's kingdom' (Mark
10.25/Matt 19.24 and Luke 18.25).[13] In the financially uncertain
existence of Jesus and his disciples there is realized that radical entering
into the salvation of God's kingdom (Matt 6.33); Jesus calls to such an
attitude in Matt 6.25–6, 28–33/Luke 12.22–4, 26–31,[14] and it is only
against such a background that the fourth petition of the Lord's Prayer
can first be fully understood: 'Give us today bread sufficient for us' (Matt
6.11/Luke 11.3).[15]

to Jesus. It is authentic. Probably we must "suspect" that more sayings are authentic than many modern sceptics like to.' Cf. also Hengel, ibid. 92–3: 'Perhaps the
very fact that there is an almost inseparable fusion of the "Jesus tradition" and
"community formations" in the Gospel-traditions of the sending out of the
disciples may be taken to imply that there was in a special way a conscious
awareness at this point of the "continuity" between Jesus' activity and the later
activities of the community' (ET 83).

12. On the origin of these sayings cf. U. Luz, *Das Evangelium nach Matthäus*
(EKKNT 1, Zürich: Benziger & Neukirchen–Vluyn: Neukirchener, 1985–) 1, 357.
—Rightly G. Haufe has stated that 'following Jesus means a radicalizing of the
first commandment, a radicalizing which has practical consequences' ('Der Ruf in
die Nachfolge (Mark. 10,17–31)', in *Stimme der Orthodoxie*, 1981, Heft 6,
55–63, esp. 59).—At Qumran there was apparently no eschatologically motivated
renunciation of possessions; cf. on this E. Neuhäusler, *Anspruch und Antwort
Gottes: zur Lehre von den Weisungen innerhalb der synoptischen Jesus-
verkündigung* (Düsseldorf: Patmos, 1962) 179.

13. On this see now E. Lohse, 'Jesu Bußruf an die Reichen. Markus 10,25
Par.', in (ed.) E. Gräßer, O. Merk, *Glaube und Eschatologie (Festschrift* for W.
G. Kümmel, Tübingen: Mohr, 1985) 159–63.

14. On the history of the tradition and the question of the origin of this saying
with Jesus cf. Luz, *Matt* (n. 12) 365–6, and H. Merklein, *Die Gottesherrschaft
als Handlungsprinzip: Untersuchungen zur Ethik Jesu* (FB 34, Würzburg:
Echter, 1978) 178–80.

15. Cf. on this H. Schürmann, *Das Gebet des Herrn: aus der Verkündigung
Jesu* (Die Botschaft Gottes 2.6, Leipzig: St. Benno, 1965[2]) 77–91, esp. 82:
'Actually it is in fact only *beggars* who take no thought for tomorrow, for
today's troubles oppress them too strongly. It is they who must live from hand to
mouth and cannot concern themselves with tomorrow.' See too J. Lambrecht, *Ich
aber sage euch: die programmatische Rede Jesu (Mt 5–7; Lk 6,20–49)* (Stuttgart:
Katholisches Bibelwerk, 1984) 131–4; G. Strecker, *Die Bergpredigt* (Göttingen:
Vandenhoeck & Ruprecht, 1984) 121–4; Luz, ibid. 345–7 (however he interprets
ἐπιούσιος as 'for tomorrow').

For Jesus as for Paul the insecure life of a wanderer with its poverty
gives expression to the fact that they have been gripped by the message
of salvation which they preach. In the case of Jesus it expresses his
unconditional, active surrender of himself to his God and Father who
ushers in the divine reign. Paul understands his way of life as one
controlled by Christ, and that means, principally, controlled by the crucified and risen one; the lowliness of the crucified one and the truly new
life of the risen one are at work in the one whom he has sent. To
emphasize this is precisely the point of the catalogues of afflictions in 2
Cor 4.8–11; 6.4–10. As the apostle of Jesus Christ Paul is numbered
amongst the 'poor, who yet make many rich' (6.10); for Christ himself
'became poor for your sake, although he was rich, so that you might
become rich through his poverty' (8.9). Certainly the poverty of Christ
does not *merely* refer to the cross. Even if one finds in 2 Cor 8.9 just as
in Phil 2.6–8 the self-emptying of the pre-existent one,[16] his earthly path
that led to the cross as the path of the one who was humble, poor and
obedient is also in view.[17] The *whole* career of Christ was for Paul
characterized by lowliness and renunciation. To that extent the apostle
may also have been aware of the similarity of his itinerant life to that of
Jesus.

There is one problem that still needs clarification in this connection.
As we have seen, Paul was quite convinced that he was right to contra-
vene the letter of the saying of the Lord which he quotes (1 Cor 9.14; cf.
Matt 10.10*b*/Luke 10.7*b*); he deliberately declined to let himself be
financially supported during his initial evangelizing (1 Cor 9.15). It is
striking that he never even discusses the problem of his apparent disobedience; apparently he pushes the authority of the *Kyrios* to one side.
Only 'apparently'; for in reality Paul sees no disobedience in his conduct;
all that matters to him is the gospel (the root εὐαγγελ- occurs seven times

16. So the overwhelming majority of exegetes, but cf. the recent challenge to
this interpretation by J. Heriban, *Retto φρονεῖν e κένωσις: studio esegetico su Fil
2.1–5.6* (Bibliotheca di Scienze Religiose 51, Roma: LAS, 1983).

17. Cf. A. Schulz, *Nachfolgen und Nachahmen: Studien über das Verhältnis
der neutestamentlichen Jüngerschaft zur urchristlichen Vorbildethik* (SANT 6,
München: Kösel, 1962) 282: 'The kenosis of the pre-existent one, his earthly
existence as one humbled, and its climactic conclusion in his saving death for the
church are all most significant for the apostle when regarded from the viewpoint
of Christ's selfless service for others.' See also Goppelt, *Theologie* (n. 3.5) 417:
'For Paul the cross is the climax of the Christ-event, but it only is such *because it
was the death of the obedient one* (Phil 2.8–9), of the one sent by God, and
because the crucified one was raised or exalted (1 Cor 15.17–22). Its significance
as God's saving act is…constituted by the statements about Christ's path trodden
both in anticipation of the cross and following on from it.'

in vv 14–18!). This should have free rein, and the 'wages' of which Paul can boast (v 15) is his preaching free of charge (v 18), his renunciation of his rights as an apostle. It is with these wages of sacrificial self-humbling (cf. 2 Cor 11.7) that Paul 'lives off the gospel' (1 Cor 9.14) as the word of the cross (1.18), so that in the last analysis he is thoroughly consistent in his fulfilling the word of the Lord.[18]

II. *Renunciation of Marriage*

1 Cor 7.7–8 shows that *Paul* was not married and that he regarded this condition as a χάρισμα, a 'gift of grace'. We can leave aside here a decision as to whether he was single or a widower;[19] at any rate at the time of the writing of 1 Corinthians the apostle was living unmarried. He was not only doing this temporarily; for in v 8 he counsels the unmarried and widows to *remain* as he himself is, and that till the parousia (cf. vv 25–35 and 40).

If Paul describes his unmarried state as a χάρισμα then this clearly shows that this state owes its nature to the activity of God; through the divine Spirit (cf. 1 Cor 12.4) God constantly strengthens the apostle's self-control (1 Cor 7.9*a* with Gal 5.23; Wis 8.21), so that Paul exists solely for the *Kyrios* (1 Cor 7.34*b*) and can preach his gospel (9.19*b*). In any case χάρισμα is to be understood in 1 Cor 7.7 too in the same sense as it characteristically has elsewhere in Paul's writings, as a 'revelation of the Spirit' (12.7);[20] for the unmarried state meets what Paul regards as the decisive criteria for *charismata* which are discussed in 1 Cor 12–14: it serves the confession of Jesus as *Kyrios* (cf. 12.1–3), in other words an undivided service in mission, and it aids the upbuilding of the church (cf.

---

18. These ideas were stimulated by the arguments of K. Kertelge's paper on 'Autorität des Gesetzes und Autorität Jesu bei Paulus', which was delivered to the 'Paulus und Jesus' seminar at the 40th General Meeting of the SNTS in Trondheim.

19. Cf. here the discussion in J. Jeremias, 'War Paulus Witwer?', in *ZNW* 25 (1926) 310–12; E. Fascher, 'Zur Witwerschaft des Paulus und die Auslegung von 1 Cor 7', in *ZNW* 28 (1929) 62–9; Jeremias, 'Nochmals: War Paulus Witwer?', in *ZNW* 28 (1929) 321–3.—On the motive for Paul's being unmarried before he became a Christian cf. the discussion in H. Windisch, *Paulus und Christus: ein biblisch-religionsgeschichtlicher Vergleich* (UNT 24, Leipzig: Hinrichs, 1934) 129–30.—C. K. Barrett, *A Commentary on the First Epistle to the Corinthians* (Black's NT Comms, London: Black, 1971[2]) 161, and W. F. Orr–J. A. Walther, *I Corinthians* (AB 32, New York: Doubleday, 1977) 209–10, are now inclined to accept that Paul was a widower.

20. Cf. K. Berger in *EWNT* 3, 1105.

14.12), for Paul can give himself to it with all his energies (cf. 2 Cor 11.28–9).

Paul had not abandoned a previous marriage when he became a Christian; he opposes such a course of action in 1 Cor 7.10–24. Rather he was called when already unmarried. But through his call this situation was shown to him in a new light, as something which, in the purposes of God, enabled him to apply himself unreservedly to missionary work.[21] Thus it is not the unmarried state in general which is seen as a gift of grace, but it in so far as it serves Christ and his church; in 1 Corinthians Paul emphasizes that it is of the essence of a χάρισμα that it aims at οἰκοδομή, 'upbuilding (of the church)', and διακονία, 'service' (1 Cor 12–14).[22] It is because his unmarried state is a matter of grace that Paul is unable to instruct the single[23] and widowed to renounce marriage (1 Cor 7.8–9); the gifts of God's grace are many and varied and cannot be got by ordering someone to practise them; they can only be desired (v 7) or prayed for (14.13). Therefore we find no call to the Corinthians to imitate the apostle in this (contrast 4.16–17; 10.33–4).

Many have remarked on the closeness of the contents of 1 Cor 7.7 to those of Matt 19.10–12.[24] This brief passage, found only in Matthew, provides an expansion of Mark 10.2–9/Matt 19.3–9. In Matt 19.10–11 the Evangelist, following on from Mark 10.10, has created a link to v 12 which is a saying of Jesus which he has received;[25] this enables him to

---

21. On the link between calling and χάρισμα cf. Berger, ibid. 1104–5.

22. Cf. on this M.–A. Chevallier, *Esprit de Dieu, paroles d'hommes: le rôle de l'Esprit dans les ministères de la parole, selon l'apôtre Paul* (Neuchâtel & Paris: Delachaux & Niestlé, 1966) 57–9 and 180–1.—Marriage is not implicitly regarded as a χάρισμα; for the latter is 'not just any activity, but one that occasions amazement and points to a vertical dimension' (Berger, ibid. 1105).

23. The precise meaning of ἄγαμοι is disputed. E. Fascher, *1 Kor* (n. 4.1) 183, supposes them to be widowers. H. Baltensweiler, *Die Ehe im Neuen Testament: exegetische Untersuchungen über Ehe, Ehelosigkeit und Ehescheidung* (ATANT 52, Zürich & Stuttgart: TVZ, 1967) 186, includes the divorced. W. Wolbert, *Ethische Argumentation und Paränese in 1 Kor 7* (Moraltheologische Studien— Systematische Abteilung 8, Düsseldorf: Patmos, 1981) 94, suggests 'older un-married persons', amongst whom widowers would then receive further, special mention.—I had no access to N. Baumert, *Ehelosigkeit und Ehe im Herrn: eine Neuinterpretation von 1. Kor 7* (FB 47, Würzburg: Echter, 1984).

24. Cf. Windisch, *Paulus* (n. 19) 128–33; Schlatter, *Paulus* (n. 4.14) 219; Fascher, *1 Kor* (n. 4.1) 182; E. Schweizer, *Das Evangelium nach Matthäus* (NTD 2, Göttingen: Vandenhoeck & Ruprecht, 1973) 250; Goppelt, *Theologie* (n. 3.5) 1, 163; G. G. Gamba, 'La "Eunuchia" per il Regno dei Cieli', in *Salesianum* 42 (1980) 243–87.

include the theme of the state of the unmarried within the context of instruction about marriage and divorce.

Can this saying in v 12 be traced back to Jesus despite the fact that it is only represented by one strand of tradition? There were tendencies amongst the earliest and early Christians to renounce marriage (cf. 1 Cor 7.1 and 7; Rev 14.4; 1 Tim 4.3), and it is precisely in such groups that this saying would attract especial interest. On the other hand the agreement between the first half of the saying and rabbinic statements (see below) points to a Palestinian origin, and the shockingly forceful language may point to Jesus as its author (cf. Matt 8.22/Luke 9.60; Matt 13.33/Luke 13.20–1; Matt 24.43–4/Luke 12.39–40; Luke 16.1–8; 18.1–8; Mark 9.43–7; 10.23); eunuchs were viewed with revulsion,[26] and self-castration was forbidden in Judaism (cf. *Sipra* on Lev 22.24; *b. Šabb.* 110*b*; Jos., *Ant.* 4.291; *Ap.* 2.270–1; Pseudo-Phocylides 187).[27] But it is precisely these people that are mentioned favourably here in connection with God's kingdom! Finally the contents of the saying matches Jesus' conduct, for, as far as we know, Jesus was unmarried (cf. Mark 3.31–5; 6.3).[28] All in all the conclusion that the saying originated with Jesus seems to be warranted.[29]

V 12 mentions three groups of people who are unmarried. The distinction drawn in v 12*a* and v 12*b* was one current in Judaism ('castrated by the sun, i.e. from birth' and 'castrated by human beings'; cf. *Yebam.* 8.4; *Šabb.* 2.1; *t. Meg.* 2.7).[30] Following those who are from birth incapable of begetting and those who are so through human agency v 12*c* as a climax speaks of those who make themselves eunuchs. This group, viewed with revulsion in Judaism, are valued positively by

25. On the redactional nature of vv 10–11 cf. A. Sand, *Reich Gottes und Eheverzicht im Evangelium nach Matthäus* (SBS 109, Stuttgart: Katholisches Bibelwerk, 1983) 51–5. Both Bultmann, *Geschichte* (n. 3.31) 25, and Baltensweiler, *Ehe* (n. 23) 103, regard v 12 as an original isolated saying of Jesus.

26. Cf. the evidence in J. Blinzler, 'Zur Ehe unfähig...', in id., *Aus der Welt und Umwelt des Neuen Testaments* (Stuttgart: Katholisches Bibelwerk, 1969) 20–40, esp. 23 n. 12.

27. The evidence can be found in Str–B 1, 807, and Blinzler, ibid. 25 n. 18.

28. Cf. here J. Schneider in *TWNT* 2, 765.4ff, and Blinzler, ibid. 23 n. 12.

29. So too Blinzler, ibid. *passim*; Braun, *Radikalismus* (n. 5.35) 112–13 n. 3; W. Grundmann, *Das Evangelium nach Matthäus* (THKNT 1, Berlin: Evangelische Verlagsanstalt, 1981⁵) 429; Baltensweiler, *Ehe* (n .23) 50; Gamba, '"Eunuchia"' (n. 24) 275–6.—Whether v 12*d* is part of the original contents of the saying is hard to decide; cf. Sand, ibid. 55.

30. Cf. Str–B 1, 806–7.

the qualification διὰ τὴν βασιλείαν τῶν οὐρανῶν, 'for the sake of the king-dom of heaven'.[31] Rightly most assume that v 12c does not refer to physical castration, but that a deeper meaning is intended:[32] it refers to those who have decided *definitively* to remain unmarried for the sake of God's kingdom; it speaks of εὐνοῦχοι and not ἄγαμοι, 'unmarried', or παρθένοι, 'virgins'.[33] That they are motivated by the reign of God shows that the βασιλεία is the reason for such conduct, just as previously v 12a and v 12b mentioned other reasons for being a eunuch. What is meant is a life thoroughly shaped by God's reign and consequently lived in its service and at the same time directed towards it.

The phrase in v 12c is hardly meant to include the disciples or even any of them;[34] for Peter at least was married and remained so (cf. Mark 1.29-31; 1 Cor 9.5), and Jesus' calls to follow him do not include any basic principle of the renunciation of marriage (Luke 14.26 is secondary compared with Matt 10.37, and likewise Luke 18.29 compared with Mark 10.29; cf. also Luke 14.20 with Matt 22.1-10). The words εὐνοῦχοι and εὐνούχισαν ἑαυτούς cannot be meant to express only a temporary re-nunciation of marriage. The plural is therefore most easily taken to refer to John the Baptist and to Jesus;[35] both gave themselves up so totally to the reign of God that fulfilling the obligatory commandment to marry[36]

---

31. Originally it would have spoken of *God's* kingdom. On the secondary character of Matthew's preference for the phrase 'kingdom of heaven' cf. Jeremias, *Theologie* (n. 5.22) 100-1.

32. Cf. Blinzler, 'Ehe' (n. 26) 26: 'elsewhere in Jesus' preaching of the kingdom of God value and worth accrue not to people's outward actions or external nature, but to their inner attitude, a person's "heart" (cf. Mark 7.15-23)'; also 28 n. 23: 'sudden switches from the literal to the figurative use of words can be found elsewhere in the Gospels: cf., e.g., Luke 9.60, "Let the (spiritually) dead bury their (physically) dead!"'

33. Cf. Gamba, '"Eunuchia"' (n. 24) 276 with n. 78.

34. Yet Blinzler, 'Ehe' (n. 26) 36-8, takes it so (but he has certainly offered an illuminating account of the background of the saying—Jesus' defence against the charge that he was neglecting the commandment of Gen 1.28); Neuhäusler, *Anspruch* (n. 12) 87-9; Baltensweiler, *Ehe* (n .23) 108-10; Gamba, ibid. 271 and 283.

35. Cf. J. Schneider in *TWNT* 2, 766.9-11. On the connection between John the Baptist's conduct and his message cf. J. Becker, *Johannes der Täufer und Jesus von Nazareth* (BibS(N) 63, Neukirchen-Vluyn: Neukirchener, 1972) 16-26, on asceticism esp. 25-6.—This is no correction of the Essene ideal of celibacy (so C. Daniel, 'Esséniens et eunuques [Matthieu 19,10-12]', in *RevQ* 6 [1968] 353-90); cf. Sand, *Reich* (n. 25) 36-7; also H. Hübner, 'Zölibät in Qumran?', in *NTS* 17 (1970-1) 153-67.

was impossible for them;[37] they were apparently already unmarried before they began their public ministries.

If we compare 1 Cor 7.7 with Matt 19.12 we have to note, negatively, that we can detect in Paul's words no echo of this saying of Jesus in either their language or their content. But, positively, we can spot a material (*sachlich*) agreement in that (1) like Jesus Paul was throughout unmarried, (2) both Jesus and Paul agree in seeing this way of life as a deliberate assent to their being gripped by God's eschatological activity, and (3) for Jesus as for Paul being unmarried is in the service of the preaching of salvation.

III. Humble Service

According to Mark 9.35/Matt 23.11 and Luke 9.48 (cf. also Mark 10.43–4/Matt 20.26–7 and Luke 22.26–7)[38] Jesus called his disciples to renounce any striving to be important, and to be ready to serve. The same thing is intended in Luke 14.11; 18.14; Matt 23.12; 18.4. It is a matter of eschatological revaluation and the true value of a human being before God. At the same time the disciple is thus drawn into the son of man's work of service (cf. Mark 10.45).[39]

There are interesting parallels in *Paul's* letters. When he writes in 1 Cor 9.19 'Although I am free from all, I have made myself the slave of all, so that I may win the majority (over to faith)', then the free apostle (9.1) in his missionary situation corresponds to the instructions of Mark 9.35. The eschatological motivation is manifest in 1 Cor 9.23: 'I do all for

36. On this see Str–B 2, 372–3.

37. That Jeremiah was unmarried (Jer 16.2) was also a sign that the prophet's message shaped his existence; it is true that this was a sign of judgment; cf. here Sand, *Reich* (n. 25) 71–2.—If the Baptist is included then this strengthens the case for treating this as a saying of Jesus; for the early church was not inclined to draw extensive parallels between John and Jesus.

38. The unrestricted formulation of Mark 9.35 may be more original in comparison with the version in 10.43–4 whose language deals with relations within the church (ἐν ἡμῖν, ἡμῶν); cf. Pesch, *Markus* (n. 3.19) 105, and his conclusion that '9.33–5...certainly goes back to Jesus'. Cf. also K. T. Kleinknecht, *Der leidende Gerechtfertigte: die alttestamentlich-jüdische Tradition vom 'leidenden Gerechten' und ihre Rezeption bei Paulus* (WUNT 2.13, Tübingen: Mohr, 1984) 176–7.

39. The literary connection between Mark 10.42–4 and v 45 is secondary (cf., e.g., A. Schulz, *Nachfolgen* [n. 17] 261–2, and Pesch, ibid. 153–4), but this does not affect the connection in their *subject-matter*.—On Mark 10.45 see below in the next section.

the sake of the gospel, so that I may be a joint partaker of it.' Paul wants to share in the salvation brought by the gospel along with those towards whom he directs his preaching; then his eschatological freedom, which he already possesses now, yet exercises in renunciation of it, will be fully realized.

A similar idea with a characteristic change of phrasing is found in 2 Cor 11.7: Paul has humbled himself that the Corinthians may be exalted. This assertion recalls Luke 14.11; 18.14; Matt 23.12; 18.4, but now it is the church, not Paul, that is exalted: the apostle's humiliation of himself by renouncing payment during his first missionary visit to Corinth effected a transfer of the Corinthians from the depths of alienation from God into saving eschatological fellowship with God. Here we meet that idea which will be considered more fully in the next section, namely that the apostle's humility benefits the churches (an idea which is also present in 1 Cor 9.19). It is true that Paul does not lose his 'exaltation' thereby, but the exalting of the church also has an eschatological significance for him; the church is in fact his 'boast' (1 Cor 15.31; 2 Cor 1.14; Rom 15.17; Phil 2.16; 1 Thess 2.19–20) or his 'crown' (Phil 4.1; 1 Thess 2.19–20).

Even if Paul does not make an explicit connection, yet he still acts in accordance with Jesus' teaching on humility; in his service he is a follower of Jesus Christ, drawn into the humble self-abasement (Phil 2.8) of the one who 'did not live to please himself' (Rom 15.3).[40] In 1 Cor 11.1 he himself draws attention to this connection. There, at the end of his discussion about eating meat offered to idols, Paul says of himself that he does not seek his own good, but that of others, to save them (10.33); he treats this way of life as an expression of the fact that he is an 'imitator of Christ'. In his attitude of renunciation for the sake of others the apostle is orientated towards Christ, who effected salvation through his selflessness. His argument in 2 Cor 4.5[41] is similar: 'For we do not preach ourselves, but Jesus Christ, the Lord, but ourselves as your slaves for Jesus' sake.' In the phrase διά Ἰησοῦν, 'for Jesus' sake', which expresses his motivation, the use of the name 'Jesus' probably serves to recall particularly his self-offering on the cross.[42] In the service of this

40. 'In a comprehensive summary the complexive aorist ἤρεσεν in Rom 15.3*a*...interprets the entire life of the historical Jesus as a perpetual self-renunciation' (Schulz, *Nachfolgen* [n. 17] 280 n. 950.

41. On this verse see esp. P. Madros, *Susceptibilité et humilité de Saint Paul dans sa seconde lettre aux Corinthiens* (Jerusalem: Franciscan, 1981) 30–2.

42. Cf. H.-J. Klauck, *2. Korintherbrief* (Die Neue Echter Bibel 8, Würzburg: Echter, 1986) 43–4.

Kyrios, who brought about salvation through lowliness, the apostle
works selflessly for the church.

IV. *Suffering Persecution*

Paul often speaks of the contempt, suffering and persecutions to which
he is exposed because of his preaching. He does so strikingly in the
catalogues of his afflictions: 1 Cor 4.9, 'devoted to death as in a play',
and similarly 2 Cor 6.9, 'as dying, and see, we live', and 11.23,
'frequently in danger of death'; 1 Cor 4.11, 'ill-treated', similarly 2 Cor
6.5, 'with blows', 6.9, 'as punished', and 11.23, 'beyond measure with
blows', which is spelled out in vv 24 and 25*a*; 1 Cor 4.12, 'reviled', v
13, 'the lowest filth',[43] and similarly 2 Cor 6.8, 'with contempt, with vile
slander...', as a seducer'; 1 Cor 4.12, 'persecuted', and also 2 Cor 4.9,
together with the incident in 2 Cor 11.32–3; finally the mention of
imprisonments in 2 Cor 6.5 and 11.23. But apart from these lists Paul also
speaks of the sufferings to which he is exposed as a messenger of the
gospel; indeed he does so in *each* of his extant letters (cf. 1 Thess 2.2,
14–15; 1 Cor 15.32; 2 Cor 1.5–6, 8–10; Gal 5.11; 6.17; Phil 1.7, 13–17;
2.17; 3.10; Rom 8.36; Philemon 1.9, 23; cf. also Col 1.24; 4.3, 18).

Several passages show that Paul sees his sufferings not only as analogous to those of Jesus (so 1 Thess 1.6; 2.14–15; cf. also 1 Cor 4.12–13
and 2 Cor 6.8 with Rom 15.3: Paul, like Christ, is exposed to abuse by
God's enemies), but also as his being drawn into Christ's sufferings. So
in 2 Cor 1.5 he speaks of his great abundance of the 'sufferings of
Christ', and in Gal 6.17 of the στίγματα τοῦ Ἰησοῦ, the 'marks of Jesus',
which he bears on his body. It is the use of the name 'Jesus' in the latter
passage[44] that clearly shows the reference to the crucifixion: by the
wounds and scars which he has incurred through the punishment inflicted
by his persecutors (cf. 2 Cor 11.24–5) he shows that he belongs to the
crucified one. In 2 Cor 4.10 he says of himself that he 'continually carries
around in his body the putting to death of Jesus'.[45] The use of the term

---

43. On the interpretation of 1 Cor 4.13*b* see now esp. Kleinknecht, *Gerechtfertigte* (n. 38) 231–2.

44. Cf. on this above all Güttgemanns, *Apostel* (n. 3.29) 126–35, and U. Borse,
'Die Wundmale und der Todesbescheid', in *BZ* Neue Folge 14 (1970) 88–111.

45. Kleinknecht, *Gerechtfertigte* (n. 38) 274, rightly supposes 'that Paul deliberately seeks to relate himself to the process of Jesus' passion and death'; cf. also
ibid. n. 103: 'It is a matter of the nature of *Jesus'* sufferings and death as a
process, i.e. a matter of his passion in contrast to the mere fact, the mere "Daß"
["that"] of his death.' On the interpretation of this see also J. Lambrecht, 'The
Nekrōsis of Jesus: Ministry and Suffering in 2 Cor 4,7–15', in Vanhoye,

παραδιδόναι, 'hand over, give up', in v 11 with its traditional Christological usage (cf. 1 Cor 11.23; Rom 4.25; 8.32), underlines the close ties between the apostolic sufferings and Jesus' fate; the violent rejection that Jesus experienced carries on into the violent rejection of his apostle during his missionary journeys (cf. περιφέρειν, 'carry around'). Similarly Paul speaks in Phil 3.10 of sharing (κοινωνία) in Christ's sufferings as a being conformed to his death[46] (cf. also 2 Cor 13.4). Of course Paul knows that sufferings are not only a characteristic of the apostle but also of every Christian (cf., e.g., 1 Thess 1.6; 2.14–16; Phil 1.29; 2 Cor 1.6–7; Rom 8.36). There is no qualitative difference between them; these are fundamentally 'the same sufferings' (2 Cor 1.6; cf. 1 Thess 1.6; Phil 1.30); every believer is thus through fellowship with Christ drawn into Christ's sufferings in a dynamic way. But for the apostle the *special measure* of his sufferings is distinctive (1 Cor 4.9a; 2 Cor 1.5; 11.23);[47] this is a concomitant of his unrestrained missionary activity. Through this especial closeness to Jesus' passion the apostle is in an unmistakable way the one authorized and sent by Christ.

Paul accords his sufferings a positive value for the churches. He does not think of these sufferings as supplementary to Christ's saving work. Yet still his sufferings are of value both for encouraging and for saving them (2 Cor 1.6); for they provide an example by which it may be seen that they are constitutive of Christian existence; that is an encouragement when faith is afflicted, and strengthens one's awareness of eschatological salvation (cf. Phil 1.28). Thus it is the apostle in his chains who emboldens other church members to fearless preaching (Phil 1.14). According to 2 Cor 4.12 'death is at work in us, but life in you'. Finally, when Col 1.24[48] says that the apostle completes representatively for the church the afflictions of Christ which still remain, then that once again makes plain the unusual measure of the apostolic sufferings, which encompass a considerable part of the affliction that is necessarily linked to the eschatological struggle.

L'apôtre (n. 3.59) 80–96, esp. 86ff.

46. Cf Heriban, *Retto φρονεῖν* (n. 16) 243: 'Christ's death takes on anew a visible form in Paul's sufferings.'

47. Cf. here Windisch, *Paulus* (n. 19) 238; E. Kamlah, 'Wie beurteilt Paulus sein Leiden?', in *ZNW* 54 (1963) 217–32, esp. 225 and 228; Kleinknecht, *Gerechtfertigte* (n. 38) 372–3.—Güttgemanns, *Apostel* (n. 3.29) 323–8, emphasizes how the apostolic existence functions as an epiphany.

48. On the authorship of Colossians cf., e.g., E. Schweizer, *Der Brief an die Kolosser* (EKKNT, Zürich: Benziger & Neukirchen–Vluyn: Neukirchener, 1976) 20–7. On the exegesis of 1.24 cf. ibid. 81–6 and now particularly Kleinknecht, *Gerechtfertigte* (n. 38) 377–80.

That *Jesus* was persecuted during his public ministry, apart from his last visit to Jerusalem, is improbable: Luke 4.28–30 should probably be regarded as a Lukan composition,[49] and Luke 13.31 likewise;[50] the repeated references to persecutions in the Gospel of John (from 5.16 on) are part of the Fourth Evangelist's style of presentation. It is true that we frequently hear of hostility (cf., e.g., the conflicts over the sabbath or the charge in Mark 3.22; also Matt 10.25*b*). But it apparently never got as far as taking steps to persecute Jesus. Thus everything is focused on his violent end.

Scholars are not agreed whether or how far Jesus spoke of this end.[51] To my mind the fact of the Last Supper provides a secure basis for statements of Jesus about his death and also about its significance for salvation.[52] Apart from the so-called eucharistic words (Mark 14.22–5/ Matt 26.26–9 and Luke 22.19–20; 1 Cor 11.23–5) there are also good reasons to suppose that Mark 10.45 too is authentic.[53] According to a saying that is found in many strands of tradition (Mark 8.34/Matt 16.24 and Luke 9.23; Matt 10.38/Luke 14.27; John 12.26; *Gos. Thom.* 55) Jesus called his disciples to follow his way in readiness for suffering and death. This saying is, like Mark 8.35–6, shaped by the experiences and language of the earliest church (αἴρειν τὸν σταυρὸν αὐτοῦ, 'to take up his cross', ἕνεκεν ἐμοῦ καὶ τοῦ εὐαγγελίου, 'for my sake and the gospel's').[54]

49. Cf. G. Schneider, *Das Evangelium nach Lukas* (Ökumenischer Taschenbuchkomm. zum NT 3, Gütersloh: Siebenstern, 1977) 110–1; J. Jeremias, *Die Sprache des Lukasevangeliums* (MeyerK Sonderband, Göttingen: Vandenhoeck & Ruprecht, 1980) 127–8.

50. Cf. Schneider, ibid. 308–9; Jeremias, ibid. 233–4.

51. On the discussion cf., e.g., J. Gnilka, 'Wie urteilte Jesus über seinen Tod?', in (ed.) K. Kertelge, *Der Tod Jesu—Deutungen im Neuen Testament* (QD 74, Freiburg-i-B., etc.: Herder, 1976) 13–50; A. Vögtle, 'Todesankündigungen und Todesverständnis Jesu', in ibid. 51–113; V. Howard, 'Did Jesus Speak about His Own Death?', in *CBQ* 39 (1977) 515–27; L. Oberlinner, *Todeserwartung und Todesgewißheit Jesu* (SBB 10, Stuttgart: Katholisches Bibelwerk, 1980); H. Schürmann, *Jesu ureigener Tod* (Freiburg-i-B., etc.: Herder, 1975); id., *Gottes Reich—Jesu Geschick* (Freiburg-i-B., etc.: Herder, 1983).

52. Cf. on this C. Wolff, *Der erste Brief des Paulus an die Korinther 2: Auslegung der Kapitel 8–16* (THKNT 7.2, Berlin: Evangelische Verlagsanstalt, 1982) 88–90; cf. also the rather different assessment in Kim, *'Son of Man'* (n. 8) 38–73.

53. Cf. here Stuhlmacher, 'Existenzstellvertretung' (n. 3.16); Kim, ibid. 38ff; Kleinknecht, *Gerechtfertigte* (n. 38) 171–3.

54. Cf. here A. Satake, 'Das Leiden der Jünger "um meinetwillen"', in *ZNW* 67 (1976) 4–19.

However a version like that of Matt 10.38 could go back to Jesus himself.[55] Basically it is true that, if following the earthly Jesus always meant 'a sharing of his life and fate'[56] too, then at the same time that ultimately involves a readiness to die.

Paul makes no reference to the sayings about following and suffering. The fact of Jesus' crucifixion is the true orientation point for him; as the messenger of the crucified and risen Lord dying and resurrection life affect him intensely. As Jesus Christ was, so too the one who is in his service is a suffering righteous one,[57] but here the idea of atonement is always associated exclusively with Christ (Rom 15.3).[58]

Certainly we can assume that Paul knew details of Jesus' passion, as the tradition of the Lord's Supper in 1 Cor 11.23–5 shows. This passage starts by speaking of the 'night in which the *Kyrios* Jesus was handed over', and the imperfect form παρεδίδετο, 'was handed over', is used, expressing the course that this process took. Furthermore there are striking agreements between the traditional passage in 1 Cor 15.3*b*–5 and the story of the passion.[59] This suggests that Paul linked the imprisonments, ill-treatment and abuse that were his lot with specific details of Jesus' passion. At any rate the analogy, even in details, is noteworthy.

V. *Summary*

The preceding discussion has sought to show parallels between Jesus and his apostle Paul with regard to their renunciation and service. Paul for his part regarded himself as moulded by the lowliness of the crucified Christ

55. Cf. P. Stuhlmacher, 'Achtzehn Thesen zur paulinischen Kreuzestheologie', in *Rechtfertigung* (n. 6.49) 509–25, repr. in id., *Versöhnung* (n. 3.16) 192–208, esp. 206–7. On the history of the tradition see J. Lambrecht, 'Q-Influence on Mark 8,34–9,1', in Delobel, *Logia* (n. 6.1) 277–304, esp. 279–82.

56. Hengel, *Nachfolge* (n. 7) 98. Cf. also here Gräßer, 'Nachfolge' (n. 8) 177–9. Braun too (*Radikalismus* [n. 5.35] 100ff) recognizes the existence of a 'martyrdom-paraenesis' that goes back to Jesus, but yet denies that it has anything to do with Jesus' death.

57. Cf. on this Kleinknecht, *Gerechtfertigte* (n. 38) 193ff.

58. Similarly Paul related statements about God's servant in Deutero-Isaiah to himself, yet understood Isa 53 Christologically; cf. on this T. Holtz, 'Zum Selbstverständnis des Apostels Paulus', in *TLZ* 91 (1966) 321–30.

59. Cf. on this Wolff, *1 Kor* (n. 52) 157. Stuhlmacher, 'Thesen' (n. 55) 204, thinks that on the basis of 1 Cor 11.23ff; 15.3ff; Rom 4.25; 5.8–9; 8.32 we may assume 'that Paul knew the basic features of the passion story that was part of the evangelistic tradition of the Jerusalem church.'

and—proleptically—by the power of the risen Christ (cf. esp. 2 Cor 4.10–11; Phil 3.10). Besides this we can detect some remarkable correspondences with individual features of Jesus' life, but it is impossible to discover from Paul's letters whether the apostle was conscious of them all or at least of some of them. One could presume that characteristics of the messenger of God active in the end-time are determinative here in each case in the life of Jesus and in that of Paul; with regard to almost all the features which we have examined there exist parallels with John the Baptist too. Yet if one is to be true to Paul's own view of himself, as apostle, i.e. representative, of Jesus Christ (cf. 2 Cor 5.20; 13.3; Gal 4.14; Rom 15.18), then one will have to see in these similarities in details, over and above the basic conformity of his life to the course of Jesus' life, the expression of a special closeness of the apostle to his *Kyrios*.

When one observes that already following the earthly Jesus meant an 'attachment to his person and his way', which was only true of certain individuals,[60] then this special link is best included under the category of 'following'. It is true that Paul does not use the word ἀκολουθεῖν, 'follow', in this sense, but what the term refers to is thoroughly applicable to him. A list of the basic features of the idea of following in the Jesus-tradition runs like this: an 'authoritative call, unconditional obedience, unreserved following, a common destiny, sending with authority'.[61] These features apply to Paul in an even more intense way in the post-Easter situation: he was called by the risen Lord to be the apostle to the Gentiles (cf. esp. Gal 1.15–16 and Rom 1.5); he followed this call to the uttermost (cf. Phil 3.4*b*–11); the persecutor of the church which God had chosen (1 Cor 15.9; Gal 1.13, 23; Phil 3.6) became the authoritative messenger of Christ (Gal 1.1), who was under the necessity of preaching the gospel (1 Cor 9.16). On the basis of this call and the resultant ties that bound him to Christ his entire existence was shaped by the person and way of Jesus Christ. In all this Paul displayed himself as a true follower.

---

60. Hengel, *Nachfolge* (n. 7) 68–70 (ET 61–3, quotation from 61).—The Pauline idea of the imitation of Christ (cf. 1 Cor 11.1) contains only part of the idea of following (cf. Hengel, ibid. 69=ET 62).

61. Gräßer, 'Nachfolge' (n. 8) 169 n. 6.

8

PAUL AND THE STORY OF JESUS

Alexander J. M. Wedderburn

In Gal 3.28 we find an intriguing statement: 'In Christ there is neither Jew nor Greek, there is neither slave nor free person, there is neither male nor female; for you are all one person in Christ Jesus.' This is intriguing for the reason that the Christ who is to be 'put on' by baptized Christians (3.27) is evidently not the earthly Jesus, for then they would all be Jews, free persons and males! It is true that this is not necessarily Paul's own formulation, for it is widely regarded as an earlier formulation which he quotes, perhaps one that had its setting in the context of early Christian baptismal rituals.[1] Yet at the same time it is also one which he seemingly endorses. This phenomenon raises a number of fascinating questions: how could the delineation of Christ have arisen in Christian faith and belief in such a form as thus both to transcend the earthly limitations and particularity of Jesus of Nazareth, and at the same time seemingly to have remained in contact with the earthly Jesus? It does seem to remain in

---

1. H. D. Betz, *Galatians: a Commentary on Paul's Letter to the Churches in Galatia* (Hermeneia, Fortress: Philadelphia, 1979) 195, rightly points out that the fact that the distinctions between slave and free, male and female were not at issue in Galatia is an argument for the use of tradition at this point; cf. D. Lührmann, 'Wo man nicht mehr Sklave oder Freier ist: Überlegungen zur Struktur frühchristlicher Gemeinden', in *WD* 13 (1975) 53–83, here 57–8 (he also points out that Paul does not need to justify this statement, but rather uses it in support of another assertion; Lührmann also seems to want to derive the assertion that the 'slave–free' distinction is transcended in Christ from the fact that Christ was both Lord and servant—68–9, and one could argue that, born a Jew, he also became as a sinner and thus on the same footing as a Gentile, but this line of argument will not explain 'neither male nor female'); W. A. Meeks, 'The Image of the Androgyne: Some Uses of a Symbol in Earliest Christianity', in *HR* 13 (1974) 165-208, here 180-1; H. Paulsen, 'Einheit und Freiheit der Söhne Gottes—Gal 3,26–29', in *ZNW* 71 (1980) 74–95, here 77–89.

contact with the earthly Jesus, for this surely remains the likeliest
explanation for Paul's retention of the Aramaic form of address to God as
'Abba' even when writing to Greek-speaking converts (Gal 4.6; cf. Rom
8.15). Or again, what were the links between the traditions about the
earthly Jesus and the characteristics, the traits, of the heavenly Christ, or
what Norman Perrin refers to as the 'faith-image' of Jesus which is
identical with the 'kerygmatic Christ'?[2] What determined which characteristics of the former were transferred to the latter, and which were
not?[3] And whence came the characteristics that were not derived from
the earthly Jesus? Following on from this is the question, what links with
the earthly Jesus were necessary if Paul's Christ were to fulfil the role
that he played in Paul's thought? In other words we are concerned with
questions of derivation and function: whence did Paul derive the features
of his Christ, and what implications did this derivation have for the role
which his Christ played in his thought?

I

Paul clearly knows of a 'story' of Jesus which is not simply the story of
the earthly Jesus, and one which indeed passes very rapidly over the
ingredients of such a story as we know it from the gospel tradition. He
tells us of God sending (out) his Son, born of woman, born under the Law
(Gal 4.4), a Son who was at the same time the Lord 'through whom are
all things' (1 Cor 8.6). Being rich he beggared himself (2 Cor 8.9), and
being in the form of God he did not hold equality with God to be a ἁρπαγ-
μός,[4] but rather 'emptied' himself and took on a servile form, a human
likeness; he humbled himself to the point of being subject to death, even
crucifixion (Phil 2.6–8). He became a 'servant of the circumcision for the
sake of God's truth' (Rom 15.8). Though he knew no sin he was made sin

2.   *Rediscovering the Teaching of Jesus* (London: SCM, 1967) 243.

3.   Obviously this was a matter of opinion among early Christians; for some
Jewishness was integral to being Christ's and so in Christ there were only Jews
(including Gentiles who had become Jews by obedience to the Law)—Judaizers
of various sorts; for others maleness was essential—cf. *Gos. Thom.* logion 114.
Our question is: what led Paul (and those whom he may have followed) in transcending these racial and sexual differences?

4.   On the meaning of this word cf. the recent studies of N. T. Wright, 'ἁρπαγ-
μός and the Meaning of Philippians 2:5–11', in *JTS* 37 (1986) 321–52, H. Binder,
'Erwägungen zu Phil 2⁶⁻⁷ᵇ', in *ZNW* 78 (1987) 230–43, C. A. Wanamaker,
'Philippians 2.6–11: Son of God or Adamic Christology?', in *NTS* 33 (1987)
179–93, and U. B. Müller, 'Der Christushymnus Phil 2⁶⁻¹¹', in *ZNW* 77 (1988)
17–44, esp. 23–4 and n. 38.

for our sakes, that we might become God's righteousness in him (2 Cor
5.21); he became a curse for us by being hanged on his cross that he
might redeem us (Gal 3.13). He was betrayed and on that night held a last
meal with his disciples (1 Cor 11.23–5). He was given up for our trans-
gressions and raised for our justification (Rom 4.25). God's own Son was
not spared by his Father, but was given up for us all (Rom 8.32). He died
for our sins, was buried, was raised on the third day, and appeared to
various disciples and Paul (1 Cor 15.3–8). He died, was raised, and was
exalted to God's right hand (Rom 8.34). God greatly exalted him, to
receive the homage of all things (Phil 2.9–11). He will descend from
heaven to be reunited with the dead in Christ and those who are still alive
(1 Thess 4.16–17).

The story of Jesus which Paul knows is clearly a narrative of events, a
'story', but it differs from being a story of the earthly Jesus in that it tells
of a 'prehistory' in Jesus' existence before his human life on earth, and it
also tells of what happened to him subsequently, after Jesus' this-worldly
life came to an end. It is also highly interpretative in character: not only
does it repeatedly speak of God's involvement in the experiences of
Jesus, either explicitly ('God sent', 'God greatly exalted') or implicitly in
divine passives ('he was given up', 'he was raised'), but it also gives
Christ a role in creation comparable to that of the divine wisdom (1 Cor
8.6), and speaks of his experiences being redemptive (1 Cor 15.3; 2 Cor
8.9; Gal 4.5) and according to the scriptures (1 Cor 15.3–4). The 'prehistory' and the sequel to Jesus' earthly life set the latter within the
perspective of a grander, divine design.[5]

Many would describe this story, or at least parts of it, as a 'myth',
particularly since it tells of Jesus' 'prehistory' and of what happened to
him after he had died.[6] If the term 'story' is used here in preference, it

5.   I am indebted to Professor R. Leivestad for the observation that Jesus already had set his own life within a grander, divine purpose; cf. also G. B. Caird,
The Language and Imagery of the Bible (London: Duckworth, 1980) 212-13.

6.   Although O. Cullmann reclassifies the biblical stories of the beginning and
end as 'prophecy' ('only prophecy', as opposed to those parts of the story which
are prophecy, but a prophecy which also 'refers to facts that can be historically
established, and... makes these facts an object of faith')—*Christ and Time: the
Primitive Christian Conception of Time and History* (London: SCM, 1962[2]; ET
of Zürich: Evangelischer, 1946) 95–9; this is, however, not an alternative to
calling them 'myths'—cf. his *Salvation in History* (London: SCM, 1967) 139
(ET of Tübingen: Mohr, 1965), even if he there claims that the 'myths' of the
beginning and the end have in the Bible been 'historicized' by being placed on the
same level as the historically controllable narratives. But for N. Perrin, 'myth' is a
'vividly pictorial way' of interpreting history—*The New Testament: an Introduction: Proclamation and Parenesis, Myth and History* (New York, etc.:

is largely because of the widely varying connotations of the term
'myth'.[7] There are for a start the varying strands that Rudolf Bultmann
wove together in his conception of 'myth', and the correspondingly varying evaluations of 'myth' which these different traditions entailed.[8] The
scene has also been further complicated by the introduction of yet further
uses and evaluations of the term 'myth', ones which are yet further removed from the popular, usually pejorative, connotations of the term, and
this means that its use is liable to invite even greater misunderstanding.
Norman Perrin did much in his writing to introduce these new dimens-
ions of the term into the general discussion of the New Testament.[9] In
addition to Bultmann's work he also drew upon that of Mircea Eliade and
that of Paul Ricoeur: for the former a 'myth' is a 'sacred history' of

Harcourt Brace Jovanovich, 1974) 32.

7. Cf. U. Bianchi, *The History of Religions* (Leiden: Brill, 1975; ET from
[ed.] G. Castellani, *Storia delle religioni*, Torino: Unione Tipografico-Editrice
Torinense, 1970[6]) 63–143; W. Burkert, *Structure and History in Greek Mytho-
logy and Ritual* (Sather Classical Lectures 47, Berkeley, etc.: Univ. of California,
1979) esp. chap. 1; Caird, *Language* (n. 5) 219–23; M. S. Day, *The Many
Meanings of Myth* (Lanham, etc.: Univ. Press of America, 1984); M. Detienne,
The Creation of Mythology (Chicago & London: Univ. of Chicago, 1986; ET of
Paris: Gallimard, 1981)—a study as elusive in meaning as its subject-matter!

8. For instance, R. A. Johnson,*The Origins of Demythologizing: Philosophy
and Historiography in the Theology of Rudolf Bultmann* (Studies in the History
of Religions 28, Leiden: Brill, 1974) esp. 30–1, disentangles three strands, those
views that derive from (1) the *religionsgeschichtliche Schule*, (2) the Enlightenment, and (3) existentialism. For the first the term 'myth' was in fact used of a
quite specific myth, that of the Heavenly Redeemer or Primal Man and the ideas
and motifs associated with this (cf. 89). For the second 'myth' was a sort of
thought and mode of expression characteristic of a primitive, pre-scientific period
of history. For the third 'myth' offers a particular understanding of human existence, even if it is expressed in a medium which is alien to its purpose. This third
view, while retaining the negative evaluation of the Enlightenment, combined it
with a positive one, in that it saw 'myth' as concerned to express an understanding
of existence, despite its chosen form; it had something of relevance to say, although in an unfortunate form. Strikingly this seems to straddle both of the 'two
camps' into which 'rationalists contemplating myth' fall according to Day, ibid.
2–3: those seeing myth as pre- or sub-rational, and those seeing it as supra-
rational.

9. Particularly in his *The New Testament* (n. 6) esp. 21–33, quoting from M.
Eliade, 'Myth' in *Encyclopaedia Britannica* 15 (1968) 1132–42 (Eliade seems
only to have been responsible for 1132–40 in the 1973 ed. accessible to me), esp.
1133 and 1135, and Ricoeur, *Symbolism* [n. 5.24]; cf. now the latter's art. on
'Myth and History', in (ed.) M. Eliade, *The Encyclopedia of Religion* 10 (New
York & London: Macmillan, 1987) 273–82; cf. also C. H. Talbert, *What Is a
Gospel? The Genre of the Canonical Gospels* (Philadelphia: Fortress, 1977) 99.

something occurring in 'primordial time'; as that history is told or enacted one is seized by its 'sacred, exalting power' (23); for the latter 'myth' is 'a narrative account of the effective origin of a symbol, which is acknowledged as representing a primary aspect of experienced reality' (24).

In a rather similar vein Walter Burkert speaks of 'myth' as '*a traditional tale with secondary, partial reference to something of collective importance*',[10] and, with a reference to Malinowski's 'charter myths', he sees 'myths' as explaining or justifying various social institutions, in much the same way as Perrin refers to 'foundation myths'.[11]

Perrin then goes on to make the interesting point that, seen in this light, 'a myth cannot be true or false; it can only be effective or ineffective';[12] it can only be the former if it rises 'out of the consciousness of the people', corresponding to 'reality as they experience it', and making sense of that reality, or a significant part of it, for them. In this account, then, a story is a 'myth' if it functions in a certain way, and to function in that way it must correspond to reality in a certain way. Even if we are eschewing the term 'myth', what Perrin says of 'myth' would be equally applicable to 'story': the story of Jesus functions in a certain way within Paul's theology, and it can only function in that way if it corresponds to reality in a certain way. That then in turn raises the questions, to which reality the story must correspond, and how it must correspond to it. Is the reality involved here at least in part a historical reality, and in what sense? Is it just the historical reality of Paul and his readers and interpreters, situated in history both ancient and modern, or is it also the historical reality of Jesus' life?[13]

---

10. *Structure* 23 (his italics); cf. his *Homo necans: Interpretationen altgriechischer Opferriten und Mythen* (Religionsgeschichtliche Versuche und Vorarbeiten 32, Berlin & New York: de Gruyter, 1972; ET—Berkeley, etc.: Univ. of California, 1983) 43.

11. Cf. Ricoeur, 'Myth' (n. 7) 273, and also G. Sellin, 'Mythologeme und mythische Züge in der paulinischen Theologie', in (ed.) H. H. Schmid, *Mythos und Rationalität* (Gütersloh: Mohn, 1988) 209–23, here 214.

12. Cf. Burkert, *Structure* (n. 10) 3: 'Just by disregarding the question of truth one may enjoy myth, or wonder, and start thinking'—for in telling a μῦθος one disclaims responsibility according to Eur., frg. 484 (Nauck[2]); Callimachus, *Hymn* 5.56; Plato, *Symp.* 177A, etc. Contrast, however, J. G. Griffiths, *The Origins of Osiris and His Cult* (Studies in the History of Religions 40, Leiden: Brill, 1980) 1, who claims that in recent hermeneutics it is recognized that those telling these stories believed that these things had happened. K. W. Bolle, too, speaks of a myth having 'an extraordinary authority'; it does not have to make a case for its validity for 'the myth *is* its validity' (Art. 'Myth: an Overview', in Eliade, *Encyclopedia* (n. 7) 10, 261–73, here 262; cf. 266.

13. Cf. Perrin, *The New Testament* (n. 6) 29: 'in the myth of the cross of Jesus

But if uncertainty about the sense of the term 'myth' is one reason for
preferring to speak of a 'story', another is that 'story' can be used to
cover those parts of the narrative that might be classed as 'myth' *and*
those that could be classed as 'history' or, better, 'historical accounts' or
'accounts of history'.[14] The term thus serves to bring together what Paul
does not separate, but mentions as together part of one continuous
narrative that begins with God before creation and reaches forward into
the divine consummation that lies beyond our present history. At the
same time it needs to be noted that the question will still remain, what
relation to one another the different parts of the story have, both those
that fall within verifiable history and those that fall outside it.

II

That in turn raises the question how such myths or stories arise as well as
that of the use made of them, for clearly, as we have seen, in this case we
have here a story that transcends the boundaries of the empirical, in that it
tells of the prehistory of this particular historical individual and also of
his destiny beyond the grave. To answer this question it may be helpful to
look at accounts of two mythical figures, accounts which are roughly
contemporary with the New Testament, Philo's exegesis of the creation
of an ἄνθρωπος made in God's image according to his *De opificio mundi*
134, and Plutarch's account of the rites of Isis in his *De Iside et Osiride*
27.

Philo's 'heavenly person' is a figure that invites comparison with

as redemptive the only criterion of truth or validity is its effectiveness on the
historicity of the life in the world of the participants in the Christian meal'.
Whether the passion narrative is 'historically factual' is, he argues, 'simply
irrelevant'. But is it? Could the myth function that way if the participants in the
Christian meal thought that Jesus never lived, let alone suffered and died? Cf.
Day, *Meanings* (n. 7) 11.

14. This may be regarded therefore as one aspect of 'the broader question of the
effectiveness of myth as a general hermeneutical category' (H. W. Frei, *The
Eclipse of Biblical Narrative: a Study in Eighteenth and Nineteenth Century
Hermeneutics*, New Haven & London: Yale Univ., 1974, 272). I have here
supplied alternatives to the term 'history' (in inverted commas) when referring to
an account of what happened, for to use that term alone would be to invite a
confusion between 'history *qua* account' and 'history *qua* event(s)', a confusion
that has muddied much theological and philosophical discussion (and a similar
ambiguity seems to attach to the word 'Geschichte'—cf. J. Barr, 'Story and
History in Biblical Theology', in *JR* 56, 1976, 1–17, repr. in *Explorations in
Theology* 7, London: SCM, 1980, 1–17, here 5–6, who makes the additional
point that 'Geschichte' can also mean 'story').

Paul's Christ-figure in Gal 3.27–8, for this figure too is described as 'incorporeal, neither male nor female, by nature incorruptible (ἄφθαρτος)' (*Op. mund.* 134); this figure is an 'idea or type or seal'. The nature of this figure as 'neither male nor female' arises from its nature as an idea, 'in the class of incorporeal species' (*Quaest. in Gen.* 1.8).[15] The logic of this is presumably that it would be inappropriate to the idea of the species 'humanity' to be exclusively either male or female, for the species embraces both male and female; however it could, of course, equally be *both* male *and* female for this role, and this would indeed be nearer to, and a more obvious exegesis of, Gen 1.27 LXX, ἄρσην **καὶ** θῆλυ ἐποίησεν αὐτούς.[16] Philo, however, opts for the less obvious alternative. Richard A. Baer points out that, although the irrational part of humanity, including the reproductive capacity, may be male or female, these categories are inapplicable to the rational part, let alone to the Logos, and still less God, in whose likeness the rational soul is created.[17] In contrast to Philo the Platonic conception of an idea of humanity that is both male and female is then later 'personalized' in what John Dillon calls the 'underworld' of Middle Platonism, in the Hermetic literature as

15. Cf. my 'Philo's Heavenly Man', in *NovT* 15 (1973) 301–20, esp. 312–13. The view of R. A. Baer, *Philo's Use of the Categories Male and Female* (ALGHJ 3, Leiden: Brill, 1970) 29, that the ἄνθρωπος formed after God's image in *Op. Mund.* 134 is 'the generic heavenly man, i.e. the rational nous in man that was patterned after the image of the Logos', depends on the assumption that Philo consistently reserves the creation of the ideas to the first day of creation only (Gen 1.1–5 in *Op. Mund.* 1–35) with subsequent days describing 'the creation of the generic sense-perceptible world' (ibid. 28). It is hard to see, however, how ἀσώματος in §134 could apply to anything 'sense-perceptible'.

16. T.H. Tobin, *The Creation of Man: Philo and the History of Interpretation* (CBQMS 14, Washington: Catholic Biblical Association of America, 1983) 110 (cf. 127), seems to explain Philo or his predecessors' preference for an interpretation that runs counter to the obvious meaning of the Gen text as being due simply to a logical inference from the fact that the ἄνθρωπος of Gen 1.27 was not composed of body and soul, but was prior to any differentiation between the sexes (as in Gen 2); such an interpretation he holds to be pre-Philonic. Philo, however also knew of the idea of a bisexual ἄνθρωπος—cf. Meeks, 'Image' (n. 1) 186 and n. 92; also *Leg. all.* 2.13 (cf. C. H. Dodd, *The Bible and the Greeks*, London: Hodder & Stoughton, 1935, 151). However J. Jervell, *Imago Dei: Gen 1,26f im Spätjudentum, in der Gnosis und in den paulinischen Briefen* (FRLANT 58, Göttingen: Vandenhoeck & Ruprecht, 1960) 64, quotes *Op. Mund.* 134 as if it referred to an androgynous being, and Dodd, ibid., argues that 'asexuality is equivalent to bisexuality'. However, would Philo really be prepared to view God as bisexual as opposed to asexual in this way?

17. *Use* (n. 15) 18–19.

exemplified by the tractate *Poimandres*:[18] in *Corp. Herm.* 1.9 Nous is
described as ἀρρενόθηλυς[19] and in §15 the Ἄνθρωπος formed by Nous is
like Nous in this respect—here the other option mentioned above is
found, i.e. both male and female, rather than neither male nor female. It is
the former option ('both...and') that would be appropriately said to
describe an androgynous being, but it is the latter tradition that seems to
be nearer to what is postulated for Christ in Gal 3.27–8 (despite the
grammatically rather awkward οὐκ...καί as opposed to the preceding οὐκ...
οὐδέ, a variation which may betray the influence of Gen 1.27)[20] and,
although this is often thought to be based on the myth of 'an androgynous
Christ-redeemer',[21] this tradition might be more aptly described as that
of a figure without the distinctive characteristics of either sex rather than
possessing those of both, asexual rather than bisexual.[22] This too is
attested elsewhere in later Christian and Gnostic literature.[23] That may
explain why Paul 'seems to avoid the discussion of the point of andro-
gyny'.[24]

It would be tempting to say that Paul, or more likely those from whom
he had inherited the baptismal tradition of Gal 3.27–8, had been
influenced by Platonizing exegetical traditions of the kind which Philo
reflects. That would be all the more probable if G. Sellin and H. Räisänen
are correct to detect in Paul's writings traces of other Hellenistic Jewish
spiritualizing interpretation of such concepts as circumcision, and
Räisänen expressly mentions the possibility that Gal 3.28 reflects such
traditions, perhaps in the Antioch church.[25] At the same time it is worth

18. *The Middle Platonists: a Study of Platonism 80 B.C. to A.D. 220* (London:
Duckworth, 1977) 176. For evidence of this tradition in Neoplatonism and other
secondary lit. on the topic cf. Betz, *Gal* (n. 1) 197; significant, though, is his
observation that the hymn containing the idea that Zeus ἄρσην γένετο, ...ἄμβροτος
ἔπλετο νύμφη ([Arist.], *De mundo* 401b 2 ['ἐν Ὀρφικοῖς']= O. Kern, *Orphicorum
fragmenta* 21a) was known to Plato (*Leg.* 4.715E), but unfortunately his
allusion to what seems quite like this Orphic hymn contains no echo of this
particular line; however it remains possible that the tradition had more ancient
roots in Platonism.

19. For parallels see ed. A. D. Nock–A.-J. Festugière 1 (Paris: Belles Lettres,
1946), 20 n. 24.

20. Cf. Meeks, 'Image' (n. 1) 181 n. 77; 185.

21. Betz, *Gal.* (n. 1) 199.

22. Cf. my *Baptism* (n. 5.45) 386 and n. 22.

23. *2 Clem* 12.2, 5; *Gos. Eg.* in Clem. Alex., *Strom.* 3.92.2; *Gos. Thom.* §22;
Naassenes in Hipp., *Ref.* 5.7.15 (although this is immediately afterwards
identified with being ἀρσενόθηλυς).

24. Betz, *Gal.* (n. 1) 200.

recollecting that the motivation that led to the characterization of the idea of humanity, Philo's heavenly ἄνθρωπος, as neither male nor female would apply equally forcibly to the person who represented all humanity in early Christian thought: just as the idea of all humanity must transcend the differences between the sexes, so too the one who is to represent all humanity and embodies the new creation of humanity cannot be limited in nature to either sex. Similarly one should perhaps see the addition of 'barbarian' and 'Scythian' to the rather similar list (but one lacking the reference to 'male' and 'female')[26] in Col 3.11 as due to the recognition that 'Greek' and 'Jew' did not cover the full range of humanity; there were others who were neither 'Greek' nor 'Jew'.[27] In other words the delineation of this new, eschatological person is dictated by the logic of the role to be performed by that person. It is not therefore essential that this idea should have reached early Christianity by way of an exegetical tradition so directly influenced by Platonism. Moreover we find no correspondence in Philo's exegesis to the other differences that are eliminated here, 'neither Jew nor Greek, neither slave nor free person'. That in itself places severe difficulties in the way of any explanation solely in terms of Platonizing exegesis, and while this sort of exegesis may have made some contribution to the formation of this tradition, we shall have to look elsewhere for an adequate explanation of the rise of this tradition (see §VI below).

Plutarch in his *De Iside et Osiride* 27 tells us that Isis did not

> allow the contests and struggles which she had undertaken, her wanderings and her many deeds of wisdom and bravery, to be engulfed in oblivion and silence, but into the most sacred rites she infused images, suggestions and representations of her experiences at that time, and so she consecrated at once a pattern of piety

25. Cf. Räisänen, "'Hellenists'" (n. 1.4) 242–306. Professor G. Sellin's suggestions on this point in his response to the original paper at Trondheim were incorporated into the revised and expanded published version of this paper (see also n. 6.8).

26. Though some MSS include it; why it is not included is harder to gauge. Was it felt to be in tension with 3.18 (P. Pokorný, *Der Brief des Paulus an die Kolosser*, THKNT 10/1, Berlin: Evangelische Verlagsanstalt, 1987, 144)?

27. 'Barbarian' and 'Scythian' are not opposites like the other pairs in the list; why 'Scythians' are singled out for mention is unclear; Pokorný may be correct in regarding this pair as a *Steigerung* (ibid.)—the Scythians would then be an example of particularly barbarous barbarians; O. Michel in *TDNT* 7, 448, refers to the widespread 'censure of their crudity, excess and ferocity', and he and E. Lohse (*Colossians and Philemon*, Hermeneia, Philadelphia: Fortress, 1971=ET of MeyerK, 1968[14], 144) aptly cite Jos., *Ap.* 2, 269: βραχὺ τῶν θηρίων διαφέροντες.

and encouragement to men and women overtaken by similar misfortunes (361DE, tr. J. G. Griffiths).[28]

Sharon Kelly Heyob notes apropos of this passage that 'Isis as mourner came to be imitated in festivals everywhere in Egypt, and eventually in Greece and Rome, too'.[29] She has already in the *Pyramid Texts* the role of a mourner of her brother and husband, along with her sister Nephthys (38), and this role she retains, as we have seen, in the time of Plutarch. Apart from this role Isis had also functioned in Egyptian piety as an ideal wife and ideal mother (1). In the Graeco-Roman period this role as wife and mother is of more importance in the spread of her cult.[30] Diodorus Siculus, Heyob notes (43), claims that the Egyptians based their marriage laws on the pattern of the marriage of Isis and Osiris (1.27.1), permitting the marriage of brothers and sisters. But 'it was especially as mother that Isis touched the hearts of the faithful' (44; cf. 74–78) and she was frequently represented together with her son Horus; 'her emotions were very human ones—love, loyalty, sorrow, compassion—and it was her human qualities with which the ordinary man (*sic*) could identify and which caused her widespread popularity' (ibid.). In the light of this it seems to me unnecessary to limit the significance of Plutarch's reference in *Is. et Os.* 27 solely to Isis' role as a mourner, for her qualities as an exemplary wife and mother were also displayed in her sufferings as portrayed in her rites.

In this case it would be too long a matter to investigate how this story arose,[31] nor would it be of great use for our present purpose, for quite

---

28. Ed. J. G. Griffiths (Univ. of Wales, 1970) 158–9:
...οὐ περιεῖδε τοὺς ἄθλους καὶ τοὺς ἀγῶνας, οὓς ἀνέτλη, καὶ πλάνας αὐτῆς καὶ πολλὰ μὲν ἔργα σοφίας πολλὰ δ' ἀνδρείας ἀμνηστίαν ὑπολαβοῦσαν [following the reading of C. B. Meziriacus; the LCL, following the reading of all codices, has ὑπολαβοῦσα] καὶ σιωπήν, ἀλλὰ ταῖς ἁγιωτάταις ἀναμίξασα τελεταῖς εἰκόνας καὶ ὑπονοίας [cf. Plato, *Resp.* 2.378D] καὶ μιμήματα τῶν τότε παθημάτων εὐσεβείας ὁμοῦ δίδαγμα καὶ παραμύθιον ἀνδράσιν καὶ γυναιξὶν ὑπὸ συμφορῶν ἐχομένοις ὁμοίων καθωσίωσεν. Betz, *Nachfolge* (n. 7.10) 128, argues that although Plutarch's text talks of a *mimesis* of Isis, Plutarch himself speaks of a συνουσία with Isis and Osiris. Yet 2.352A which he cites speaks of a γνῶσις of Osiris and says of him, not of his devotees, that he is μετ' αὐτῆς (Isis) ὄντα καὶ συνόντα.

29. *The Cult of Isis among Women in the Graeco-Roman World* (EPRO 51, Leiden: Brill, 1975) 42 ; cf. 52.

30. Ibid. 42; cf. 52; R.E. Witt, *Isis in the Graeco-Roman World* (London: Thames & Hudson,1971).

31. Cf. from the perspective of the rise of the story of Osiris (and after all it is with this aspect of the story of Isis that Plut. is here concerned) Griffiths, *Origins* (n. 12); Heyob, ibid. 38, notes that already in the *Pyramid Texts* the story of Isis, Osiris and Horus is presupposed and alluded to.

clearly it had arisen long before Plutarch's time. But its usefulness for him is surely significant. It is in his eyes of relevance to mortals because the experiences of Isis referred to in this story are analogous to human experiences which indeed the vast majority of humanity shares, namely bereavement and sorrow and the like, as well as the faithfulness and devotion with which the goddess meets the demands made upon her.

In these two instances we have thus seen mythical material functioning in two different ways, which we may describe, for want of better terms, as respectively *'theoretical'* and *'practical'*. Philo's characterization of the 'heavenly ἄνθρωπος' is an example of the former, for it is a description that arises out of the logic inherent in his speculations; it is, moreover, not a description of actions that can be imitated, nor of a character that can readily be imitated; its Christian version, however, does seem to have its practical implications, in that it can be inferred that sexual differences, in particular involving status, can, or should, be transcended. Yet these implications remain a relatively indirect inference from the theorizing with regard to the nature of Christ. The Isis myth describes, on the other hand, some very human actions of the goddess— all too human in some cases, it is true, and at times somewhat larger than life, but still recognizably akin to the deeds of mortals—and these actions are carried out in this world, quite specifically in the land of Egypt and the Levant—, and Plutarch argues that her story has very practical implications, for people can imitate the goddess, can be consoled when they find themselves placed in a similar situation to hers. Here the relation to human actions is a far more direct one; it is one of imitating actions of the goddess which are clearly analogous to human ones, whereas in that of Philo's sexless ἄνθρωπος the possible human implications are far from immediate and Philo himself does not seem to draw any. The example of Isis shows that to be imitated the actions of the deity must be narrated in anthropomorphic, this-worldly terms. That is not to say that these actions are historical; far from it. But they should be depicted as if they were a piece of human history.

III

The account given by Perrin which was quoted in §I also helps us further with our problem in that he attempts to answer the question of the relation of those parts of the story that are outside history to those parts that are within it with regard to the New Testament in general, and in so doing modifies his position with regard to the truth or falsity, the efficacy or inefficacy of myths, by pointing out that the New Testament claims that Jesus *'exemplified the reality that the myth claims to mediate'* (ibid. 29, his italics); so historicity is relevant to the functioning of a myth when it bears on an aspect of history which is claimed to embody the myth (31). That is to say that it is not only relevant to know *that* Jesus lived and died, but also in some respects to know *how* he lived and died. So Perrin argues with regard to both Paul and Jesus, and in particular the conversion of the former and the tradition of the latter's last meal with his disciples, that

A Paul hostile to the Christian mission to the Gentiles would be fatal to the myth of origins of the Christian church, and a Jesus carried to his cross railing against God and his fate would destroy the myth of the cross as redemptive, but the narrative details of the supper or of Paul's conversion do not matter except as expressions of the myth (31).[32]

Yet this distinction requires greater precision, for one could claim that other cultures and religions also used myths involving characters exemplifying the reality that the myths mediated, without the question ever being raised whether these characters did in fact exemplify it; it was enough that they exemplified it within the narrative of the myth. Obviously this is particularly true of narratives set within 'primordial time, the fabled time of the "beginnings"',[33] for then it makes no sense to ask historically whether they really exemplified the myth. Moreover it was often observed that such stories had an exemplary function; in the words of K. W. Bolle, 'a myth functions as a model for human activity, society, wisdom, and knowledge';[34] hence the protests of philosophers, from Xenophanes onwards,[35] at the corrupting influence of the examples

32. Earlier, in *Rediscovering* (n. 2) 244, he had argued that our 'faith-image', our kerygmatic Christ, must be 'consistent with the historical Jesus'; our historical knowledge of him validated the Christian kerygma, not, however, as kerygma, but as Christian.

33. Eliade in *Encyclopaedia Britannica* 15 (1968) 1133, cited by Perrin, ibid. 23; C. J. Bleeker, 'Die aktuelle Bedeutung der antiken Religionen', in *Perennitas: studi in onore di Angelo Brelich*, promossi dalla Cattedra di Religioni del Mondo Classico dell' Università degli Studi di Roma (Roma, 1980) 37–49, here 37–8; Bolle, 'Myth' (n. 10) 262, 265; Ricoeur, 'Myth' (n. 7) 273. But n.b. Bolle's treatment of 'eschatological myths' (ibid. 264)—these are, however, 'renewals of the real origin' and so linked to the primordial; Bianchi, *History* (n. 5) 141–2 sets the narrative of myth in either 'the age of the world's beginning, or...the last of time'; also see Ricoeur's extension of 'myth' to *Heilsgeschichte* in virtue of its function (ibid. 280).

34. Ibid. 261; cf. Talbert, *Gospel* (n. 7) 99: myth 'reveals the exemplary models for all human activities here and now'..

35. Cf., e.g., Xenophanes B 1.19–20 in H. Diels–W. Kranz, *Die Fragmente der Vorsokratiker* 1 (Berlin: Weidmann, 1960⁹) 127—a concern for words that

actually offered by the widely respected stories told in the works of Homer and Hesiod; at the same time Plato utilizes mythology in the service of his philosophy and of the inculcation of virtue.[36] So one has here too stories of figures who are claimed to exemplify something, and for their critics they are bad examples. The crucial difference in the case of Christianity is that the central character in the 'myth' is a figure of the recent past, and, moreover, a figure whose goodness or badness was and still is a matter of controversy, and that it is claimed that this person and no other is central to the Christian 'myth'. This 'myth', in other words, is shaped by this figure, even if the accounts of him may in turn be shaped by the 'myth' as well. The example offered can thus be judged, not just on the basis of the story offered (does it tell of a good example?), but also on the basis of facts ascertainable independently of the story (is the story true to life, and was the example offered in the story in fact as edifying as the story would have us believe?). Yet this is not a feature unique to Christianity, for many more recent religious movements have given a messianic or quasi-messianic significance to historical figures, and some have found a cognitive dissonance between their mythical assertions about their leader or founder and the historical reality of that person's life, which they can only resolve by either denying the apparent historical reality or by denying the relevance to his or her mythical status of , e.g., charges of immorality. C. H. Talbert also points out that this was paralleled in the ancient world too: communities like cities and philosophical schools needed a 'myth of origins for their historical existence' and had 'to speak of a historical founder in mythical terms';[37] others might interpret those historical founders' lives differently and so these lives needed to be defended, by re-telling their story in a proper way.

Perrin also betrays at this point a certain imprecision in the way in which he conceives of figures embodying the reality of a myth. This emerges more clearly in his treatment of the 'foundation myth of Christian origins' (30); this involved 'an abandonment of Jerusalem and a movement to Rome'. Acts portrays this, and in doing so distorts the facts, for Paul's witness in Jerusalem took place some time after his conversion, and his eventual arrival in Rome was as a prisoner about to be put to death. Here Paul's role as 'the exemplary Christian apostle' (31) is not impaired as long as he is allowed to preach for two years in Rome 'openly and unhindered', but what becomes of this role if the historical facts are otherwise? In this account it becomes apparent that one needs to

---

promote ἀρετή instead of tales of the Titans, etc.

36. Cf. Detienne, *Creation* (n. 7) chaps 4–5.

37. *Gospel* (n. 9) 100.

be clear which historical facts are relevant to which 'myth' or to which aspect of a 'myth'. For the 'myth' of the 'abandonment of Jerusalem and a movement to Rome' is, as such, unaffected by the circumstances under which Paul arrives in Rome, and the 'myth' of Paul as 'the exemplary Christian apostle' would remain unaffected by Paul's imprisonment and even by his martyr's death if one accepted Paul's characterization of 'the exemplary apostle' as one who shares the sufferings and the humiliation of Christ.[38] It is only if one's 'exemplary Christian apostle' is one who must be able to preach 'openly and unhindered' that the functioning of this 'myth' is endangered by the possibility that Paul's fate in Rome was different to that portrayed in Acts.

Now such talk of a historical figure exemplifying or embodying a myth echoes the claims of two recent studies of Paul's theology, those of Daniel Patte and Gerd Theißen, which lay considerable stress on the importance in that theology of the role of Christ as a model.[39] For Patte[40] it is fundamental to Paul's faith that there is a relationship between past, present and future experiences which can be expressed in terms of certain 'types' or patterns of experience that both promise similar experiences in the future and are themselves fulfilled in other experiences of a like pattern. This belongs to the level of the system of convictions which undergirds Paul's text and shapes his argument, rather than to the level of the logic of Paul's argument; this argument is subservient to his basic convictions and presuppositions, and the latter in their turn provide the framework for the former. Yet in contrast to some of his earlier statements[41] he is prepared to speak of the two as necessary

---

38. See, e.g., 1 Cor 4.9–13; 2 Cor 4.7–12; 6.3–10.

39. D. Patte, *Paul's Faith and the Power of the Gospel: a Structural Introduction to the Pauline Letters* (Philadelphia: Fortress, 1983); Theißen, *Aspekte* (n. 3.55). Worthy of note, too, is how L. E. Keck (*Future* [n. 5.38] 180–7) sets alongside one another entrusting oneself to a person and appropriating that person as a model, and interprets Christian discipleship accordingly.

40. Although at times the ideas and even the language of Patte's study are rather similar to those of Theißen's, yet the former is clear that he is not attempting to analyse Paul's psychology (*Faith* 41).

41. Cf., e.g., his *What Is Structural Exegesis?* (Philadelphia: Fortress, 1976)— there he stresses that structuralist 'exegesis no longer aims at what the author meant' (14), and that an unconscious element built into our very nature as human beings imposes itself upon the writer (17, 25). These elements of structuralist exegesis are far from prominent in his work on Paul, concerned as it is with Paul's faith, with structures of thought of which Paul is to a varying degree conscious, and which are by no means integral to all human nature; he seeks therefore to penetrate beyond the text itself, using it as evidence for something which gave rise to it.

for each other, as the two sides of the one coin, as it were: Paul's convictions need to be expressed in theological statements to be intelligible, but the latter are meaningless unless set in the context of the convictions undergirding them (202–3).[42]

In Paul's thought Christ provides a normative pattern or 'type' for all Christian experience (240; cf. 320); although Paul himself also has a similar role (cf. 139), faith in Christ is yet central. God may be at work in the experience of every human being, but these manifestations are insufficient of themselves to bring about faith, for they are in themselves ambiguous (239). Christ, and particularly Christ's death and resurrection, has a pre-eminent place among the 'types' which validate present experiences, in that these experiences can be viewed as fulfilments of these 'types', along with other 'types' provided by the experiences of former believers and various Biblical figures like Abraham (238).[43] At the same time Patte resists the suggestion that Jesus Christ is thereby a complete and final revelation of God; rather he is a 'type', a 'promise' of future, Christ-like experiences, ones which follow the same 'type' or pattern as his (139; cf. 157).

Theißen's exposition of Paul's thought likens the role of Christ there to that of a model within learning theory, distinguishing here between 'real models' like Paul, whom his converts have actually seen, and 'symbolic models' like Christ, of whom they only hear (19=ET 9); both are to be imitated. Further, commenting on the speed with which 'the historical Jesus' came to be regarded as a pre-existent divine being, he suggests that 'in the experience of the first Christians, there appeared with Christ a reality that had always existed [as "preexistent tendencies within human beings"] but that had just then entered consciousness'.[44] Apropos

42. M. E. Boring, 'The Language of Universal Salvation in Paul', in *JBL* 105 (1986) 269–92, here 274, perhaps interprets Patte's book on Paul in terms of what he thinks a typical structuralist should say when he argues that for Patte Paul's convictions are what Paul 'really thinks'. On my reading of this later book of Patte's it is far from clear to me that he is in fact making quite this claim.

43. Patte is prepared to speak of a 'sacred history' consisting of a series of experiences undergone by various Old Testament figures, Jesus, the churches in Judaea, Paul, subsequent believers, and believers at the end of time, a history of God's revelatory interventions; these are causally connected: Paul's converts are converted due to Paul's experience and proclamation of the gospel, and Jesus is exalted and acknowledged by all because he was obedient even to death. For Paul this 'sacred history' has three main periods, of the promises, of the Law, and of faith (*Faith* 194–6).

44. *Aspekte* 26=ET 16 (quoted here)—this within a discussion of Jungian archetypes, which he interprets in terms of 'genetically preprogrammed dispositions—adaptive structures that correspond to an archaic phase of our existence

of the phenomenon of glossolalia he seeks to bring together the perspectives of learning theory and of psychodynamic theories by speaking
of Christ as an external model who 'activates and brings to consciousness
a preexistent structure within believers—an open "program" that lets the
organism strive for wholeness and fulfillment'. It may be, he argues, that
historical figures can only have this religious significance if they 'address
preexistent psychic structures and form them anew'; experience, including presumably encounter with historical figures, must be 'integrated
cognitively into a symbolically interpreted world' if they are to achieve
'permanence, stability, clarity, and communicability' (340=ET 340–1).
Along similar lines he argues that 'the historical Jesus' became for Paul
the embodiment of pre-existent wisdom, the embodiment, that is, of a
psychic tendency programmed into us in the course of human evolution
(380=384), a tendency to 'self-realization, individuation, form, or
totality' (386=390). Conversely, may one not then say that seeing this
mythical figure embodied in Jesus enabled this historical person to be
interpreted as someone who met a profound human need, a human need
built into the very nature of human beings? At the same time Theißen
rightly sees that Jesus' assumption of certain roles results in the
transformation of the mythical figures which hitherto had embodied them.
So he says of Christ's assumption of the role of judge that the resultant
judging by this judge is now seen as ultimately salvific (107=102).
Theißen links this transformation with the fact that Jesus was himself
condemned, thus being fitted to represent all within us that is condemned
(109=103), but one could surely also argue for the influence here of the
tradition of a Jesus who was the friend of sinners and who welcomed in
God's name those condemned by his contemporaries, receiving them into
his company and thus into the realization on earth of God's reign.[45] For
when Paul looks ahead to the Christian's judgment he sees at God's right
hand Jesus Christ who died (but he does not stress here his having been
condemned), who is characterized by his intercession for us and his love
for us (Rom 8.34–5).[46] That means that Christ's being for us, on and at
our side, is here as important for the transformation of the impending
judgment as is that of his taking our place and identifying himself with

---

but that are now unconscious since adaptation to the changed conditions of the
contemporary environment requires conscious acts of a completely different type'.
These predispositions 'are always shaped by cultural influence and can be
reinforced, modified, or even suppressed by cultural factors' (22=13).

45. Cf. chapter 6 above, esp. 130–6.

46. Cf. Theißen 117–18=111–12, referring to this text from Rom 8.

us, and it is perhaps in fact arguably even more important; at least it is more in the forefront of his conscious thinking.

Both these scholars' accounts imply that the *manner* of Jesus' life, death and resurrection is of fundamental importance as well as the mere fact that he lived, died and rose again. Correspondingly, if Paul or his converts came to doubt the historical veracity of the account given of Jesus' story as far as it relates to historically verifiable or falsifiable data, this would introduce into Paul's thought a serious dislocation, for the 'faith-image' of Christ would then become a fictional one, divorced from historical reality, an ideal projection of human aspirations or, more particularly, of Paul's conception of what faith in God should be. It must be admitted that this is theoretically possible, but at the same time it is appropriate to ask whether it is not more plausible to say that this figure became such a normative model or 'type', and at the same time such a revolutionary one, through actually being such a person.

It is in fact the 'revolutionary' character of Jesus' role as a model that is perhaps our best warrant for holding that it is unlikely to be the product of something other than his actual life on earth. If the story were portrayed in terms that simply reinforced existing models, then it would be at least as plausible to suggest that the story of Jesus had been recast in terms of these models to give expression to them. But the story told of Jesus is every bit as paradoxical and subversive of established values as is the apostolic existence of his servant Paul. Thus Theißen, as we have seen, refers to the transformation of the role of the eschatological judge by the identification of that figure with Jesus, and Weder speaks of the element of surprise in God's revelation that is contained in the event of the cross.[47]

But there is another aspect of this which bears upon the relation of the story to empirically verifiable history: for such a model to function effectively as a model it must be seen that the model was in some way or other a successful one. Otherwise the incentive to follow it is removed. So, if it could be shown that Jesus in fact died disillusioned and despairing, then much of the value of the story of Jesus is undermined. This was the sort of scenario with which Albert Schweitzer was apparently left at the conclusion of his *Quest* : in a famous passage he describes how Jesus, knowing he is the Son of Man, throws himself upon the 'wheel of the world' to set it moving on its last turn, but instead of bringing ordinary history to a close its revolution crushes him. The wheel rolls on, leaving hanging upon it 'the mangled body of the one immeasurably great Man, who was strong enough to think of Himself as

---

47. *Kreuz* (n. 5.4) 234–5.

the spiritual ruler of mankind and to bend history to his purpose.... . That is His victory and His reign.' Schweitzer's reconstruction of the historical Jesus leaves him as 'a stranger and an enigma' for us, and it is 'not the historical Jesus, but the spirit which goes forth from Him and in the spirits of men strives for new influence and rule' which overcomes the world. We cannot ascribe to him the thoughts and ideas of our century, but must simply rediscover the power of the 'world-negating spirit of Jesus'.[48] Schweitzer rescues himself from the dilemma of this apparent failure by describing the one thus destroyed as 'the one immeasurably great Man' and calling his destruction a 'victory' and a 'reign', thus underlining both that his life was an example to be followed and that it was successful. It would be quite possible for lesser persons than the author of this great study of Jesus to shrink back from the denial of the world that Schweitzer so impressively embraced and exemplified in his own life, and to pass the verdict of 'impressive but tragic and mistaken' upon Jesus' career.

But for Paul, at any rate, Jesus' life and death seemed of no value without their vindication in his resurrection; thus he declares that 'if Christ has not been raised, our faith is void' and 'if it is only in this life that we have put our hope in Christ, we are more pitiable than all (other) people' (1 Cor 15.17, 19). Whether or not we hold this to be true, it is apparent that Paul at least was not content with a life lived in this world in a 'world-denying' spirit without the rewards and vindication offered by a world beyond. For us, however, it may rather be a question of what constitutes a 'successful' life; should we not rather allow the nature of Jesus' life to dictate to us what counts as 'success' in God's eyes?

IV

It is easy to assert that Paul's proclamation of Christ is controlled by the reality of the earthly life of Jesus and that, as Ernst Käsemann puts it, Paul and John 'recall' the earthly life of Jesus and 'encapsulate his history into the Gospel'.[49] So too Weder maintains that for Paul the question who the living Christ is is inseparable from the question who the Jesus was who died on the cross, and that Christ's identity is decisively shaped by Jesus' historical existence in poverty and weakness.[50] It is

48. *Quest* (n. 2.16) 369, 397, 399–400.

49. 'Blind Alleys in the "Jesus of History" Controversy', in id., *Questions* (n. 5.18) 23–65, here 64—ET from *Exegetische Versuche und Besinnungen* 2 (Göttingen: Vandenhoeck & Ruprecht, 1965²) 31–68.

50. *Kreuz* (n. 5.4) 236–7.

another thing to find the evidence that one might expect from this of Paul doing that 'recalling' for such a purpose or of him showing how that historical existence in fact determines the identity of Christ.[51] Rom 8.34, for instance, which was mentioned above, might be evidence of his doing that: the Christ whom we shall meet at the final judgment is the same Jesus Christ that died for us.

That such an appeal is for the most part implicit rather than explicit may stem from the fact that it was simply assumed at that stage that Christian beliefs were in fact shaped or to be shaped by that historical reality. In other words there was then no question or possibility envisaged of cutting loose from that foundation story, nor was there any conception that Christian tradition had in any way loosened its hold upon that story. It was believed that they stood in a continuous tradition, received 'from the Lord' (1 Cor 11.23), and that they should stand there. Not yet had an awareness arisen that there could be any problems over the identity of the earthly Jesus and the one who was now Christ and Lord, and consequently it was not realized how divergent Christian messages could apparently appeal with equal force to the same tradition, or at least to different parts of it. At least the rise of such an awareness is surely implied if Käsemann is right[52] to claim that the Christian Gospels arose when they did in order to sift out true expressions of the Christian message from perversions of it.[53] Otherwise one can at least see such a

51. Hence Betz, *Nachfolge* (n. 7.10) 137–8 could plausibly claim that the imitation of Christ for Paul was related, not to the public ministry of Jesus, but to the event of the incarnation, crucifixion and installation as *Kyrios* of the pre-existent Christ as described in the Christ-myth (cf. 160–1). That is true as far as it goes, but we then have to ask what controlled the story told in the Christ-myth and gave it features which could be regarded as imitable.

52. Yet most perhaps interpret the nature and purpose of the Gospels otherwise, and as less polemical or corrective of error in their intent. However Talbert, *Gospel* (n. 9) 98, also states that 'our gospels belong to the debates over the legitimacy of the various forms of kerygma in early Christianity, that is, to the arguments over which Jesus is the "true" Jesus and which way of life is the "true" Christian way'; they 'often include...alien traditions and try to neutralize or re-interpret them by inclusion in a new whole' (cf. 119–23); cf. also Keck, *Future* (n. 5.38) 119–20.

53. 'Blind Alleys' (n. 49) 40–65, e.g. 41—the Gospels as a genre perhaps represent a relatively late reaction against an enthusiasm that thought itself 'able to do without the earthly Jesus'. Cf. also his 'The Problem of the Historical Jesus', in id., *Essays on New Testament Themes* (SBT 41, London: SCM, 1964) 15–47, here 30–4—ET of *ZTK* 51 (1954) 125–53=*Exegetische Versuche und Besinnungen* 1 (Göttingen: Vandenhoeck & Ruprecht, 1960) 187–214.

realization surfacing by the time of the writing of 1 John (1.1–3; 2.22; 4.1–3).

Yet if this 'recalling' is for the most part implied rather than explicit how can we be so sure that it is in fact taking place? We have more than once seen in the course of these essays that often the most that we can do is to point to a common pattern found both in the story of Jesus and in the life and message of Paul. Then, as I did earlier in chapter 6, it is possible to argue that the presence of a similarity in two phases of one and the same religious movement is more likely to be causally explained rather than being explicable as the occurrence of two separate and not directly related phenomena: Paul acts and preaches as he does because a tradition has come down to him either that Jesus acted and preached in a similar way or that such acting and preaching is the Christian way to act and preach.[54] That was the case, I argued, with regard to Jesus' welcoming acceptance of sinners in God's name and Paul's acceptance of Gentiles into the church. It was also the case with the phenomena outlined by Dr Wolff in chapter 7. For there we saw that he detected four aspects of Jesus' and Paul's ministries in which both ran parallel to one another: both ministries were characterized by deprivation (poverty, homelessness, hunger, and the like), by celibacy, by humble service, and by enduring persecution. Not all of these similarities were necessarily the result of a deliberate imitation by Paul of the circumstances of Jesus' ministry, yet Dr Wolff argued that if Paul was conscious of being Christ's apostle or representative, it was surely probable that Paul saw these common features as expressions of his nearness to his Lord, although he grants that it is possible that he was unaware of this. That Paul was aware that the character of his ministry bore a resemblance to that of Jesus seems to me intrinsically plausible, even probable; is it not, after all, likelier that Paul was convinced that this was the appropriate form for his Christian ministry to take because he saw this form of ministry as following the lines of the pattern of ministry which he detected within the traditions concerning the earthly ministry of Jesus? Similarly it could be argued that the lists of qualities that should characterize the Christian life such as we find in 1 Cor 13.4–7 or Gal 5.22–3 stem ultimately from the remembered character of the earthly Jesus,[55] even if when Paul wrote

---

54. Bearing in mind once more Professor N. Walter's valuable distinction, apropos of Rom 14.14*a* , between a conscious reference to tradition known by Paul to be Jesus-tradition and a more general appeal to what seemed to be a necessary corollary of the gospel of Christ—chapter 3, here 57.

55. J. D. G. Dunn, *Jesus and the Spirit: a Study of the Religious and Charismatic Experience of Jesus and the First Christians as Reflected in the New Testament* (London: SCM, 1975) 321, suggests that these passages were 'charac-

these passages he was, if anything, influenced more by the whole story of Jesus that extended back before, and forwards beyond, his earthly life and by the model for Christian conduct which it offered.[56]

V

We noted earlier that the story of Jesus was for Paul one that began before, and ended beyond, the scope of human history. Any story of any complexity, however, contains within itself some elements that are more important than others, more constitutive of it, and certain episodes or a single episode in it may be considered as typical or representative of the story as a whole. Thus Hans Weder speaks of Jesus' *Geschichte* being for Paul 'summarized and concentrated' (*zusammengefaßt und konzentriert*) in his death on the cross.[57] Yet at the same time it must be recognized that this is a deliberate act of selection by an interpreter, in this case Paul; such episodes do not select themselves, nor do the stories summarize themselves. It is open to others to turn the spotlight on other episodes, the teaching of Jesus, the miracles performed by him, or the like. So when Jesus' opponents summarized his story in terms of his 'sorcery'[58] they are selecting another aspect of that story, Jesus' miracles, and are giving it an unfavourable interpretation. Equally versions of the Christian message which represented Jesus in terms of a 'divine man' or a teacher were focussing on other elements in the story and thus giving a different interpretation of the whole by their selection.

---

ter sketches' of Christ and then speaks of the Spirit being marked by 'the image or character of *Jesus*'—'the yardstick is *Jesus*' (my italics). W. Schrage too (*Ethik des Neuen Testaments*, GNT 4, Göttingen: Vandenhoeck & Ruprecht, 1982, 202) observes how many of the characteristics that Paul attributes to love are also predicated of *Christ* (not, however, the earthly Jesus—see the reff. in n. 76 below). However E. Larsson, *Christus als Vorbild: eine Untersuchung zu den paulinischen Tauf- und Eikontexten* (ASNU 23, Uppsala & Lund: Gleerup & Kopenhagen: Munksgaard, 1962) 210–21, makes out a case for such 'Christian virtues' being modelled on the character of God as well as that of Christ. However we can surely also say that these particular characteristics of God were singled out and thrown into prominence for Paul by the nature of God's representative, Jesus Christ.

56. So O. Wischmeyer, *Der höchste Weg: das 13. Kapitel des 1. Korintherbriefes* (SNT 13, Gütersloh: Mohn, 1981) 115, speaks of the Christology implicit in the former passage, responsible for the 'entirely new evaluation' of ἀγάπη there.

57. *Kreuz* (n. 5.4) 229.

58. So in *b. Sanh.* 43*a* Jesus is condemned to death for sorcery and for seducing Israel. That that was already an interpretation of Jesus' activity during his life-time is implicit in the Beelzebul controversy (Mark 3.20–30 par.).

At the same time it must be noted that the selection of an aspect or
episode of a story as central to, and typical of, the whole may be highly
significant and far-reaching in its effects, in that all other aspects of the
story are subordinated to that one feature. In doing that such a selection
may 'filter out' interpretations that concentrate on other aspects of the
story, and the element focussed on becomes a starting-point and central
focus for the interpretation of the story, in the light of which all other
possible interpretations can be evaluated. Paul's chosen point, around
which the rest of the story is oriented, is one unambiguously set within
the range of human history, the crucifixion of Jesus, even if it must at the
same time be stressed that it is this event as seen and interpreted in the
light of a perspective that transcends history: this crucifixion is interpreted in the light of Paul's (and other early Christians') belief that the
one crucified had been raised from the dead and exalted by God. Paul's
focus on the crucifixion means that he does not, for instance, concentrate
on the descent of the pre-existent Christ into the world nor focus upon
discourses of the risen Christ with his disciples.

We need not here go into the question whether for the Fourth
Evangelist the cross of Jesus is but one feature of 'the absolute minimum
of the costume designed for the one who dwelt for a little while among
men', a traditional feature that has, however, ceased to be a thing of
shame, but has become the place for 'the manifestation of divine self-
giving love and his victorious return from the alien realm below to the
Father who had sent him'.[59] It is enough for our purpose to note that
Paul's preaching of Christ, at any rate, is in the starkest possible contrast
to this interpretation of Johannine Christology. He sets the cross at the
centre-point of his story of Jesus; this cross is far from being rendered
innocuous in his eyes, for he recognizes that it is 'an offence to Jews, and
folly to Gentiles' (1 Cor 1.23).

It also needs to be noted that, although assertions about the non-
historical parts of the story of Jesus are not in themselves empirically
falsifiable, they could be rendered open to question if their continuity
with the historical parts is in doubt, and they could then no longer
function effectively in the way that they do in Paul's thought. If Jesus had
behaved self-assertively in his earthly life, appeal to the example of his
self-denial in his incarnation (2 Cor 8.9; Phil 2.6–7) would be, if not
falsified, at least obstructed and vitiated: Paul's converts could then
reasonably ask which example of Jesus they were to follow, and could
claim that they preferred to follow the self-seeking earthly Jesus rather
than the self-denying heavenly one. Indeed the example of the earthly

---

59. E. Käsemann, *The Testament of Jesus: a Study of the Gospel of John in the
Light of Chapter 17* (London: SCM, 1968=ET of Tübingen: Mohr, 1966) 10.

Jesus was, it might be claimed, more relevant to them for they too were but creatures of flesh and blood, not denizens of the heavenly realm.[60] That choice is not on offer if the character claimed for the heavenly Christ is in harmony with that of the earthly Jesus. (It would in fact be hard to find an epistemologically adequate basis for asserting that the character of the heavenly Christ was different.) If this example seems too hypothetical, then it should be recalled that S. G. F. Brandon presented a reconstruction of Jesus' life in which the pacifist Jesus was dismissed as a fabrication of the Evangelists and the historical Jesus was one who was closely allied with the Zealot movement;[61] if that were historically true, could we still as plausibly and convincingly place love in the central position that it occupies in Paul's theology (e.g. Rom 5.5–8), Christology (e.g. 2 Cor 5.14) and ethical teaching (e.g. Gal 5.22)? Certainly Paul, as we have seen, expects the character and disposition of the exalted Christ whom Christians will meet on the day of judgment to be that of the Jesus who died for ungodly and sinful humanity; that same Jesus, now alive again, will rescue from wrath those whom he reconciled to God by his death (Rom 5.6–10); when at the end Christians stand before God's throne they will meet there that Christ who was the Jesus who died for them and who now intercedes for them, and the last word concerning them will be his, a word of love (8.34–5).

So, however much Paul, or Christians before him, drew upon various speculations, for instance about God's wisdom, that lay to hand in their world, to provide them with the means to interpret the status and significance of the Jesus whom they acknowledged as Lord, yet the fact that these speculations were introduced to interpret this particular historical figure remained at least a potential, or indeed an actual, control upon those interpretations, and the selection of the crucifixion of that figure as the centre of his story exercised a powerful influence upon the form which those interpretations could take.

---

60. It is at this point that a tension emerges in the thought of the Letter to the Hebrews, since, on the face of it, how can we combine the assertion that Christ is like us in all respects (2.17) and even tempted in all respects like us (4.15) with Christ's pre-existence (1.2)? To be conscious of the latter in the manner of John 17.5 would be incompatible with exposure to the full range of human temptation; is this then a pre-existence of which Jesus was unaware? This question is not posed, let alone answered. But it should be if the story of Christ is to function as the author of Hebrews wants it to, as a consolation to humans (2.18; 4.16) and an example for them to follow.

61. *Jesus and the Zealots: a Study of the Political Factor in Primitive Christianity* (Manchester Univ., 1967) esp., e.g. 338–56.

VI

The question of the function of the story of Jesus in Paul's thought needs, however, to be distinguished from the question of its function in the traditions upon which he drew. Just as the motives that led Paul to echo traditions moulded by wisdom speculations (e.g. 1 Cor 8.6) need not be the same as had originally had led early Christians to utilize those speculations to expound the significance of Christ,[62] his purpose in appealing in Gal 3.27–8 to the baptismal tradition that in Christ there is neither Jew nor Greek, neither slave nor free person, neither male nor female, need not be that of those who had first formulated this idea. For a start, as we have seen, he is only interested in this context in the superseding of the Jew–Greek distinction, which he appropriately mentions first, whereas those whom he quotes were evidently also interested in the distinctions between slaves and free persons, and between males and females. Unfortunately we know nothing for certain about the origins of this striking formulation, and any suggestions that we can make must remain conjectural.[63] We saw above (§II) that it was doubtful whether a Platonizing

---

62. Cf., e.g., Wolff, *1 Kor* (n. 7.52) 8: the motive for transferring to Christ wisdom's role as mediator in creation arose from early Christians' conviction that a new creation had been introduced by Christ's resurrection; they wished to show that the original creation had all along been oriented towards this fulfilment. Paul's purpose in referring to this, on the other hand, was to show that everything in heaven and on earth owes its being to the will of one God expressed through the one Lord, in contrast to the pagan belief in many deities (ibid. 10).

63. But some such suggestions are called for, since, as Betz notes (*Gal.* [n. 16] 189), 'v 28 leads to the field of political and social ideals and practices', defining 'the religious, cultural, and social consequences of the Christian baptismal initiation'; in n. 68 he mentions the attempts of some commentators to evade such implications. One can clearly see an example of how the transcending of the distinction between Jew and Greek would work out in practice in the sort of table-fellowship evidently existing in Antioch before the intervention of 'certain people sent by James' as reflected in Gal 2.12, but the implications of the transcending of the other differences are less clear. The women of Corinth may have drawn inferences from 'neither male nor female' (cf., e.g., Wolff, ibid. 67), but, if 1 Cor 11.16 is to be believed, they were the first to do so. Lührmann, 'Sklave' (n. 1) 70, speaks of an 'anticipation of eschatology subject to the conditions of this world', but the question is how this 'anticipation' worked out in practice. In his later article, 'Neutestamentliche Haustafeln und antike Ökonomie', in *NTS* 27 (180–1) 83–97, here esp. 93, he seems to think in terms simply of people of all these sorts sitting down together at table together. That would be significant enough, but was that all there was to it? W. Klaiber, too, is clear that this eschatological statement has 'considerable significance for the social situation in the Church's communal life' (*Rechtfertigung und Gemeinde: eine Untersuchung zum paulinischen Kirchenverständnis*, FRLANT 127, Göttingen: Vandenhoeck & Ruprecht, 1982,

exegesis after the manner of Philo could account for the presence in the tradition of the transcending of all three pairs of differences. I argued rather that it was more likely that this stemmed from the idea that Christ represented all humanity, transcending the distinctions between different groups and classes of humanity. But that does not answer the question of the group responsible for the origins of this tradition, nor that as to how this conviction found expression in the life of the community in which it originated, or, put bluntly, what sort of community resulted when this was proclaimed at its initiation rites. As regards the first question my inclination would be to look for its authors in the same circles which I suggested[64] were responsible for drawing creative and radical inferences from Jesus' openness towards 'sinners' and who responded equally openly and welcomingly themselves to the 'sinners' around them; these 'sinners' now included Gentiles, and in a centre like Antioch-on-the-Orontes they would have found themselves surrounded by those who were 'sinners' of this sort. If this openness and refusal to discriminate against non-Jews were incorporated in their baptismal rites, then it seems that they may well also have viewed this rite as a 'new creation', and that Paul alludes to this tradition later in Galatians in a rather similar formulation to that of 3.28, in 6.15. If this 'new creation' were viewed as restoring a condition that had obtained at the beginning or had originally been intended by God then it would be natural for exegetical traditions concerning the first created human being to have played a part; that would account for the abolition of the distinction between male and female, but the abolition of that between slave and free or Jew and Greek takes us beyond anything which, to my knowledge, is paralleled in Hellenistic Jewish material; indeed it is less likely that we should find there the abolition of the latter distinction, with its resultant threat to Jewish privilege and distinctiveness;[65] Christians were surely more likely to have been responsible for this.

In Phil 2.6–11 Paul holds out to the Philippians the example of Christ's obedience, that they too might be obedient.[66] But Professor

---

103); cf. Paulsen, 'Einheit' (n. 1) 88–9, 93–5. But A. Cameron, '"Neither Male nor Female"', in *Greece and Rome* 2nd ser. 27 (1980) 60–8, rather misses the point when she accuses Paul in Gal 3.28 of 'refraining from a real assessment of male and female roles' (64); if that charge is to be levelled it is to be levelled at those who formulated what Paul quotes for a a more specific purpose.

64. See chapter 6.

65. But contrast Betz, *Gal.* (n. 1) 191.

66. Cf. the argument of Prof. Reumann's paper at the Göttingen meeting that 2.6–11 looked forward to the exhortation of v 12; at the same time it was noted in the discussion that the appeal for ταπεινοφροσύνη in v 3 is echoed by the

John Reumann argued plausibly in a paper on '*Imitatio* (*Christi*) in
Philippians with Special Reference to Christology' which he presented to
the 'Paulus und Jesus' seminar at Göttingen in 1987 that this hymn 'in its
pre-Philippians form did not have *imitatio Christi* or ethics of any sort as
its aim. It was soteriological and Christological' (p. 20).[67] That would
explain why the person that originally composed the passage was apparently also interested in the rewards of that obedience, since as much of
the passage is taken up with a description of the subsequent exaltation of
Jesus. Those rewards are not a matter of imitation by believers, for the
gaining of them must remain a matter of a promise to be realized solely
by the divine activity of grace.

These different possible interpretations of one and the same story
illustrate in some measure the truth of Burkert's observation that myths'
reference to 'something of collective importance' is 'secondary' and
'partial'.[68] The story that functions as a myth can be interpreted in many
different ways,[69] but it exists prior to, independent of, any of the various
possible interpretations. At the same time it owes its continued existence
and its status to its function within the community that hands it down.
The foundation of myths is to be located in '*basic biological or cultural
programs of actions* ' and 'actions or sequences of actions' are the stuff
of myths.[70] Yet at the same time we have to add that the story that
functions as a myth may be retold so that a different programme of
actions is held out for imitation.

In other words, whereas in many cultures myths function as a
foundation for the *status quo* of society and an endorsement of its
structures and values, myths can also be a tool for the critical questioning
of those structures and values. Indeed, the Christian story can also
function in a conservative way, but it is in its essence so paradoxical and
so subversive of many accepted values that it is eminently suited to a
critical role.[71] But which of these two roles it in fact plays is integrally

---

ἐταπείνωσεν of v 8; these need not be alternatives, for those who are humble-
minded will be ready to obey, to give heed to others, especially God's appointed
apostle.

67. Cf. E. Käsemann, 'Kritische Analyse von Phil. 2,5–11', in *Versuche* 1 (n.
53) 51–95, repr. from *ZTK* 47 (1950) 313–60, here 356: this was true too of
Paul's understanding of the hymn. But contrast the views of G. Strecker and H.-
M. Schenke mentioned in Müller, 'Christushymnus' (n. 4) 18.

68. *Structure* (n. 7) 23; 'secondary' because the myth has a meaning in itself
that is not to be derived from its application, and 'partial, since tale and reality
will never be quite isomorphic in these applications'.

69. Cf. ibid. 4–5.

70. Ibid. 18, 24, his italics.

linked to the question of which aspects of the story are thrown into prominence. (A Christian culture which observes Sunday strictly as 'holy' would feel itself supported by a telling of the story of Jesus which emphasized his participation in synagogue worship, but threatened by one which emphasized his freedom with regard to sabbath observance.) Paul's concentration on the cross as the centre of Jesus' story, on something, that is, which was 'offensive' and 'foolish' by usual standards, enables him to use that story with potentially revolutionary effect.[72] The world had been crucified as far as he was concerned and he as far as it was concerned,[73] and the result was a 'new creation' (Gal 6.14–15). It is from these roots in the paradoxicality of God's dealings with us in the story of Jesus Christ that there springs Paul's equally paradoxical understanding of human, and especially apostolic, existence.[74]

It must be noted that this revolutionary teaching, which outdoes the Cynics' recoining of language and values in its paradoxicality,[75] does not arise in the first instance either out of the other-worldly parts of Jesus' story or out of theorizing as to how or what he should be, but out of the most brutally this-worldly part of the story of Jesus, his death on a cross. From this viewpoint Paul evaluates both the rest of Jesus' earthly life and the other-worldly part of his story, and all must be consistent with this.

To conclude: in the preceding study I have tried to show how certain features of Paul's characterization of Christ could be described as 'theoretical', as the result of theorizing and arising out of the need to give expression to the function which his Christ was perceived to have: Christ had to be like this to do what he did; he needed to be amongst other things a universal representative of all humanity, and so his nature was described in such terms as would set out this all-inclusive role, even if this description did not fit the particularity of the individual Jesus of Nazareth. The central character in the story was invested with characteristics that arose, not from the story itself, but from the function that the

---

71. Cf. Theißen, *Aspects* (n. 3.55) 52, on the revolutionary and conservative roles of religion in general. It is this former quality of Jesus' story which, for Keck, prevents the early Christian preaching of Jesus from being classified as 'propaganda'—*Future* (n. 39) 110–1.

72. 'Potentially', because, in my view, 1 Cor 11.2–16 is a sad reflection of how incompletely Paul was able to see the full scope of the revolution that was implicit in the story of Jesus as interpreted in Gal 3.27–8.

73. On this interpretation of the datives cf. my *Baptism* (n. 5.45) 43 n. 1.

74. See n. 38 above.

75. For an example of this see my *Baptism* (n. 5.45) 381–9.

story was now being made to fulfil. But Christ was also appealed to for 'practical' purposes, as Paul urged Christians in the name of this Christ to adopt certain courses of action and to behave in certain ways. Appeal was then made to the 'story' of Jesus who was now the Christ, but not just to the earthly story of this Jesus, but just as much, if not more, to the story of the pre-existent one who was sent by God and who was exalted to be at God's right hand;[76] the narrative presupposed is not confined to the earthly course of the life of Jesus of Nazareth from his birth to the grave. Not that Paul recognizes any discontinuity or breaks in the story here: it is for him all one story of one person, and he seems to have been blissfully unaware of the problems of the relationship of the eternal and preexistent to the incarnate that were so to exercise later theologians. But the story of the other-worldly one is told in this-worldly terms, as indeed it ultimately must be if it is to be told at all, and implicitly the other-worldly parts of the story are of a piece with the this-worldly; for we can say with some justification that those parts of the story are in large measure projections backwards and forwards of the patterns of action and the attitudes of the earthly Jesus.[77] Much the same has happened in the case of the story of Jesus as C. H. Dodd argues led to the adaptation and inclusion of the mythical stories at the beginning of Genesis; they were used as 'symbols of truth learned in history'. Although 'nominally' prehistory they in fact 'apply the principles of divine action revealed in the history of a particular people' in a universal way.[78] So too Christians' experience of the earthly life of Jesus formed the basis of their projection backwards into prehistory and forward into an eschatological consummation of that which they had seen in Jesus and of the divine activity which they believed they had discerned in his life. At the same time setting this earthly life within this larger context enabled them to interpret the significance of that earthly life in a manner which they considered appropriate.[79] Thus the whole story hangs together as the coherent story

---

76. Cf. Schrage, *Ethik* (n. 55) 163, 198–9, citing Phil 2.5–11; 2 Cor 8.9.

77. 'In large measure', for one could say that the fact that God sent Jesus was not such a projection, but that he was willing to be sent was, in that such obedience and self-denial characterized his earthly life.

   J. P. Mackey speaks of the future predictions contained in the story as an 'extrapolation from "the story so far"' (in J. D. G. Dunn, J. P. Mackey, *New Testament Theology in Dialogue*, London: SPCK, 1987, 29). Equally, though, those parts of the story concerned with events before Jesus' appearance on earth can be regarded as 'extrapolations' from that earthly life.

78. *The Bible Today* (Cambridge Univ., 1946) 115, endorsed 'wholeheartedly' by Ricoeur, *Symbolism* (n. 5.24) 242 n. 4.

of one person, and for Paul it coheres around a central point which is the obedient suffering of crucifixion by this one person. In other words, this central, and earthly, part of the story is then a yardstick or control upon the way in which the rest of the story can be told if it is to be one coherent story.

---

79. However for Sellin, 'Mythologeme' (n. 11) 211, those stories which are properly called 'myths do not interpret reality, but form a non-negotiable frame-work for the appropriation of reality'; Paul does not tell myths, although his theology presupposes at certain fundamental points the ontology of the mythical (222).

9

POSTSCRIPT

Alexander J. M. Wedderburn

If, at first sight, the preceding chapters seem to have left more questions unanswered than they have solved, then this is perhaps as much as anything due to the complexity of the issues raised and the nature of the evidence which is available to us in our search for solutions. Yet at least some questions have, to my mind, received fairly unequivocal answers: Professor Walter has made out a strong case for considerable caution in assessing the amount of Jesus-tradition which Paul knew *as Jesus-tradition*, and the amount which we can say with confidence that he knew is small indeed; on the other hand Dr Wolff has shown the exegetical implausibility of appealing to 2 Cor 5.16 in order to show that Paul was on principle averse to acquiring knowledge of, or showing an interest in, the earthly Jesus. These may be somewhat negative conclusions, but they do clear the ground for further questions.

The questions on which the remaining essays have concentrated have centred around the theme of continuity, continuity in the content and the basis of the messages of Jesus and Paul, continuity in the outworking of those messages in the lives and the missionary practice of both Jesus and his followers, including Paul, continuity in attitudes and actions despite the discontinuity in the verbal form which their messages took. Dr Wolff and I have both pointed to various similarities, and I have argued that this should not be regarded as a coincidence; rather Jesus and Paul both stand within a historical movement, an ongoing tradition of teaching and practice which mediated certain features of the former's life and teaching to the latter. We may be unsure of the intervening links, for here we have to read between the lines of the New Testament, but the fact that this was a historical movement gives us cause to think that some such concrete links did indeed exist and that Paul gained much of his knowledge of Christianity from something or some one more tangible than a heavenly

voice;[1] I have sought to make out a case for identifying the most
important link as the group of the Hellenists around Stephen whom Paul
had persecuted, whose Christian traditions and version of Christianity he
then largely adopted as his own after his conversion. This case may, of
necessity, have to remain hypothetical, but without it the problem of continuity becomes an even more intractable conundrum.

Yet, even if this hypothesis is accepted, problems remain in considerable numbers. With regard to this question of the historical links
they stem in large measure from the fact that no New Testament writer is
concerned to spell these links out for us: the author of Acts is far too
concerned with the roles of prominent figures like Peter and Paul to
appreciate the significance of this largely anonymous group of Greek-
speaking Jewish Christians, and far too concerned to show the early
Christians in general as loyal to the Jewish Law to appreciate how disloyal this particular group of Christians must have seemed to be in the
eyes of contemporary Jews if we are adequately to explain the persecution to which they were subjected. And, when Paul comes to speak of
such matters, he is far too concerned with stressing the divine authority
for his message to worry about the human channels through whom he had
come to learn of Christ and to discover the nature of that Christian gospel
which he had initially so vehemently rejected (cf. Gal 1.11–16).

The situation is further complicated by the fact that Paul and his converts and readers shared a certain heritage and certain presuppositions
which remain unspoken and unwritten in Paul's correspondence; we are
left to guess at what they were. We have seen how this works in the case
of Paul's use of sayings of Jesus and how some scholars have felt able to
argue that Paul knows far more Jesus-tradition than he actually uses. Yet,
as I pointed out,[2] this argument has to come to terms with the fact that
there are many cases where Paul is involved in arguments where his case
would have been greatly helped by appeal to sayings of Jesus which we
know; yet no use is made of them in such contexts. That should warn us
against any too glib assumption that Paul knew much more than he
actually quotes as sayings of the Lord.

The same lack of knowledge on our part lies behind the repeated
observation that Paul's letters do not allow us to say with any certainty

---

1. A criticism that might well be levelled against Jüngel's *Paulus* (n. 2.1) is
that to relate Paul's message (for Jüngel one of justification) to that of Jesus in
terms of 'two speech-events (*Sprachereignisse*) following one another as events
belonging to one speech-history (*Sprachgeschichte*)' (263) runs the risk of dis-
embodiment; for it is people who speak and they do so within certain historical
contexts and their utterances are in large measure conditioned by those contexts.

2. N. 6.1

how far Paul was conscious of the points of contact which we feel able to detect between what he writes and what we know of the Jesus-tradition. We are for the most part unsure how far a similarity which we detect, be it in the words Paul uses or in the manner of his life, is a conscious imitation of, or following of, Jesus-tradition, or how far Paul was merely being carried along by a stream of Christian tradition that ultimately stemmed from Jesus. Did he know this tradition simply as Christian tradition, or was he aware of its points of contact with actual sayings or actions of Jesus?

In the last chapter we saw yet another, related, instance of this: we do not, for the most part, see Paul demonstrating the continuity between what he does or teaches and the teachings and actions of the earthly Jesus; the nearest that he perhaps comes to doing so is in his appeals to Jesus' death for us in Rom 5.6 and 8 and 8.34—not that this is any bare historical fact, for it is the bare fact drastically re-interpreted as a saving death for humanity and as a manifestation of the essential nature and will of God; it is around this event in history that Paul claims to orientate his message, however differently others might interpret that event (1 Cor 1.18, 23). Yet mostly Paul seems to assume that, once stated, it should be plain to his readers that a certain piece of instruction or a certain course of action is what is appropriate for the followers of Jesus Christ—despite the fact that there were plainly others around who claimed to follow Jesus Christ and who taught and acted in a decidedly different fashion. In the last chapter I also suggested that this apparent incaution and lack of thorough argumentation on Paul's part indicates a stage in the development of the Christian tradition at which the possibility of losing touch with the historical origins of that tradition had not yet been realized or felt to be a real problem. This seeming innocence and blindness to the danger of such a loss of control would also have been encouraged by the lively sense of the spiritual guidance of the risen Christ which Paul and other early Christians shared; this led to the danger, to which Paul himself was not immune, that ecstatic experiences and pronouncements in the name of Christ were deemed to be sufficient in themselves and self-authenticating; the dangers were beginning to become apparent by the time that Paul wrote 1 Corinthians, but his response is not always to argue explicitly what the nature of the Spirit's work and leading must be if it is with any plausibility to be identified with the Spirit of Jesus Christ; he is prepared to set inspiration against inspiration, ecstasy against ecstasy, as if that provided any fully cogent argument that his position was the truly Christian one (cf. 1 Cor 2.16; 7.40; also 14.37). Whether the guidance came from a shared Christian tradition (cf. 1 Cor 11.16) or from inspiration, Paul seems to have felt that it ought to be plain enough,

without further argument, what belonged within the Christian tradition
and what did not. He belonged to an age of innocence, before it was fully
realized how great were the problems with which those must wrestle who
seek to determine what the 'mind of Christ' (1 Cor 2.16) is within their
own situation.

What is clear is that even in Paul's day it was not enough simply to
repeat the words and ways of Jesus; the situation and the time had
changed. However much we may detect points of contact at a deeper
level in the conduct and attitudes of Jesus and his followers in the time
after his resurrection it seems clear that following Jesus in this new
period of history did not simply involve copying the words and actions of
Jesus of Nazareth. Clearly Paul for one felt himself to be under no such
constraints; indeed so far was that from being the case that some have, as
we have seen, found it difficult to see what, if anything, bound Paul to
Jesus, or what they had in common. If the former is not to be regarded as
having re-founded Christianity, then we cannot shirk the task of
discovering that which is common to them. But at the same time the
differences between them may provide us with a valuable hermeneutical
model as we in our turn seek to live within the same tradition, discovering for our day what is that will and nature of God that is revealed
in Jesus Christ. In chapter 5 above I tried to suggest some of the reasons,
both negative and positive, that had led Paul to formulate his message in
terms different to those which had been used by the earthly Jesus; in
chapter 6 we saw how the Hellenists may have been forced by their
circumstances, in particular their being approached by interested non-
Jews, to ask themselves how Jesus would have responded to such a
situation; I argued that they found their answer in the way in which Jesus
had treated the 'sinners' of his world. Yet in the last chapter we saw the
Christian tradition also boldly appropriating for the Christ whom they
proclaimed characteristics which transcended the historical limitations of
the earthly life of Jesus of Nazareth, and claiming for him qualities which
befitted the role which they believed that he was playing within the
purposes of God. So the suggested actions of the Hellenists, and after
them of Paul, reflect a deliberate recalling of the earthly Jesus, but at the
same time went beyond anything expressly endorsed by him, even if it
seemed to them to be in sympathy and continuity with his attitudes and
actions; in other words, they had to ask themselves 'What would the
Jesus whom we knew, or who has been handed down to us by the
tradition concerning his life, have done in the situation in which we find
ourselves?' The development of a Christology of Christ as an all-
inclusive, universal representative figure, on the other hand, seems rather
to ignore the characteristics of the earthly Jesus; he has, for such

Christological affirmations, become more than a historical figure, and transcends the limitations inevitably placed upon any historical figure. And yet, at the same time, we also saw that it was possible, even likely, that free rein was not given to all sorts of fantasy and self-gratifying speculation; we might say that such affirmations had still to be felt to be in continuity with the will and purposes of the earthly Jesus, however much they left the limitations of his particular historical existence behind; in the case of this particular Christological development we could say that such a Christ was felt to be an expression of the same openness and availability to all shown by Jesus that had led the Hellenists to their policy with regard to Gentiles.

All of these developments in the history of early Christian thought and practice provide valuable starting-points for our reflections on a Christian faith and Christian ethical teaching for today. If the arguments of the preceding chapters have at all facilitated the use of these starting-points for such reflections and made them more accessible, that is reason enough for setting them down in print.

INDEX

INDEX OF NEW TESTAMENT PASSAGES CITED

INDEX OF AUTHORS CITED

DATE DUE